Believers Church Bible Commentary

Elmer A. Martens and Willard M. Swartley, Editors

BELIEVERS CHURCH BIBLE COMMENTARY

Old Testament
Genesis, by Eugene F. Roop
Exodus, by Waldemar Janzen
Judges, by Terry L. Brensinger
Jeremiah, by Elmer A. Martens
Ezekiel, by Millard C. Lind
Daniel, by Paul M. Lederach
Hosea, Amos, by Allen R. Guenther

New Testament
Matthew, by Richard B. Gardner
Mark, by Timothy J. Geddert
Acts, by Chalmer E. Faw
2 Corinthians, by V. George Shillington
Colossians, Philemon, by Ernest D. Martin
1 and 2 Thessalonians, by Jacob W. Elias
1–2 Peter, Jude, by Erland Waltner and J. Daryl Charles

Old Testament Editors
Elmer A. Martens and Allen R. Guenther (for *Jeremiah*), Mennonite
    Brethren Biblical Seminary, Fresno, California

New Testament Editors
Willard M. Swartley and Howard H. Charles (for *Matthew*),
    Associated Mennonite Biblical Seminary, Elkhart, Indiana

Editorial Council
David Baker, Brethren Church
Lydia Harder, General Conference Mennonite Church
Estella B. Horning, Church of the Brethren
Robert B. Ives, Brethren in Christ Church
Gordon H. Matties, Mennonite Brethren Church
Paul M. Zehr (chair), Mennonite Church

Believers Church
Bible Commentary

Judges

Terry L. Brensinger

HERALD PRESS
Scottdale, Pennsylvania
Waterloo, Ontario

Library of Congress Cataloging-in-Publication Data
Brensinger, Terry L.
    Judges / Terry L. Brensinger.
        p. cm. — (Believers church Bible commentary)
    Includes bibliographical references (p.   ) and index.
    ISBN 0-8361-9104-8 (alk. paper)
    1. Bible. O.T. Judges Commentaries. I. Title. II. Series.
BS1305.3.B74   1999
222'.3207—dc21   99-43081

BELIEVERS CHURCH BIBLE COMMENTARY: JUDGES
Copyright © 1999 by Herald Press, Scottdale, Pa. 15683
    Released simultaneously in Canada
    by Herald Press, Waterloo, Ont. N2L 6H7. All rights reserved
Library of Congress Catalog Card Number: 99-43081
International Standard Book Number: 0-8361-9104-8
Printed in the United States of America
Cover, maps, and page makeup by Merrill R. Miller
09 08 07 06 05   10 9 8 7 6 5 4 3 2

To order or request information, please call
1-800-759-4447 (individuals); 1-800-245-7894 (trade).

Website: www.heraldpress.com

To Reinhold A. Barth,
whose sermon from Judges softened
my then-rebellious heart

Abbreviations

Copyright page names Bible versions: GNB, KJV, NIV, NRSV, RSV

*	The Text in Biblical Context
+	The Text in the Life of the Church
//	parallel to
=	parallel to
x	times
ca.	circa, about
cf.	compare
[Chronology]	typical reference to essays that precede the Bibliography
e.g.	for example(s)
esp.	especially
Heb.:	Hebrew text
LXX	Septuagint, Greek translation of OT
notes	Explanatory Notes
NT	New Testament
par.	parallel to
OT	Old Testament
TBC	The Text in Biblical Context
TLC	The Text in the Life of the Church

Contents

Series Foreword 11
Author's Preface 13

Approaching Judges 15
Judges Within the Old Testament 15
Theology of Judges 16
The World of the Judges 17
Surveying the Book of Judges 19
Selected Issues in Judges 21

1. Principal Cause:
   The Disobedience of Israel, 1:1—3:6 23
The Conquest Abandoned:
   A "Political" Introduction, 1:1—2:5 26
Joshua's Death, 1:1a 27
Judah's Accomplishments, 1:1b-21 28
The Northern Tribes' Failures, 1:22-36 32
The Messenger's Rebuke, 2:1-5 34
   * A Unified Community 35
   * Incomplete Obedience 36
   + On Not Stopping Halfway 37
The Covenant Forsaken:
   A "Theological" Introduction, 2:6—3:6 39
A Generation's Faithfulness, 2:6-9 40
A New Generation's Unfaithfulness, 2:10-19 40
The Lord's Indictment, 2:20—3:6 42

     * Divine Tests and the Possibility of Failure 43
     * Learning from Failed Tests 44
     + Tests Failed or Passed 44

2. Worsening Effect:
The Deterioration of Israel, 3:7—16:31 47
The Pattern Established: Othniel, 3:7-11 50
     * Exemplary Models 52
     + Empowered and Obedient 52
The Pattern Affirmed: Ehud and Deborah, 3:12—5:31 . 54
A Positive Portrait: Ehud's Escapades, 3:12-31 55
     * Deception 58
     * Much with Little 59
     + Productivity or Fruitfulness? 59
     + Never Too Small 60
A Positive Portrait: Deborah's Adventures, 4:1—5:31 61
     * Women in Leadership Positions 66
     * Reluctant Responses and the Plan of God 67
     + If Only 68
     * Liberation and Singing 73
     + Songs from the Liberated Soul 74
The Pattern Threatened:
**   Gideon and Abimelech, 6:1—10:5** 76
An Ambiguous Portrait (Scene 1): Gideon's Quests, 6:1—8:32 . 77
     * Desperate Situations 86
     * Requesting Signs 86
     + God's Presence During Difficult Moments 87
     + God's Patience During Weaker Moments 87
     * Divine Works and Human Downsizing 93
     * Compassionate Responses 94
     + Self-Emptying for Faithful Service 94
     * Seeking Revenge 102
     * Dealing with Public Affirmation 103
     + Taming Anger 104
An Ambiguous Portrait (Scene 2):
   Abimelech's Atrocities, 8:33—10:5 105
     * Speaking in Parables 117
     * Grasping for Power 118
     * Stable Administrators 119
     + Power in Serving 119
     + Balanced Leadership 120

The Pattern Ignored:
Jephthah and Samson, 10:6—16:31 121
A Negative Portrait: Jephthah's Undertakings, 10:6—12:7 . . . 122
  * Wearying God 126
  + A God in Pain 127
  * Making Vows 138
  * Human Sacrifices 139
  + The Longevity of Words 140
  + The Impact of Words 140
Negative Portraits:
  Ibzan's, Elon's, and Abdon's Operations, 12:8-15 141
A Negative Portrait: Samson's Stunts, 13:1—16:31 . . . 143
  * Barrenness 149
  + Life from Barren Places 150
  * Just One More Time! 159
  * Refreshment for the Weary 160
  + Dealing with Emotional Fallout 160
  * Self-Control 167
  * Misused Abilities 168
  + Misdirected Ambitions 169
  + Perverted Sexuality 169

3. Final Outcome:
The Depravity of Israel, 17:1—21:25 171
The Danites' Alternate Conquest, 17:1—18:31 174
  * Idolatry 179
  * False Security in Religious Rites 179
  + On Misreading God 180
  * Opportunism 188
  * Sin's Snowballing Effect 189
  + Curtailing Corruption 190
  + Exposing Corruption 190
The Death of Morality, 19:1—21:25 192
  * Domestic Violence 198
  + Abusing Our Own 199
  + Hospitality 200
  * Ratings on Wrongs 203
  + Sensitivity and Balance 204
  * God as Commander-in-Chief 209
  * In-House Fighting 209
  + Denominational Divisions 210
  * The Danger of Human Solutions 215

* The Influence of Leadership 216
+ God at the Center 217
+ The Crisis of Leadership 217

Outline of Judges 219
Essays 223
    Ancient Near Eastern Texts 223
    Archaeological Periods 224
    Asherah 225
    Ashtoreth 225
    Baal 226
    Breakdown of the Judges Cycle 226
    Canaanites 227
    Chronology 227
    Envelope Structure (Inclusio) 229
    Formation of the Book 229
    Hero Stories 231
    Historicity and Truth 232
    Holy Spirit in the Old Testament 232
    Localized Accounts 233
    Prohibition Against Images 234
    Role of the Judges 235
    Sea Peoples 236
    Septuagint 236
    Theophany 237
    Violence and War in Judges 237
Maps for Judges 240
    Tribal Allotments and Judges 240
    The Ancient Near East in the Time of the Judges 241
    Israel in the Time of the Judges 242
Bibliography 243
Selected Resources 251
Index of Ancient Sources 252
The Author 259

Series Foreword

The Believers Church Bible Commentary Series makes available a new tool for basic Bible study. It is published for all who seek more fully to understand the original message of Scripture and its meaning for today—Sunday school teachers, members of Bible study groups, students, pastors, and other seekers. The series is based on the conviction that God is still speaking to all who will listen, and that the Holy Spirit makes the Word a living and authoritative guide for all who want to know and do God's will.

The desire to help as wide a range of readers as possible has determined the approach of the writers. Since no blocks of biblical text are provided, readers may continue to use the translation with which they are most familiar. The writers of the series use the *New Revised Standard Version*, the *Revised Standard Version*, the *New International Version*, and the *New American Standard Bible* on a comparative basis. They indicate which text they follow most closely, as well as where they make their own translations. The writers have not worked alone, but in consultation with select counselors, the series' editors, and the Editorial Council.

Every volume illuminates the Scriptures; provides necessary theological, sociological, and ethical meanings; and, in general, makes "the rough places plain." Critical issues are not avoided, but neither are they moved into the foreground as debates among scholars. Each section offers explanatory notes, followed by focused articles, "The Text in Biblical Context" and "The Text in the Life of the Church."

The writers have done the basic work for each commentary, but not operating alone, since "no . . . scripture is a matter of one's own interpretation" (2 Pet. 1:20; cf. 1 Cor. 14:29). They have consulted with select counselors during the writing process, worked with the editors for the series, and received feedback from another biblical scholar. In addition, the Editorial Council, representing six believers church denominations, reads the manuscripts carefully, gives churchly responses, and makes suggestions for changes. The writer considers all this counsel and processes it into the manuscript, which the Editorial Council finally approves for publication. Thus these commentaries combine the individual writers' own good work and the church's voice. As such, they represent a hermeneutical community's efforts in interpreting the biblical text, as led by the Spirit.

The term *believers church* has often been used in the history of the church. Since the sixteenth century, it has frequently been applied to the Anabaptists and later the Mennonites, as well as to the Church of the Brethren and similar groups. As a descriptive term, it includes more than Mennonites and Brethren. *Believers church* now represents specific theological understandings, such as believers baptism, commitment to the Rule of Christ in Matthew 18:15-20 as crucial for church membership, belief in the power of love in all relationships, and willingness to follow Christ in the way of the cross. The writers chosen for the series stand in this tradition.

Believers church people have always been known for their emphasis on obedience to the simple meaning of Scripture. Because of this, they do not have a long history of deep historical-critical biblical scholarship. This series attempts to be faithful to the Scriptures while also taking archaeology and current biblical studies seriously. Doing this means that at many points the writers will not differ greatly from interpretations which can be found in many other good commentaries. Yet these writers share basic convictions about Christ, the church and its mission, God and history, human nature, the Christian life, and other doctrines. These presuppositions do shape a writer's interpretation of Scripture. Thus this series, like all other commentaries, stands within a specific historical church tradition.

Many in this stream of the church have expressed a need for help in Bible study. This is justification enough to produce the Believers Church Bible Commentary. Nevertheless, the Holy Spirit is not bound to any tradition. May this series be an instrument in breaking down walls between Christians in North America and around the world, bringing new joy in obedience through a fuller understanding of the Word.

—*The Editorial Council*

Author's Preface

The book of Judges might well have been written during our own life-time. Indeed, the situations described and the themes developed ring today with such force and clarity that the modern reader rarely escapes taking part in the story line. With a deepening sense of antic-ipation, we mount the stage. We share the joy and utter excitement of both divine blessing and human potential. Painfully, so too do we experience the increasing frustration of watching our own individual and communal dreams unravel. In many ways, the book of Judges is a book for the contemporary world.

In spite of its profound relevance and its equally enjoyable literary qualities, few people list Judges among their favorite books of the Bible. "There is too much bloodshed," one dismayed reader announces. "Nothing but a collection of stories," another cynic pro-claims. Such comments, of course, merely reflect the crying need on the part of many people to look anew at these old but living pages. Within the book of Judges, virtually limitless treasure lies waiting to be discovered. In at least a small way, I hope that this commentary will help bring some of these treasures to light.

As is typical of the Believers Church Bible Commentary series as a whole, the present volume does not include the complete text of the book of Judges. Biblical texts that do appear here are taken from the NRSV unless otherwise noted.

Throughout the writing of this commentary, recent books on Judges by Lawson Stone and Barry Webb proved to be especially helpful. While I refer to their work at various places in the following pages, I mention them here for the readers' careful consideration.

I am pleased to express my deep appreciation to the many people who provided valuable assistance in bringing this project through to completion. I am grateful to Elmer Martens, the editor, for his thorough and timely comments. I offer similar words of thanks to those who read the manuscript in its formative stages—Christa Ann Vogel, Eric Seibert, Christine Heidel, Louis Astuto, Professor Lawson Stone, and Professor William Jolliff. I am also indebted to Messiah College and the Ecumenical Institute for Theological Research (Tantur). The administration, faculty, and staff of Messiah College provided a wide range of supports, including funding, secretarial assistance, and simple encouragement. Ann Bonsell, secretary for the Biblical Studies, Religion, and Philosophy Department, was particularly helpful in preparing the final copy of the manuscript. The people at Tantur in Jerusalem not only made available to my family a wonderful setting in which to work, but also a warm and caring community in which to live.

Finally, I offer profound but inadequate words of appreciation to my wife, Debra, and my three children, Timothy, Jordan, and Julie. Not only did they travel halfway around the world with me, but they patiently supported me when my own resources ran frightfully low. In a real way, this is our project. Together, we give thanks to the Lord for its completion.

—*Terry L. Brensinger*
  Messiah College
  Grantham, Pennsylvania
  May 1999

Approaching Judges

In the book of Judges, we find such well-known characters as Deborah, Gideon, and Samson. Yet the book of Judges is far more than a random collection of seemingly isolated stories. What we actually find here are overarching themes, a developing plot, and a forceful message. The more carefully we explore the background and organization of Judges, the more persuasive the message becomes.

Judges Within the Old Testament

According to the layout of our English Bible, the book of Judges forms one part of what we typically call the "Historical Books." By implication, the books of Joshua through Esther deal primarily with the retelling of *history* (a less-than-popular word in many circles). Importantly, however, the Hebrew Bible actually places Judges among the "Former Prophets." The ancient scribes, therefore, did not so much see in Judges a mundane collection of dates and facts, but rather a religious and indeed prophetic interpretation of their past *[Historicity and Truth]*.

To develop this notion a bit further, eventually there came a time in the life of ancient Israel for a serious and reflective examination of the past. No doubt many such moments occurred from time to time. Yet a particularly comprehensive examination apparently took place during the years immediately preceding and following Jerusalem's destruction in 586 B.C. The closing period of reform and triumph under king Josiah (ca. 640-609) and the utter decay thereafter forced the community to evaluate prayerfully just what went wrong.

Out of this crisis grew not so much new traditions, but assessments of older and either forgotten or neglected ones. In the view of most

15

scholars, such assessments and reassessments of ancient stories and records eventually led to an overarching written presentation of Israel's experiences from the time of Joshua through the fall of Jerusalem. This presentation is included in a multivolume work encompassing the books of Joshua, Judges, 1–2 Samuel, and 1–2 Kings; it lays out a moving and interpretive account of Israel's journey with God *[Formation of the Book]*.

In this overall work, referred to by scholars as the "Deuteronomistic History," the book of Judges covers the period from the death of Joshua to the rise of the monarchy (ca. 1200-1020 B.C.) *[Chronology]*. Thus, Judges bridges the important gap between the conquest of the land of Palestine and the formation of what might actually be called the nation of Israel.

Theology of Judges

As the foundation for this theological interpretation of Israel's past, the writers of the Deuteronomistic History used the fundamental principles of what now is the book of Deuteronomy. "The book of the law" supporting Josiah's reforms (2 Kings 22–23) was likely an early form of Deuteronomy. The various stories, records, and traditions from the Israelites' earlier years were measured against the teachings of Deuteronomy. These teachings can be consolidated into a comprehensive formula: *obedience to God results in blessing, but disobedience results in disaster.*

On the basis of this formula, the Deuteronomistic History presents the unmistakable conclusion that Israel's eventual downfall and Jerusalem's destruction resulted, not from any weakness or unfaithfulness on God's part, but from the community's own sinfulness. Throughout the multivolume work, the writers have attempted to demonstrate persuasively the validity of their conclusion. They have sought, quite simply, to show that disaster stems from disobedience and that brighter prospects lie in God alone. As a result of such a sermonic and prophetic demonstration, it was hoped that subsequent generations might thankfully learn and live differently.

In specifically bridging the gap between the conquest and the monarchy, the book of Judges reiterates this basic Deuteronomistic formula and uses it to explain the dreadful turn of events following the time of Joshua. Israel's ever-increasing sinfulness repeatedly reduces otherwise promising situations into chaotic nightmares *[Breakdown of the Judges Cycle]*. Over and over, the Israelites turn out to be their own worst enemy by abandoning God in favor of other deities. Furthermore, only by altering their ways and truly returning to God can the Israelites hope for genuine and lasting change in the days ahead. As Judges clearly demonstrates, God must remain at the center for everything to hold together.

The World of the Judges

To better understand the period of the judges and with it the book of Judges, one must at least briefly consider both the ancient Near East in general and Palestine in particular during that time. However, insofar as the book of Judges provides a theological interpretation of the period in question, it is somewhat difficult to reconstruct a clear picture of the actual historical context. This is so not because the stories in Judges totally lack historical value, but because the writer has selected and arranged the materials with a religious and in fact sermonic purpose in mind [Historicity and Truth]. It is a blessing that various archaeological discoveries and extra biblical texts provide helpful information that further illuminates the ancient world during the twelfth and eleventh centuries B.C. [Chronology].

The Ancient Near East at the Time of the Judges

At the beginning of the Iron Age (1200-586 B.C.), the ancient Near East found itself in a power vacuum of sorts [Archaeological Periods]. The Assyrians to the northeast in Mesopotamia, strong throughout the waning years of the Late Bronze Age (1550-1200), now underwent a period of temporary decline. Likewise, the power and position of the Egyptians to the south had been greatly reduced [Map, p. 241]. In fact, the Amarna Letters vividly indicate that Egyptian influence in Palestine was rapidly crumbling already during the fourteenth century B.C. [Ancient Near Eastern Texts]. These two developments, together with the absolute destruction of the Hittite empire to the north, left the entire region without any dominant power. This absence of outside forces had significant effects on the ongoing affairs of Palestine itself.

Palestine at the Time of the Judges

Typically the primary "gameboard" upon which the surrounding nations played war, Palestine during the twelfth and eleventh centuries B.C. now experienced far-greater freedom and maneuverability. Such freedom, however, hardly resulted in peace and tranquillity. Rather than suffering at the hands of outside antagonists, the various inhabitants of Palestine frequently turned upon each other. Included among them were the Canaanites, Philistines, and Israelites [Canaanites; Sea Peoples].

While the fertile valleys and coastal plains were primarily occupied by the Canaanites and later the Philistines, far-less populated at the onset of the Iron Age were the mountains that run north to south through the center of the region. Importantly, however, archaeological surveys indicate a significant number of new, smaller settlements there and in other formerly less-populated areas beginning around 1200 B.C. (Mazar: 334). While no artifactual remains specifically link such a development with the arrival of the Israelites, the context closely mirrors the picture presented in Judges. Centered in the hill country and along the fringe areas, the Israelites faced the formidable task of extending their control into the already-occupied areas below [Maps].

In contrast to the city-state structure characteristic of the Canaanites, the Israelites displayed a more rural, tribal arrangement. The Old Testament, in fact, refers to three basic social units operating among the Israelites prior to the monarchy: the extended family, the clan, and the tribe (Mayes: 46-51). Rather than centering power in a ruling class, varying degrees of authority rested within these units. Apparently nothing, however, superseded tribal authority and thereby connected the various tribes. Like the Canaanites, no all-embracing governmental structure was in place.

At this point, many contemporary readers of Judges need to readjust their thinking. Too often, people envision the Israelites during this period as a large, cohesive unit. Accompanying this misconception are images of refined organization, national leaders, and readily available lines of communication. It may be true that previous figures like Moses and Joshua provided a unifying "glue" of sorts for earlier generations, but no such individuals rose to prominence at the time of the judges. Rather, what we find are more localized leaders and a somewhat disjointed collection of tribes, apparently held together by nothing more than a common understanding of their identity [Localized Accounts]. Not until the rise of the monarchy in the face of increasing external pressures does this situation change significantly.

For the Israelites during this period, life was difficult and undoubtedly mundane. People generally clustered in small villages, temporarily moving when necessary to small dwellings on their farmland. Daily responsibilities depended upon the season, but common activities included sowing, pruning, harvesting, threshing, and grazing. The average diet consisted of in-season produce with only an occasional serving of meat. Communication of any kind was laboriously slow, and people rarely saw anyone outside of their own tribe. Such a life was often trying and overridden with routine.

Occasional celebratory festivals provided much-needed relief throughout the year. But more frequently, the ordinary rhythm of a difficult life was eased by neighborly get-togethers and the simple retelling of stories. For such gatherings, characters like Ehud, Gideon, and Samson vividly came to life. Such stories were refreshing for both heart and soul.

Surveying the Book of Judges

The book of Judges divides rather cleanly into three primary units. Precisely how these units relate to each other, however, has raised an endless number of questions among students and scholars alike (Buber; Brettler; Exum, 1990; Stone: 459-477). Before turning to an examination of the book's finer parts, therefore, an overview of the entire landscape may prove helpful.

Judges 1:1—3:6

The opening unit of Judges, discussed in part 1 of the commentary, consists of two introductions which highlight the cause of Israel's problems depicted later in the book. The first of these introductions, 1:1—2:5, presents a glimpse of Israel's attempts to finalize the conquest of the land after the death of Joshua. According to this presentation, the Israelites fared relatively well in the southern regions, but showed increasingly less success as they moved further north. As a result of their ultimate failure, the Israelites found themselves in the unenviable and unexpected position of living among the Canaanites on an ongoing basis. Such a situation did not result from divine indifference or military weakness, however, but from human disobedience.

Given the continuing presence of Canaanites in the land, the second introduction, 2:6—3:6, reflectively examines the anticipated consequences. In this way, 2:6—3:6 is in fact a summary statement of all that *will* transpire throughout the judges' period. These remaining Canaanites will serve to test the religious commitments of the Israelites, and the expected outcome looks bleak. Indeed, past disobedience now gives way to a seemingly unbreakable habit of unfaithfulness involving each of the following steps:

1. The Israelites do evil in the eyes of the Lord.
2. The Lord summons various foreign oppressors.
3. The Israelites cry out for assistance.
4. The Lord raises up a deliverer.
5. The oppressor is defeated.
6. The land has rest.

This sequence of events, so neatly condensed here, will be repeated with alarming regularity throughout the book.

Judges 3:7—16:31

Following the introductory materials, the next major unit, examined in part 2 of the commentary, demonstrates Israel's resulting struggles during the period of the judges. In so doing, a thematic arrangement of several otherwise independent hero stories appears *[Hero Stories]*. These stories, though different in various ways, are carefully linked together through the use of standard introductory and concluding statements. As a result of this linkage and the positioning of the stories, one fundamentally important conclusion emerges: Israel's condition grew increasingly worse as the period progressed.

To present persuasively such a conclusion, the writer repeatedly makes careful use of the sequence of events summarized in 2:6—3:6. In the account of Othniel, the initial judge, every step in the sequence is unmistakably present. Thus, Othniel fulfills his calling with noteworthy efficiency. In subsequent episodes, however, erosion sets in and the sequence gradually breaks down. Along the way, the Israelites commit even greater atrocities; the calling of deliverers either slows down or draws mixed responses; and the Lord himself grows weary and even distant. By the time 3:7—16:31 comes to an end, the sequence is practically unrecognizable *[Breakdown of the Judges Cycle]*. Clearly, things have gone from good to bad to worse.

Judges 17:1—21:25

In a manner parallel to the opening unit of Judges, 17:1—21:25 consists of two distinct sections. Each of these sections, discussed in part 3 of the commentary, recounts various stories intended to relieve any lingering doubts concerning the legitimacy of the writer's conclusions. At the close of the previous unit, the people of Israel appeared to be pitifully asleep in their own habitual waywardness. In that context, two questions continue to beg for answers. First, has the end of the road finally been reached, or can the crisis still worsen? Second, how might this dreadful tendency to sin ultimately be broken? Both of these questions receive attention in this closing unit of the book.

Concerning the first question, 17:1—21:25 wastes no time in demonstrating that Israel's condition did indeed worsen by the end of the period. Structurally, no signs of the sequence of events outlined in 2:6—3:6 remain. Furthermore, the tribal confederation itself reacts with sheer horror and disbelief at the news of the concubine's gruesome murder (19:30). Finally, the recurring expression *all the people did what was right in their own eyes* underscores the absolute anarchy characterizing the times.

In short, this closing unit serves as the climax of the book, for it depicts the frightening end of a long, downward spiral.

With respect to the second question about breaking the dreadful tendency to sin, the writer unashamedly suggests that the corrective for Israel's woes is the institution of kingship (a conclusion that later events will undermine). In his mind, kings would succeed where judges had failed. Repeatedly we readers are reminded that *in those days there was no king in Israel* (18:1; 19:1; 21:25). The book actually closes with this reminder. As a result, Judges concludes with a forward glimpse to the Davidic monarchy, just as it began with a backward glance at the charismatic leadership provided by Joshua.

Selected Issues in Judges

In recounting Israel's declining religious journey from the time of Joshua to the rise of the monarchy, the book of Judges raises various key issues that continue to confront contemporary readers. Of these issues, two seem to draw the most attention.

Violence

The stories in Judges frequently depict what appears to be excessive violence in all levels of Israelite life. There are the familiar war narratives that describe Israel's battles with many of the surrounding nations. In at least one of these descriptions, even grotesque violence is not simply restated but actually celebrated (5:24-31). Still other accounts portray "in-house" conflicts: Israelites wage war against and virtually exterminate fellow Israelites (12:1-6; 20:1-48). Finally, selected episodes portray similar violence within domestic contexts, violence that culminates in the actual dismembering of an unnamed woman (9:1-6; 11:34-40; 19:22-30). The book of Judges, therefore, often depicts a society in violent conflict with itself and with others.

God in Politics

In Judges, God's involvement in what we today call "politics" is apparent from start to finish. The God of Israel plays a direct role in the affairs of the nations, summoning one foreign leader after another to deal with his disobedient people. Further, this same God actively participates within Israel's own political arena. He selects and ultimately empowers certain leaders, people whose political and military exploits will make them heroes among the population at large. Throughout Judges, God is not simply establishing an alternative community by totally separating his people from the rest of the world. On the contrary, both God and the Israelites often work through the political and social structures of the day to bring about God's purposes.

For many readers, past and present, such violence and political involvement raise varying responses. Some people, for example, inappropriately use biblical texts like these in Judges simply to justify various contemporary acts of violence, warfare, and political activity. For them, little if any chronological and cultural distance exists between ancient Israel and the modern world. Others, including many in the believers church tradition, struggle with the same texts and somewhat apologetically conclude that they and other related Old Testament passages lack the authority and importance now assigned to the "peacemaking" and "separation of church and state" passages of the New Testament. For these people, a seemingly uncrossable chasm lies between the Old Testament past and the New Testament present.

Still others, including David Gill, attempt to interpret such texts within their historical and cultural contexts and to demonstrate how they ultimately fit into the overall flow of biblical teaching:

> The Bible reveals a historical progression in its word on violence as on other matters. The fact that violence is not a part of God's creation and not a part of the New Jerusalem is of considerable importance. (877)

In this third approach, taken in this commentary, these texts in Judges are neither the final word for today nor a dusty relic from the distant past. Instead, they are an act in an unfolding drama, a scene in a developing and more comprehensive picture that encompasses the whole of the Bible (TBC and TLC after 19:1-28) *[Violence and War in Judges]*.

Part 1

Principal Cause: The Disobedience of Israel

Judges 1:1—3:6

OVERVIEW

Two distinct introductions comprise the opening unit of Judges. The first of these, 1:1—2:5, swiftly surveys the increasing failure of the various tribes of Israel to dislodge the Canaanites. While religious overtones are clearly and expectedly attached to the events, particularly in 2:1-5, the primary emphasis here rests upon Israel's worsening political and military involvements. In this way, 1:1—2:5 provides the crucial context for understanding the ongoing presence of Canaanites in the land—Israel has abandoned the conquest.

By way of contrast, attention shifts in 2:6—3:6 to a more reflective theological consideration of Israel's failure itself. This second introduction probes the deeper religious implications of the unsuccessful conquest, and in so doing summarizes in advance a sequence of events that will be repeatedly replayed throughout part 2 of the book. Fundamentally, Israel has forsaken the covenant.

These differences in basic orientation, however, must not conceal the noticeable symmetry between the two introductions. Clearly, the writer has arranged the material in parallel sections. Each introduction follows the same essential pattern, beginning with faithful compliance, moving through increasing disobedience, and concluding with divine condemnation (Stone: 460-464). This is shown in the outline charted on the next page.

OUTLINE

Joshua's Leadership Ends, 1:1; 2:6

A Political Introduction	*A Theological Introduction*
Judah's Accomplishments, 1:1-21	The Former Generation's Faithfulness, 2:6-9
The Northern Tribes' Failures, 1:22-36	A New Generation's Unfaithfulness, 2:10-19
The Messenger's Rebuke, 2:1-5	The Lord's Indictment, 2:20—3:6

Judges 1:1—2:5

The Conquest Abandoned: A "Political" Introduction

PREVIEW

A strong start is important, but completing a task is the key. Judges 1:1—2:5 depicts a triumphant beginning, but a beginning that soon gives way to tragedy. In briefly recounting the events of the conquest following the death of Joshua, the author explains the continuing presence of Canaanites in the land. Following a strong start, Israel's various tribes lost momentum and, in essence, abandoned the conquest.

The material here is arranged geographically, beginning with the southern tribe of Judah and moving progressively northward (O'Connell: 10-19). In the process, no less than four key elements emerge that set the stage for the narratives that follow:

1. The conquest under Joshua has not been brought to completion, and considerably more work remains to be done after his death (1:1; Josh 13:1).

2. The Israelites have ultimately failed in driving out various Canaanite groups (1:21, 27, 29-36). After considerable success in the south, such failure becomes increasingly characteristic of the various tribes as the account moves northward.

3. This failure was not so much a military shortcoming as it was

disobedience to God (2:2).

4. The outcome of this failure will be an ongoing political and theological struggle between the Israelites and the Canaanites (2:3).

OUTLINE

Joshua's Death, 1:1a

Judah's Accomplishments, 1:1b-21
1:1b-3	Simeon Assists Judah
1:4-7	Judah Captures Adoni-Bezek
1:8	Judah Conquers Jerusalem
1:9-18	Judah Overtakes Many Foes
1:19-21	Judah and Benjamin Suffer Setbacks

The Northern Tribes' Failures, 1:22-36
1:22-26	Joseph Overtakes Bethel
1:27-36	The Remaining Tribes Experience Defeat

The Messenger's Rebuke, 2:1-5

EXPLANATORY NOTES

Joshua's Death 1:1a

The opening line of the book of Judges immediately sets the material within its intended context. *After the death of Joshua* seeks to separate what follows from all that was associated with the life of Joshua. Similar major transitional phrases occur in Joshua 1:1 and 2 Samuel 1:1, suggesting that the flow of Israel's history from Moses to the Davidic kingdom is envisioned in four general periods:

1. The era of Moses (through Josh. 1:1)
2. The era of Joshua (through Judg. 1:1)
3. The era of Judges and Saul (through 2 Sam. 1:1), in which Saul serves as a bridge to the Davidic kingdom
4. The era of the Davidic monarchy (through 2 Kings 25)

As such, the period of the Judges is included within a larger block of material that distinctly follows the conquest and settlement of the land under Joshua (rather than being a mere continuation of it) and also leads to the Davidic kingdom.

Assuming that the context of Judges follows Joshua's death, however, two problems emerge. For one thing, Joshua is still alive in Judges 2:6 (see notes on 2:6-9). For another, comparisons with the book of Joshua indicate that a number of the events described in

Judges 1 actually occurred "before" the death of Joshua. Without referring to implicit connections, note the following parallels:

1. Judges 1:10, 20; and Joshua 14:13-15; 15:13-14
2. Judges 1:11-15; and Joshua 15:15-19
3. Judges 1:27-28; and Joshua 17:11-13
4. Judges 1:29; and Joshua 16:10

Such apparent chronological discrepancies have led various commentators to conclude that Judges 1:1a was merely attached as an introductory statement for the entire book (Moore: 5; Cundall: 51; Soggin: 20). Yet the overall shape of the book in general and the opening chapters in particular suggest greater intentionality than that (Stone: 226-233; Webb: 82-83). By reusing familiar materials from the book of Joshua, the writer is able to formulate here an important contrast between the periods preceding and following Joshua's death.

The all-embracing success of Israel during the conquest under Joshua is continued by the tribe of Judah after his death, as the parallel success stories illustrate (1:10, 11-15, 20). Likewise, the occasional "blemishes" or shortcomings under Joshua are now characteristic of the central and northern tribes after his death, as the parallel stories of failure illustrate (1:27-28, 29). The point, in other words, is that while Judah has maintained the Israelite success story typical of the book of Joshua, the other tribes have consistently failed (Mullen: 53-54). As a result, a significant qualitative difference is emphasized between these two major periods. The general success before the death of Joshua has given way to general failure after his death.

Understanding this progression enables one to grasp the increasingly dismal picture portrayed in the rest of the book of Judges. As has been aptly put elsewhere, the question of the book of Joshua positively concerns the magnitude of the land that Israel would occupy. Now, however, the question of Judges negatively centers on why Israel has not been able to drive out the Canaanites (Polzin: 148).

Judah's Accomplishments 1:1b-21

Following the reference to Joshua's death, a reference which involves visions of the glorious conquest under his leadership, attention shifts to the subsequent adventures of individual tribes and their efforts to subjugate the land. First in the account are the southern tribes, which are generally swallowed up under the heading of "Judah," the dominant tribe. Here, the success of Joshua's era is essentially sustained.

1:1b-3 Simeon Assists Judah

In this new period following Joshua's death, a collective Israel appropriately requests the guidance of the Lord concerning their next move. Precisely how they did so and the ceremony involved go unspecified. To communally inquire (*ša'al*) of the Lord, however, typically involves seeking an oracle through various means, including the sacred lots Urim and Thummim (Num. 27:21; 1 Sam. 14:41-42). Most importantly, Israel is at this point unified in their request and offensive in their thinking: *Who shall go up first for us against the Canaanites, to fight against them? [Canaanites]*. Essentially the same question appears elsewhere in the book of Judges (20:18), but under entirely different circumstances!

The Lord's response to the opening request is clear and immediate. Judah, the southernmost tribe, is to assume the leadership position. Additionally, mention is made of the fact that for all intents and purposes, the battle is already over: God has secured the land for his people. By special request, however, assistance comes from the Simeonites, blood-brothers of the tribe of Judah (Gen. 29:31-35). This relationship, in addition to the fact that Simeon's inheritance lies within the territory allotted to Judah (Josh. 19:1), clarifies such an allegiance.

1:4-7 Judah Captures Adoni-Bezek

An initial victory for Judah occurs at Bezek, a site of uncertain location. While 1 Samuel 11:8 also refers to a Bezek, the geographical context there is apparently too far north to be of help here. Another alternative, not without problems of its own, is Tell Bezqa', near Gezer. At this point, verification lies beyond reach.

At Bezek, Judah defeats the Canaanites and the Perizzites, the latter typically being understood as an ethnic group. However, the term *perazot* also occurs in the Old Testament with reference to unwalled villages (Esther 9:19; Ezek. 38:11; Zech. 2:8). Insofar as the Canaanites have generally inhabited the major cities of Palestine, Boling raises the intriguing possibility that this name-pair may be an ancient antecedent of the modern "city slickers and country bumpkins" (Boling: 54). Given the manner in which opponents or oppressors are described in the book of Judges, such an all-encompassing expression, elevating the enemy and thereby magnifying the victory, would be stylistically consistent.

The treatment of Adoni-Bezek, apparently the ruler or lord (*adoni*) of Bezek, serves both to humiliate and incapacitate him. Beyond that, however, thumbs and big toes had priestly significance in both the Old Testament (Exod. 29:20; Lev. 8:23) and the texts from Ugarit (Gray: 236). Insofar as Canaanite kings doubled as priests, Adoni-Bezek is

here desecrated and removed from his priestly position. As he himself
had done to countless others, so too is the principle of the *lex talionis* ("eye for eye" law of retaliation) now applied to him (cf. Exod.
21:22-25; 1 Sam. 15:32-33; Matt. 5:38-48). All that remains is for
him to retreat and die in Jerusalem, the city next in line for the attackers from Judah.

1:8 Judah Conquers Jerusalem

In spite of the straight formal account, other references to the
Israelite conquest of the important city of Jerusalem indicate a bit
more complexity. Both Joshua 15:63 and Judges 1:21 suggest that
first Judah and then Benjamin have been unable to dislodge the
Jebusites who lived there. Apparently at some point between these
two attempts, Judah attacks and takes the city (Judg. 1:8). Yet
2 Samuel 5:6-10 informs us that it was not ultimately until David's
time that Jerusalem came under Israelite control.

Two possible solutions emerge without totally discrediting the historical value of these texts. First, after an initial failure (Josh. 15:63),
Judah launches a later and more-successful campaign (Judg. 1:8).
Then, after Judah moves on without actually occupying the city,
Benjamin attempts unsuccessfully to remove the Jebusite population
remaining there (Judg. 1:21). That task was only completed much
later during David's reign (2 Sam. 5:6-10). Second, some suggest that
Jerusalem encompassed both the fortified eastern city as well as the
unfortified western hill (Hubbard: 136-137). In this case, while Judah
successfully destroys the western hill (Judg. 1:8), no one prior to David
was able to capture the fortified portion of the city (Josh. 15:63; Judg.
1:21).

1:9-18 Judah Overtakes Many Foes

From Jerusalem, Judah's campaigns branch out throughout the
south. The hill country (between Jerusalem and Hebron), the Negev
(semiarid area south of Hebron), and the Shephelah or western
foothills (between the seacoast and the hills)—these constitute the
three major regions within Judah's territorial allotment *[Map, p. 240]*.
The Judahites, in other words, faithfully launch attacks in all areas of
their domain. That the writer specifies Hebron is significant because
of its later role as David's first capital (2 Sam. 5:5). In this way, both
Jerusalem and Hebron are highlighted among Judah's war trophies.
To capture Hebron, the people of Judah needed to defeat the three
sons of Anak (1:10; cf. 1:20; Josh. 15:14); this only adds to the
accomplishment. The Anakites, in the minds of the Israelites, were

renowned for both their size and strength (Deut. 9:2).

From Hebron, the battle moves on to Debir, most likely the important *Tell Beit-Mirsim*, located some 10 miles southwest of Hebron. In this context, readers find the story of Caleb and Othniel, also appearing with slight variation in Joshua 15:13-19. Whether Othniel is Caleb's younger brother or nephew is a complex question (Malamat, 1968:163-173). Of greater importance is the manner in which Othniel follows in the footsteps of the elderly Caleb. Caleb, associated with Joshua and the faithfulness of that generation (Num. 14:6; Josh. 15:13), passes on to Othniel the mantle, land, and water, not to mention his daughter Acsah! Here is a particular example of the smooth and harmonious inner workings of Judah's campaign (Hamlin: 31-33).

Before concluding this stylized recount of Judah's efforts, a brief digression informs us of Kenites entering the land and residing in the Negev region (1:16). While the Kenites are occasionally associated in some uncertain way with the Amalekites, Israel's archenemies (Exod. 17:16; 1 Sam. 15:4-6), their own relationship with Israel is generally more cordial. In fact, a leading Kenite assisted Moses along the way to Canaan, receiving in return a promise of land (Num. 10:29-32; on the relationships between Reuel, Jethro, and Hobab, see Soggin: 22-23). As such, the Kenites' inclusion here further enhances Judah's position by characterizing the Judahites as keepers of such a promise.

Judah's efforts come to a close with a successful attack on the Canaanites of Zephath, probably situated near Arad, and alleged victories over the Philistine cities of Gaza, Ashkelon, and Ekron (see notes on 1:19-20). The name change of verse 17 is a clear play on words. "Hormah" is related to the Hebrew *herem* ("to devote to the ban" or "to dedicate to destruction"), a term used elsewhere in the Old Testament in connection with the total annihilation of God's enemies (notes on 20:48; 21:11; cf. Josh. 6:17; 7:12; 22:20; 1 Kings 20:42). Zephath's name change, in other words, brings to a climax the process by which Judah not only defeated the Canaanites, but in fact freed the land of their polluting effects. What began with the desecrating of a particular Canaanite king (1:4-7), now ends with the total destruction of the Canaanite community.

1:19-21 Judah and Benjamin Suffer Setbacks

As a way of verifying what 1:2 anticipated, God has indeed been with Judah throughout these various campaigns. His presence enables them to continue the successful precedent established by Joshua. In spite of these testimonies of victory, however, Judah's efforts are not without blemish. Apparently less successful are attacks on the coastal plain, an admission that is somewhat difficult to reconcile with verse 18. Gaza, Ashkelon, and Ekron were three major Philistine cities situated precisely on the coastal plain [Map, p. 242]. Perhaps we are again to understand this as a reference to some sort of military victory without an accompanying displacement of the population. It must be noted, however, that the LXX (Septuagint) reads *Judah did not take* . . . in verse 18, an ancient textual variant that fits nicely with the picture presented in verse 19 [Septuagint].

According to verse 19, Judah is unsuccessful in the plains because the people living there are equipped with iron chariots that provide a huge advantage on relatively level terrain. Why such chariots pose difficulties for God, however, remains a mystery; tension exists here between divine ability and human inability. This flaw in Judah's otherwise praiseworthy record, along with the failure of the Benjaminites at Jerusalem, serves to lead us into the more comprehensive failures ahead.

The Northern Tribes' Failures 1:22-36

With the generally glowing testimony of Judah's exploits, a noticeable shift begins to occur as the account moves further north. What begins on a relatively positive note becomes increasingly more discouraging.

1:22-26 Joseph Overtakes Bethel

Before tracing the many failures of the northern tribes, the writer first recounts an isolated northern victory. In this way, Judah's lone failure (1:19b, 21) is balanced by the northern tribes' lone success. According to Joshua 18:22, Bethel had been assigned to Benjamin, not to the house of Joseph (Ephraim and Manasseh). Perhaps Benjamin later participated in resettling the area, but at this point had not yet joined in this more northern effort (Soggin: 29).

Bethel has a long history of importance in the Old Testament, appearing already in the narratives of Abraham (Gen. 12:8). By the time of Joshua, it had become a major Canaanite city-state and important cult center. Still later, Bethel served as one of Jeroboam's shrines (1 Kings 12:28-30), a shrine mentioned regularly in prophetic critiques of Israel's idolatrous ways (e.g., Amos 4:4). Finally, during Josiah's reforms toward the end of the seventh century, Bethel's sanctuary was ultimately destroyed (2 Kings 23:15). Even its name ("house of God"; Gen. 28:19), incorporating the general term 'el rather than the distinctively Israelite name Yahweh, underlines the city's religious significance in the region.

In their victory over Bethel, the house of Joseph benefited from the services of an unnamed "outsider" in much the same way that Joshua's troops benefited from Rahab at Jericho (Josh. 2:1-21; 6:22-25). In return for his services, this man was promised preferential treatment for both himself and his entire family. Following the battle, he fled to the land of the Hittites, no doubt his ancestral home. While the Hittites are generally associated with the area of Anatolia, the designation "land of the Hittites" also referred at times to the general region of Syria *[Map, p. 241]*. We are therefore left with an admittedly vague geographical picture. The city of Luz offers no assistance; its location remains totally unknown.

1:27-36 The Remaining Tribes Experience Defeat

The survey of campaigns comes to a close with a swift narration of the various northern tribes' failures to dislodge those living in seventeen specific city-states. Characteristic of the section is the statement, appearing seven times, that a tribe *did not drive out the inhabitants of . . .* Careful consideration of the passage, however, reveals more than a mere catalogue of squandered opportunities. Rather, what emerges is a description of *ever-worsening events*.

The situation depicted begins with the failure of Manasseh and Ephraim in the central region to gain control over six city-states, all of which lay along and therefore were a part of the major trade routes of the day. Zebulun, Asher, and Naphtali to the north fail similarly. Although at times the Israelites are able to impose forced labor upon the Canaanites, they nevertheless coinhabit the area. While the account repeatedly refers to a failure to "drive out," emphasis seems also to fall on acts of compromise. Even the imposition of forced labor implies an agreement of sorts. Rather than driving them out, the Israelites "worked things out" with the Canaanites.

The final tribe referred to is Dan, a southern tribe that eventually moved to the northernmost position (18:1-31). In addition to not displacing the Canaanites within their territory, the Danites were themselves confined to the hill country. Whereas the earlier tribes allowed the Canaanites to remain, here the Canaanites allow the Danites to remain! Rather than seeking the Lord for direction (1:1), the Danites seek the Canaanites for permission.

In a particularly insightful analysis of this section, Barry Webb traces this progression and ties it in with 1:22-26 (Webb: 99):

A long and arduous road led from the victory by the house of Joseph at Bethel, to the failure of the Danites. What began with success ended with bitter defeat.

Rather graphically, then, Judges 1:1-36 portrays a continually deteriorating situation with respect to Israel's efforts to drive the Canaanites from the land. The success prior to Joshua's death is essentially sustained afterward by the southern tribes ("Judah"), but Judah's single setback then gives way to the constantly deteriorating failures so characteristic of the northern tribes. By the end of the process, it becomes clear, on one level at least, why Canaanites remain in the land rather than driving them out, the Israelites "worked things out."

In terms of the land itself, it appears that Israel has failed to occupy three major geographical areas: the southern coastal plain (1:19), the central coastal plain (1:27, 31), and the valley of Jezreel (1:27, 33) *[Map, p. 242]*. Apart from isolated defeats, the Israelites' efforts are far more effective in the southern and central hill regions. Israel, then, is forced to inhabit the less desirable and less productive mountainous areas, leaving the Canaanites to dwell in the more fertile valleys and plains.

The Messenger's Rebuke 2:1-5

With this rather dismal showing, the tribes of Israel once again gather in some collective sense. However, the mood is understandably different from that in 1:1. Rather than a positive inquiry as to the plan of attack, what occurs is a major confrontation with God; others will follow (6:7-10; 10:10-16)! In this case, the "angel of the Lord," a divine representative of God seen frequently prior to the later flourishing of prophets, confronts the community. Usually, the angel of the Lord has brought either good news or instructions for a task (Gen. 16:7-12; 19:12-13; Num. 22:21-35; 1 Kings 13:18; 2 Kings 1:3-4).

Neither appears here. Instead, we find a stern rebuke that resembles a prophecy of disaster.

Gilgal, situated somewhere in the vicinity of Jericho and the Jordan, has served as the sanctuary and home base for Israel during the conquest under Joshua (Josh. 4:19-20; 5:10; 9:6; 10:6-9, 15, 43; 14:6). The location of Bokim, the name of which captures the Israelites' reaction to the rebuke ("weeping"), is unknown, though the LXX links it with the sanctuary at Bethel *[Septuagint]*. Since the people sacrifice to the Lord (2:5), likely a shrine is present.

Fundamental to the rebuke is the emphasis on the Lord's prior act of deliverance and his covenantal faithfulness. Given his unwavering commitment to Israel, one expects a response of gratitude and obedience. Such a desired combination of God's faithfulness and Israel's obedience would have resulted in the Canaanites' departure from the land *[Canaanites]*. Instead, what remains is a disastrous situation characterized by ongoing tension and conflict.

Importantly, however, both the acts of compromise with the Canaanites as well as the resulting consequences are couched in theological language. That is, Israel's failure is not primarily the result of military or political incompetence, but of sin. Similarly, the ongoing struggle anticipated in the future is problematic, not because of loss of property or political unrest, but because of religious syncretism. Like the sirens wooing Odysseus to the rocks, the gods of Canaan will lure Israel into faulty beliefs and practices.

In the final analysis, the transition from the success of Joshua to the turmoil of Judges can be attributed to one thing: faithlessness. The Israelites have simply grown weary of serving God in the midst of formidable opposition, and they defected to the other side. Faithlessness of this magnitude cannot easily be swept away, even with weeping and sacrifices. Subsequent stories in the book of Judges indicate only too well that outward activities need not involve a genuine change of heart.

THE TEXT IN BIBLICAL CONTEXT

A Unified Community

As the narrative begins, the people of Israel demonstrate commonality of mind and singularity of purpose. They have a divinely inspired task to complete, and they begin their work as an organized team. Equally unified efforts appear elsewhere, as when the wandering Israelites collectively construct the tabernacle and their later descendants rebuild Jerusalem's walls (Exod. 35:4-29; Neh. 4:6). Such harmony, to be sure, is in keeping with God's preferred method of operation. The psalmist savors it, Jesus prays for it, and Paul continually encourages it (Ps. 133:1; John 17:21; Rom. 15:5; 2 Cor. 13:11; Eph. 4:3; Phil. 2:2). Unity, after all, is both more pleasant and more effective than conflict and division ("In-House Fighting," TBC after 20:48; "Denominational Divisions," TLC after 20:48).

Incomplete Obedience

At this stage of the conquest, the various tribes demonstrate partial or incomplete obedience. They begin with notable success, but their success soon fades into escalating failure. Rather than driving out all the Canaanites, as they had been commanded, Israel stops halfway.

Incomplete obedience like this reminds the reader of other episodes in which biblical characters settled for less than what God expected. King Saul, instructed to destroy totally the Amalekites and all of their possessions, chose instead to spare the best for himself and his army (1 Sam. 15). Various Judahite kings, ones who customarily obeyed the Lord, consistently left selected tasks undone. Joash, Amaziah, Azariah, and Jotham, for example, failed to remove the high places where unacceptable sacrifices were offered (2 Kings 12:3; 14:4; 15:4, 35). In Amaziah's case, the Chronicler specifically informs us that "he did what was right in the sight of the Lord, yet not with a true heart" (2 Chron. 25:2). Finally, Jesus himself accused certain Pharisees and teachers of partial obedience—claiming to love God while at the same time remaining far from him (Mark 7:6-7).

Although demonstrated in Scripture, incomplete obedience is never the envisioned goal. Israel, both collectively and as individual members, was repeatedly instructed to observe all of God's laws and commands (Exod. 19:5; Deut. 5:1; 6:25; Josh. 1:7). In this light, Amaziah and his omissions stand in stark contrast to Josiah, who "did what was right in the sight of the Lord, and walked in the ways of his ancestor David; he did not turn aside to the right or to the left" (2 Chron. 34:2).

Similarly, the NT solicits unwavering commitment and disciplined perseverance. Jesus informs his disciples of the need to stand firm to the end (Matt. 10:22), and Paul likens the Christian life to a race in which finishing victoriously supersedes all else (1 Cor. 9:24-27). In the case of Jesus' own ministry, complete obedience, even under the most difficult of circumstances, enabled him to say, "It is finished" (John 19:30). For the would-be conquerors from Israel, however, incomplete obedience and abandoning the conquest bring divine condemnation.

THE TEXT IN THE LIFE OF THE CHURCH
On Not Stopping Halfway

Perplexing and troublesome situations do not bypass the people of God. Challenges present themselves, at times in ways that stretch all of us to the limit. Opportunities to compromise or simply to lose heart arise, and in the worst moments the logical thing to do is give up and accept defeat.

In such situations, Christians today are, like Israel of long ago, involved in a conquest of sorts. To be sure, the enemy is no longer the Canaanites, but an even more formidable host of forces, temptations, and habits. Yet the call of Christ, as liberating as it is, echoes the Old Testament in demanding total commitment and complete obedience. God's grace and mercy, Paul writes, must not be taken as an invitation to engage in partial or incomplete obedience (Rom. 6:15).

Complete obedience, so prevalent a theme in Scripture, has been the goal of many believers throughout the centuries. The pages of history repeatedly portray members of God's community who refused to stop halfway. Martin Luther declared: "Hear and obey! This is the greatest service of God" (Luther, 1967:84). In the Anabaptist tradition, simple but complete obedience has typically been stressed as a fundamental aspect of the Christian life. As Hans Denk expressed it in the sixteenth century, "No one may truly know Christ without following him in life." To do so precludes abandoning the faith in the face of adverse circumstances. Genuinely following Christ prohibits stopping halfway.

Michael Sattler demonstrates as well as anyone this fundamental conviction lived out under even the worst of circumstances. As a result of his Christian witness, Sattler endured one weighty accusation after another. Indeed, he and those with him were threatened with virtually every means of death known at the time: the gallows, fire, the sword, and drowning. Undaunted, Sattler sent a letter to his followers in which he wrote:

> I surrendered myself entirely to the Lord's will, and prepared myself, together with all my brethren and my wife, to die for [Christ's] testimony's sake. (Van Braght: 347)

Soon thereafter, Sattler's execution proved that he meant it. Even at the cost of own life, Sattler refused to stop halfway.

The situation depicted in Judges 1:1—2:5, however, goes well beyond a simple description of isolated individuals, emphasizing instead the increasing disobedience of the community as a whole.

Likewise, the church is summoned to make a collective stand for God within the world, regardless of the consequences. In the face of stern opposition, the early church faithfully served the advance of God's kingdom in all directions. One sometimes wonders today if such corporate momentum has too often been lost.

What became of the church during Hitler's rise to power (see TLC after 2:6—3:6)? Where was the combined energy of the church when apartheid infested South Africa? In the West, has the community of faith essentially "worked things out" with North American culture rather than obeying the sometimes confrontative call of Christ? Collectively, the church must embrace a position that, like Sattler, refuses to stop halfway. Today, as in the past, nothing less than complete obedience will do.

Judges 2:6—3:6

The Covenant Forsaken: A "Theological" Introduction

PREVIEW

Given the swift survey of events in chapter 1 as well as the anticipation of trouble in 2:1-5, now 2:6—3:6 provides a capsulized description of the problems awaiting Israel. Thus 1:1—2:5 seeks to demonstrate the "why" of the problem (Israelite failure to drive out the Canaanites); next 2:6—3:6 summarizes and explains the ongoing and ever-worsening struggle that ensues. In so doing, the general understanding of history emerges that is so foundational to the book of Deuteronomy (cf. Deut. 28) and so characteristic of the books of Joshua—2 Kings (see "Theology of Judges," p. 16, above).

According to this view, the affairs of God and people are integrally connected; nothing is left either to chance or to secondary causes. More precisely, obedience to God and his covenant yields favor and blessing, while disobedience yields judgment and punishment. On this basis, Israel's difficulties during the period of the judges stem directly from their own unfaithfulness to the Lord and his covenant. Israel alone is to blame for each crisis.

In spite of the differences in perspective between 1:1—2:5 and 2:6—3:6, it is important to note once again the clear stylistic parallelism between the two introductions. Both follow the same basic pat-

tern, beginning with faithfulness and success and concluding with disobedience, failure, and condemnation (see p. 24).

OUTLINE

A Generation's Faithfulness, 2:6-9

A New Generation's Unfaithfulness, 2:10-19

The Lord's Indictment, 2:20—3:6

EXPLANATORY NOTES

A Generation's Faithfulness 2:6-9

A simple comparison between 2:6 and Joshua 24:28 suggests that
verse 6 recaptures the original narrative or flow of events. Following
the introductory material in 1:1—2:5, the next verse, 2:6, returns to
the scene at which the book of Joshua left off.

In the same way that Judah continued the success of the conquest
in chapter 1, so too do Joshua and his entire generation continue to
serve the Lord throughout their lifetimes. Importantly, this collection
of faithful Israelites *had seen all the great work that the Lord had
done for Israel* (2:7). Some of them, though young, participated in
the great exodus from Egypt (Exod. 33:11), and all shared in the initial victories over the Canaanites *[Canaanites]*. This seemingly inno-
cent observation immediately raises the question as to what will happen when such eyewitnesses are no longer alive. That time will come
soon enough: Joshua now dies and is buried in the central hills of
Ephraim, the land of his inheritance.

A New Generation's Unfaithfulness 2:10-19

Following the deaths of Joshua and his contemporaries, a new generation moves into position. Without hesitation, the writer intensifies the
suspicions already raised in verse 7. This new generation had not witnessed firsthand God's previous saving deeds, nor did they know
(*yada'*) him in any genuine sense of the term. In the Old Testament, as
often in the New (e.g., Phil. 3:8), to "know" people typically suggests
more than simply knowing "about" them. Instead, knowing someone
involves experiencing that person. In fact, the verb *yada'* is occasionally used even to capture the intimacy of sexual intercourse (Gen. 4:1;
1 Kings 1:4). The generation that succeeded Joshua no doubt heard
various stories concerning previous events, but they did not know the
Lord (cf. 1 Sam. 3:7). To them, he was merely one of the characters.

The picture painted here is frighteningly similar to the opening verses of Exodus. There, a new pharaoh rose to power in Egypt who did not know (*yada'*) Joseph (Exod. 1:8). Much of Israel's favorable position in Egypt had rested on Joseph's relationship with the former ruler. When that relationship and its implications faded into the past, years and years of miserable slavery resulted. If "not knowing Joseph" meant slavery, one can only begin to imagine what "not knowing the Lord" might lead to. Trouble lies just ahead.

What follows is exactly that. The increasing failures of the central and northern tribes in chapter 1 become the dismal precursors for this new generation. Beginning with Israelite unfaithfulness, a series of events transpires. This briefly outlined series or cycle of events, a cycle which will be replayed throughout the book of Judges with alarming regularity and increasing intensity, includes several stages:

1. The Israelites do evil in the eyes of the Lord, most notably worshiping the gods of the people around them (2:11-12a) *[Baal; Asherah]*. As elsewhere in Scripture (Jer. 3:1; Hos. 1:2ff.), such unfaithfulness is a clear violation of the first two commandments and amounts to nothing less than spiritual prostitution (2:17)—forsaking God and running off with a divine harlot. When Israel does so, that action involves more than just a shift in thought or attitude; it further implies that the Israelites comprehensively came to terms with the Canaanites rather than driving them out.

2. As a result of Israel's disobedience, the Lord grows angry and allows his people to suffer oppression at the hands of various enemies (2:12b-15a). Israel provoked (*ka'as*) the Lord to anger on numerous occasions throughout the Old Testament, typically by worshiping foreign gods (Deut. 9:18; 2 Kings 17:17; Jer. 32:30; Hos. 12:14 [Heb.: 12:15]). In the book of Judges, however, such provocation appears with rhythmic predictability.

3. Under the awful weight of oppression, Israel cries to the Lord for his assistance (implied in 2:15b, though explicit in following accounts: 3:9; 4:3). Crying (*za'aq*) in this sense involves more than mere weeping or sobbing. In Judges 12:2, for example, Jephthah summoned (*za'aq*) the Ephraimites to assist him in a fierce struggle with the Ammonites. To cry out to someone, most frequently to the Lord, amounts to a distress signal arising from great difficulty and need (1 Kings 22:32; Ps. 22:5; Isa. 57:13; Lam. 3:8). The cries of a woman about to give birth perhaps conjure up the necessary images most vividly (Isa. 26:17).

4. Hearing their cries, God mercifully raises up a judge or deliverer to free the people from their enemy (2:16a) *[Role of the Judges]*.

5. These judges save Israel from the oppressor.

6. The land experiences periods of peace (2:16b). Such peace, however, always proves to be temporary, as 2:17-19 clearly indicates. Before too long, Israelite stubbornness reasserts itself, and the cycle recurs.

In similar fashion to 2:10, much of this cycle unmistakably calls to mind the exodus. When confronted by the weight of Egyptian oppression, the enslaved Israelites cried out to the Lord (Exod. 2:23). Moved by their woeful petitions, God subsequently raised up Moses as an instrument to secure their deliverance (Exod. 3–12). By drawing upon such imagery, then, the writer here clearly suggests that what repeatedly happens during the period of the judges approximates the exodus from Egypt: these are miniature and localized versions of the OT's central salvation event [Localized Accounts].

The Lord's Indictment 2:20—3:6

To complete the stylistic parallelism with the angel's negative evaluation (2:1-5), there is here the Lord's direct indictment. At the risk of redundancy, the writer leaves absolutely no room for doubt. All of the trouble surrounding Israel cannot be attributed either to the oppressors' military superiority or to God's impotency. Israel's troubles come from nothing less than their own *persistent* refusal to keep the Sinai covenant and follow the Lord (2:20). In response to such unfaithfulness, the Lord finally withdraws all support in the ongoing confrontation with the Canaanites [Canaanites]. That God's support is fundamentally important in conquering the land has already been made clear (1:2, 19a; 2:3). To remove it, therefore, is to leave the present generation entrenched in their own evil desires.

In bringing these introductory sections to a close, the writer seeks to clarify one final trouble spot. Given all of the difficulty associated with the remaining Canaanites, later readers might well ask why the Lord did not remove all of them while Joshua's generation was alive. In other words, with the success that Israel experienced under Joshua's leadership, why did the Lord not allow him to finish the task and save the next generation all of this difficulty (2:23)? In response, two answers are provided:

• Canaanites remain in the land in order to "test" (*nasah*) subsequent generations of Israelites (2:22; 3:1). The verb *nasah* involves the implementation of an actual test so as to attain knowledge or information (Brensinger: 111-112). The Lord used Isaac to test Abraham, for example, in order to probe the depth of his faith (Gen. 22). Similarly, the Babylonian envoys served as a test for the potentially proud Hezekiah (2 Chron. 32:31), a test on which he fared far worse than did Abraham before him! Here in Judges 2:20—3:6, the Lord leaves the Canaanites as a means of examining and reexamining the Israelites' commitment to him. The manner in which they deal with the Canaanites will reveal a great deal about their deepest convictions and allegiances.

• Canaanites also continue dwelling in the land to serve a pedagogical purpose. They remain to teach the new generation of Israelites a lesson. This generation has not witnessed the previous saving acts of the Lord (2:10), including the exodus and the wars of conquest. As a result, the adventures of the previous generation have become secondhand stories to those who now need firsthand experience.

Here the desired goal, however, is not actual military expertise: many of the miraculous stories themselves characteristically emphasize the Lord's strength and Israel's weakness. Instead, this new generation needs to learn for themselves the lessons given earlier through the exodus and conquest, lessons concerning the Lord's superiority over the nations and their gods. By faithfully following the Lord into further battles against the remaining Canaanites, such lessons can be relearned.

Sadly, by coming to terms with the Canaanites, this new generation has both failed the test and forfeited the lessons. Therefore, rather than a glimpse of faithfulness and victory, 3:5-6 depicts a community of faithless compromise.

THE TEXT IN BIBLICAL CONTEXT

Divine Tests and the Possibility of Failure

The scene in Judges 2:6—3:6 is discouraging and simply disastrous. Disobedience not only occurs but also becomes an infectious, all-too-familiar habit. Admittedly, the recurring cycle of disobedience, pain, crying out, and deliverance rings true to much of human experience. Yet to make matters worse, the Lord knows perfectly well beforehand that such a dismal outcome is a real possibility (2:22; cf. Deut. 31:16, 20-21). Indeed, God allows the circumstances that enable all of this to take place! God leaves the Canaanites in the land to test and teach his chosen community.

By testing his community, however, the Lord in fact reveals something significant about himself. For a test to be genuine, both success and failure must be possible outcomes. Every teacher who knows the joy of evaluating outstanding achievement also knows the pain and frustration of witnessing failure. To give a test, then, implies taking a risk. From all indications, God stands willing to do just that, preferring to use freedom rather than excessive restraint. Whether with Adam and Eve (Gen. 2:16-17), Job (Job 7:17-18), or Jesus himself (Matt. 4:1-11), God allows testing that can result in failure. As a parent increasingly grants freedom to a growing child, so God's acts of nurturing make room for difficult situations and varying human responses. While this approach at times seems arduous and even unfair, only the possibility of failure provides honest insight and the opportunity for true obedience to shine.

Learning from Failed Tests

Beyond divine tests and Israel's dismal showing, perhaps the note that rings even louder here in Judges 2:6—3:6 is the fact that God can use failed tests too. As the writer reflects on this discouraging period, his conclusions indicate that the painful and frequently failed tests in Canaan did in fact bring increased understanding for later generations. Because of the various lessons learned, the members of the community now realize more clearly their own role and responsibility in what has transpired (2:20; cf. Lam. 1:5, 14; 3:39). Furthermore, they have caught a renewed glimpse of God's plans and intentions, not to mention his direct involvement in all the affairs of their lives (2:21—3:4; cf. Lam. 3:21-24, 40-42). With this new or rekindled insight, the sins so prevalent during the period of the judges (3:5-6) will hopefully not be repeated. As a result, Israel may now rise to greater heights in their commitment to the Lord and his covenant.

So too was it with Peter. Having failed an important test by denying the Lord three times (John 18:15-27), Peter experienced restoration and renewed his commitment (John 21:15-19). Within a short period of time, he preached enthusiastically in Jerusalem, the same city that had just witnessed his denials. Unlike Judas, who considered failed tests to be terminal and therefore hung himself (Matt. 27:3-10), Peter acknowledged his failures, learned from them, and moved on.

THE TEXT IN THE LIFE OF THE CHURCH
Tests Failed or Passed

People rarely list test-taking among their favorite activities. Yet many individuals and communities can look back at a trying experience with gratitude and satisfaction. As righteous as Job was (Job 1:1-5), his painful period of insult and testing resulted in even further blessing (Job 42:12-17). Likewise, James instructs scattered Christians to rejoice when their faith is tested (James 1:2-3). Such testing, he reasons, produces perseverance and strength. Difficult testing grounds can change people in ways that carefree living cannot. In the absence of trying situations, individuals as well as communities grow weak and flabby.

To see this principle illustrated, one need only be reminded of the many occasions throughout the history of the church when times of testing resulted in renewed fervor and growth. The persecutions of the first three centuries, for example, culminating with the atrocities under Diocletian during the early fourth century, led many to an unwavering and self-sacrificial faith. Tertullian concluded that

> your [government officials'] tortures accomplish nothing, though each is more refined than the last; rather, they are an enticement to our religion. We become more numerous every time we are hewn down by you: the blood of Christians is seed. (Tertullian: 125)

Similar comments could be made concerning the persecution of the Anabaptists during the sixteenth century. Out of desperation over the general ineffectiveness of countless executions, the Count of Altzey reportedly said, "What shall I do? The more I execute, the more they increase" (Van Braght: 364). Even in our own day, stories of thriving Christians often emerge from extremely difficult social and political contexts. Faithfulness in the face of testing is indeed a glowing witness.

If difficult testing grounds make possible growth and a penetrating testimony, however, they also can result in defeat and failure. The pages of history verify such woe by revealing moments when the church fared dismally during times of crisis and testing. Indeed, the persecutions alluded to above often came at the hands of other segments within the organized church. What was for some a passed test, in other words, was for others a bloody failure.

Likewise, when given the opportunity to proclaim a prophetic critique in the face of Hitler's devilish policies, the church in Germany all too often remained silent and at times even supportive of the Nazi regime. According to Dietrich Bonhoeffer,

> [The church] was silent when she should have cried out because the blood of the innocent was crying aloud to heaven. She has failed to speak the right word in the right way and at the right time. She has not resisted to the uttermost the apostasy of faith, and she has brought upon herself the guilt of the godlessness of the masses. (113)

As a result of such a dismal showing, the potential glow of a faithful performance gave way to the enduring bleakness of a horrifying failure.

Times of crisis and testing, then, provide an arena in which the community of faith can demonstrate either unbending godliness and vitality, or unmatched bankruptcy and weakness. Tests, after all, can be passed or failed. Thankfully, however, even failed tests can often be redeemed. "God," in the words of James McClendon Jr., "uses all that we have been, including our failures, to equip us for all that we shall become" (18). Lingering questions remain: Precisely how will the church deal with its more pitiful showings? What lasting lessons may be learned from them?

Part 2

Worsening Effect: The Deterioration of Israel

Judges 3:7—16:31

OVERVIEW

With the introductory materials firmly in place, the writer now proceeds in the major section of the book to illustrate the ongoing problems besetting Israel during the period of the judges. What was briefly explained and summarized in 1:1—3:6, Israel's failure to dislodge the Canaanites and the recurring cycle of evil, oppression, and deliverance, is now demonstrated through a series of intriguing and captivating stories. As so typical of Hebrew narrative, readers frequently find themselves behind closed doors, listening in on private conversations, observing personal encounters, and receiving privileged information (Bar-Efrat: 17). Just to assure that no one gets lost in the stories themselves, however, selected introductory and concluding comments are added to each in order to show the underlying principle running throughout—Israel's unfaithfulness brought the Lord's condemnation [Formation of the Book].

While these various stories concerning the judges are in some ways independent units, it is a mistake to conclude, as some have done, that they are merely preserved here in a rather haphazard or unorganized manner. On the contrary, a careful reading suggests that the writer deliberately arranged the stories to demonstrate the worsening conditions during this period (O'Connell: 266-267; Stone: 464-477; Webb: 174-179). In other words, the overall situation clearly deteriorates as the book moves along. To see this most vividly, one need only trace the various stages of the cycle (cf. 2:6—3:6) through each of the stories. The sequence flows smoothly and effectively with the first judge, Othniel; yet the entire plan is in disarray by the end of the Samson narratives [Breakdown of the Judges Cycle]. Evil escalates, oppression intensifies, and the Lord's patience and mercy wear increasingly thin.

48

OUTLINE

The Pattern Established: Othniel, 3:7-11

The Pattern Affirmed: Ehud and Deborah, 3:12—5:31

The Pattern Threatened: Gideon and Abimelech, 6:1—10:5

The Pattern Ignored: Jephthah and Samson, 10:6—16:31

Judges 3:7-11

The Pattern Established: Othniel

PREVIEW

Modeling is a basic component of character development. As a case in point, students frequently refer to the ways they have been influenced by former teachers, often more so by example than by actual course content! Yet models do more than simply inspire positive or negative behavior. They also may serve as standards by which those who follow are measured or evaluated. One such model appears here in 3:7-11.

Given the recurring problems of Israelite unfaithfulness and resulting oppression described in 2:6—3:6, God raises up judges to provide a solution. The first judge, Othniel, swiftly and effectively does just that. As subsequent narratives will demonstrate, however, Othniel's example becomes an increasingly difficult one to follow *[Breakdown of the Judges Cycle]*.

OUTLINE

An Exemplary Portrait: Othniel's Example, 3:7-11

EXPLANATORY NOTES

Following the theological summation in the preceding section (2:6—3:6), Judges 3:7 returns in principle to 2:11, where we were first informed that the Israelites have done evil in the eyes of the Lord.

Now, however, the general cycle of events outlined in 2:6—3:6 receives greater specificity as actual participants are inserted in the story line.

The sin of which the Israelites are accused is abandoning the Lord in favor of the Baals and Asherahs *[Baal; Asherah]*. In response, God brings them under the domination of a certain Cushan-Rishathaim ("Cushan of Double-Wickedness"), probably a name contrived by his enemies, to highlight his reputation. Although described as the king of Aram Naharaim ("Aram of the two rivers"), an apparent geographical reference to northern Mesopotamia, the unlikelihood of such a distant foe tormenting southern Israel at this time has led some to read "Edom" for Aram (Soggin: 46). In any case, this somewhat mysterious foe has ruled over Israel for eight years.

While under such oppression, the Israelites cry out to the Lord for assistance (cf. 2:10-19). Without delay, the Lord provides Othniel to act on their behalf. In an admittedly brief and otherwise undeveloped account, three details illuminate Othniel's position as the opening judge: (1) his established reputation is based upon prior exploits (1:11-15); (2) he is from the south, a geographical tidbit that matches well with Judah's dominant position in chapter 1 (cf. 2:9 and 1:12-13); and (3) his activities precisely fit the mold for judges described in 2:16—*raised up* and *delivered/saved*. With the help of the Lord's Spirit, Othniel quickly and easily subdues the enemy *[Holy Spirit in the OT]*. What results is a forty-year period of peace.

Of particular importance in this opening report, an account frequently dismissed with only limited comment, are the complete picture that it presents of the cycle outlined in 2:6—3:6, and the relative ease with which Othniel finishes his task. In rapid succession, the Israelites sin, God sends an oppressor, the Israelites cry out, God raises a judge, the enemy is defeated, and the land has rest. Quickly and decisively, Othniel completes his assignment, and the problem is apparently solved.

In short, Othniel is a model or paradigm of sorts, demonstrating how judges are supposed to operate (Klein: 33-34). The writer refrains from forming explicit comparisons himself (that task is left for attentive readers). Yet those judges that follow Othniel and the circumstances surrounding their activities must be carefully scrutinized to discover whether or not they measure up to the pattern presented here.

THE TEXT IN BIBLICAL CONTEXT
Exemplary Models

Othniel's exemplary judgeship calls to mind other instances in Scripture when individuals function as standards for evaluation. Perhaps most notably, the writer of 1 and 2 Kings consistently assesses all the kings of Israel and Judah against David, the consummate king. Rarely, however, do they even begin to measure up (1 Kings 15:3, 11; 2 Kings 14:3; 18:3; 22:2). In fact, none of Israel's Northern Kingdom monarchs ever make the grade, being likened instead to the "negative" model of disastrous kingship, Jeroboam I (1 Kings 12:25-33; 15:25-26, 34).

In the NT, the apostle Paul employs modeling when dealing with immature Corinthian Christians (1 Cor. 4:16; cf. Phil. 2:19-20). In the context of various quarrels and struggles within the congregation, he exhorts them to follow his own example as the spiritual father of their church. Rather than emulating a host of potential leaders, the people should evaluate their own attitudes and behaviors according to the standard set by Paul himself.

Yet even Paul clearly recognizes that he is not the final model or example against whom believers should measure themselves. In so doing, he raises this idea of evaluative models to its highest level by urging that Christian standards are ultimately rooted in the example set by Jesus himself. The self-emptying attitude that Jesus demonstrated in his incarnation and crucifixion shines as a permanent model of how his followers should envision their own tasks and relationships (Phil. 2:1-11).

THE TEXT IN THE LIFE OF THE CHURCH
Empowered and Obedient

The decisive achievements of Othniel can be attributed primarily to his apparent obedience and divine empowerment. The implied swiftness with which he responds to the Lord's summons demonstrates the type of commitment and compliance that Scripture celebrates. Some, including Moses (Exod. 3–4) and a few of Othniel's fellow judges (Judg. 4:8; 6:36-40; 11:30-31), require more convincing. Others, such as Jonah, even say no.

Yet as desirable as it is, obedience falls short without genuine empowerment. "I am sensible indeed," declared John Wesley, "that without [the Spirit of God,] we can do nothing" (Wesley, 1985:53). In Othniel's case, the *Spirit of the Lord came upon him* (3:10), and only then did he "judge" Israel *[Holy Spirit in the OT]*. According to the biblical ideal, both obedience and divine empowerment are necessary for godly service (Zech. 4:6). Obedience without divine empowerment, as self-driven activists often illustrate, is ultimately resourceless. Divine empowerment without obedience, as later judges will all too clearly demonstrate, is mournfully fruitless.

Judges 3:12—5:31

The Pattern Affirmed: Ehud and Deborah

OVERVIEW

Strategizing by using deceit, as in the case of Ehud, is hardly new. Strategizing "under God," as exemplified by Deborah, is another alternative. Despite such varying approaches, however, the stories of both Ehud and Deborah sustain the success depicted in the preceding account. In other words, each stage of the cycle outlined in 2:6—3:6 clearly appears, and the stories move through to completion with relative ease. Admittedly, various points of slippage begin to emerge, and they must be noted.

For example, the character and techniques of Ehud are not without obvious blemish. Similarly, mysterious ambiguity surrounds the identity of the hero in the Deborah narrative. Nevertheless, such deviations from the paradigm are relatively minor; they do not signal the type of serious deterioration evident in later accounts. At this stage of the overall narrative, the pattern generally remains intact.

OUTLINE

A Positive Portrait: Ehud's Escapades, 3:12-31

A Positive Portrait: Deborah's Adventures, 4:1—5:31

A Positive Portrait: Ehud's Escapades

Judges 3:12-31

PREVIEW

Shrewdness and obesity highlight Ehud's personal conquest of the Moabite king Eglon (3:15-25). Accordingly, the narrative reaches a climax in verse 21, when Ehud's craftiness and Eglon's apparent naïveté facilitate the latter's assassination. The concluding section (3:26-30) then broadens the landscape; Ehud's victory over Eglon becomes Israel's victory over the now-leaderless Moabites.

OUTLINE

Crisis Introduced, 3:12-15a

Ehud Pays Eglon, 3:15b-19

Ehud Slays Eglon, 3:20-25

Ehud Leads Israel, 3:26-30

Shamgar Handles the Philistines, 3:31

EXPLANATORY NOTES

Crisis Introduced 3:12-15a

Again the Israelites do evil in the eyes of the Lord. While the precise nature of their crimes goes unspecified, the fact that the accusation is repeated twice in verse 12 highlights the gravity of the situation. In this case, the resulting oppression comes at the hands of the Moabites and their accomplices east of the Jordan.

Although genealogical traditions link the Moabites with the Israelites through Lot, Abraham's nephew (Gen. 19:37), the OT typically depicts tension between the two. The Moabites, for example, refused to allow the wandering Israelites to pass through their territory while en route to Canaan (Judg. 11:17). In fact, the Moabite king Balak hired Balaam, a Mesopotamian diviner, to curse the Israelites in an attempt to thwart their advances (Num. 22–24). In later years, occasional biblical references indicate that relations fared no better (2 Kings 3; 13:20; 24:2). As a result, various Israelite prophets denounced their Moabite neighbors on more than one occasion (Isa. 15-16; Jer. 48; Zeph. 2:8-11).

What transpires here in Judges 3, then, is by no means an isolated affair. On this occasion, Eglon, the Moabite king, has captured Jericho, the City of Palms, and subjugated Israel for a period of eighteen years. Only when Israel cries to the Lord is hope forthcoming—hope in the form of a Benjaminite named Ehud.

Already in these introductory verses, various elements evoke our curiosity and heighten the suspense for the impending confrontation between the Moabite king and Ehud. The name *Eglon*, for example, means "fat calf," amusingly appropriate given the king's noteworthy physique (3:17). Furthermore, the tribal designation *Benjaminite* literally means "son of the right hand," an intriguing designation for someone who was either left-handed (*'ṭṭer yad yeminu*) or, as Halpern has argued, "one of a breed of men schooled in the use of the left hand for war" (Halpern, 1988:35; cf. Judg. 20:16; 1 Chron. 12:2). Somewhat mysteriously, the stage is set for Ehud to pay and then slay the fatted calf (Alter: 39).

Ehud Pays Eglon 3:15b-19

As part of their oppressed condition, the Israelites have been regularly required to pay tribute to Moab. On this occasion, Ehud assumes the responsibility of delivering it to Eglon. While Ehud's divine appointment is apparent, no mention is made of divine empowerment (cf. 3:10). Instead we find a man notorious for his own cunning and scheming. With a double-edged sword concealed under his clothing, Ehud faithfully presents the tribute to Eglon and heads for home.

After dismissing those who have accompanied him, he doubles back with a supposed message for the unsuspecting and seemingly naive king. Not only does Eglon provide his undivided attention, but he further aids the hero's cause by sending away the royal servants. Ehud and Eglon are left alone.

Ehud Slays Eglon 3:20-25

The contrast between the deceptive Ehud and the easily deceived Eglon—remember, however, that he has subjugated Israel for eighteen years—reaches new heights in the climactic murder scene. With Eglon sitting in his private upper room, Ehud approaches, purporting to have a privileged word from God. That Ehud cleverly employs the general term *elohim* (god) rather than the distinctively Hebrew name *Yahweh* in part explains Eglon's overly anxious response: he perhaps took Ehud for an enemy collaborator.

Yet a foolish response it was. Within a moment, the double-edged sword fully penetrates Eglon's sizeable belly, apparently dumping his feces on the floor. In 3:22 the obscure phrase *wayyeṣe' happaršedonah* (*and he/it came out at the [?] or and [?] came out;* cf. NRSV's *and the dirt came out*), omitted in the LXX and not translated in the NIV, may refer to the king's anus *[Septuagint]*. This understanding is further strengthened by 3:24, which implies the stench of human waste.

His (graphically described) work completed, Ehud leaves the scene of the crime. The rather comical and perhaps confusing events of escape and discovery are clarified by architectural details unmentioned in the biblical text itself. Palaces such as the one envisioned here consisted of two floors: a lower audience hall and an upper chamber. Included in the upper chamber was a toilet that emptied into a latrine-like closet on the lower level.

After killing the king, Ehud locks the doors of the upper chamber, lowers himself through the toilet (not a porch, as in the NIV), exits the audience hall on the lower level, and strolls right past the royal servants who have earlier left the room (Halpern, 1988:33-44). Assuming that the king is now free, the servants return and find his chamber door locked. The stench leads them to the natural conclusion that he is relieving himself, but the passage of time suggests otherwise. Embarrassed, they unlock the door and find Eglon dead on the floor. By that time, Ehud is nowhere in sight.

Ehud Leads Israel 3:26-30

With Ehud's personal conquest of Eglon completed, the Israelites living in the central hills now gather in a corporate effort to defeat the leaderless Moabites. Under Ehud's supervision, they strike down their adversaries who, while perhaps being accomplished soldiers, are also, like Eglon, noticeably well-fed (*šamen*)! What results is an unprecedented eighty-year period of rest, magnifying the completeness of this latest Israelite victory. The Moabite oppression has been dealt with decisively. No mention is made at this point, however, of Ehud's death. Only in 4:1 does this episode officially come to an end.

Shamgar Handles the Philistines 3:31

Following the story of Ehud is a brief and seemingly interruptive note about Shamgar's activities. Notably lacking in this account are the typical expressions denoting a judge's rise to power. Even the other so-called minor judges (10:1-5; 12:8-15) either "arose" (*wayyaqam*) or "judged" (*wayyišpoṭ*) *[Role of the Judges]*. Shamgar, however, simply *was (hayah)* after Ehud. Nevertheless, the writer finds in his activities a useful connection to Israel's ongoing struggle with the inhabitants of the land.

That Shamgar appears again in 5:6 as a chronological marker suggests that he was at one time relatively well-known. By now, however, his story remains largely hidden. Even the stylistic descriptions attached to the other minor judges, including such things as tribal affiliation and years of service, are generally lacking here. Quite simply, by using some sort of farming tool (the precise meaning of *malmad*, typically translated *oxgoad*, remains uncertain), an otherwise forgotten Shamgar helps to relieve Israel of Philistine pressure.

Perhaps one reason so little remains of Shamgar's story has to do with Shamgar himself. According to P. C. Craigie, the designation *son of Anath* appears elsewhere in texts outside of the Bible, specifically those from Mari, Ugarit, and Egypt. When it does, it refers to either the person's home ("from Anath") or craft, such as a soldier associated with the war goddess Anat (Craigie, 1972:239-240). Such a designation, when coupled with the fact that *Shamgar* is a non-Israelite name, makes it likely that he is actually not an Israelite. Rather, Shamgar is perhaps a local Canaanite or mercenary who is himself oppressed by the neighboring Philistines *[Sea Peoples]*. In this case, he *delivered/saved Israel* by helping to remove a common enemy.

THE TEXT IN BIBLICAL CONTEXT

Deception

Except for the mention in 1 Chronicles 8:6 (cf. 7:10), Ehud appears nowhere in Scripture outside of Judges 3:12—4:1. Yet while he himself fails to capture the attention of other biblical writers, his most notorious personal characteristic, deception, is witnessed more often than one might wish. Jacob, himself a marvelous deceiver, utilized his skills on Isaac (Gen. 27) and Laban (Gen. 30). Following him are no less competent connivers like Tamar (Gen. 38), the men of Judah (1 Sam. 11:1-11), Michal (1 Sam. 19:11-17), and in accounts very similar to the Ehud narrative, Joab (2 Sam. 3:26-30; 20:4-10). In these and other instances, deception is the catalyst that brings good for the people of God. The apparent implication, then, is that deceitful behavior is productive and perhaps even appropriate.

This list of skillful deceivers notwithstanding, biblical writers also recount episodes in which deception is negatively portrayed. Abraham, for example, brought trouble upon others by concealing the true identity of his wife (Gen. 12:11-20; 20:2-18). The deceiving tactics of Ananias and Sapphira cost them their very lives (Acts 5:1-11).

Furthermore, the Scriptures reserve harsh language for those who deceive (Pss. 5:6; 55:23; 101:7; Rom. 1:29). Jeremiah, in fact, associates false prophets with the art of deception (5:31). Finally, Jesus himself listed deceit among the dastardly things that come out of the human heart (Mark 7:22). While deception might at times be productive, productivity is no clear indication of rightness.

Much with Little

3:31 Shamgar, as forgotten as he might be, remains a forceful example of someone who accomplished a lot with a little. As such, he fits nicely within the developing biblical motif in which God accomplishes a great deal through seemingly under-equipped people—the Israelites with their trumpets at Jericho (Josh. 6), and David with his stones and sling (1 Sam. 17:40). The writer of Judges himself thrives on the theme, as the upcoming story of Gideon particularly illustrates.

Later still, the apostle Paul speaks in a similar vein when he describes the motley crew left with the responsibility of carrying on the work of the Lord (1 Cor. 1:26-31). Yet this idea should come as no surprise; it is precisely the way God has chosen to complete his all-embracing task of redeeming the world. Rather than employing brute strength or manipulative coercion, he used the death of his incarnate Son on a Roman cross.

THE TEXT IN THE LIFE OF THE CHURCH

Productivity or Fruitfulness?

In the ongoing tension between human initiative and divine empowerment, Ehud resorts to his own crafty capabilities. In fact, God himself is referred to in the narrative in only the most superficial sort of way. From all indications, Ehud's success rests more on the art of deception than upon divine guidance and empowerment.

Given the emphasis on productivity in today's world and the resulting pressure to succeed in all undertakings, both the church collectively as well as its individual members often face the same tension between human initiative and divine empowerment. The demands of ministry and the strength of opposing forces seemingly far surpass the magnitude of Israel's Moabite oppressors. To make matters worse, the supposed call of every Christian involves changing the world, often single-handedly! Successful churches reproduce, and they regularly do so in great numbers. Committed believers conquer their foes and live without apparent weakness. Yet as unrealistic and indeed unbiblical expectations result in increased pressure and tension, deceptive strategies often replace divine anointing. Production, it is supposed, is far more important than obedience!

In the midst of this nerve-wrenching jungle, Henri Nouwen draws a crucial distinction between productivity and fruitfulness (Nouwen: 57-64). Productivity implies human advancement and elevates personal accomplishments; fruitfulness implies divine enabling and elevates God-given growth. In addition, productivity stresses the need to achieve; fruitfulness encourages a vibrant connection with the vine, a relationship that enables growth to occur (John 15:1-11). Christians, according to Nouwen, are called to be fruitful rather than productive. In this release from productivity and godless competition, deception gives way to fruit-bearing honesty and dependence upon the Lord.

Mother Teresa stands as a welcome reminder of biblical fruitfulness. On one occasion, she remarked that God called her to be faithful, not successful. While being faithful, however, Mother Teresa's "fruitfulness" quietly and humbly has stretched to the most destitute around the world. No gimmicks. No deception. If God can even use a deceiver like Ehud, how much more can he use those who place their diligent efforts under his lordship?

Never Too Small

It has often been said that you can be too big for God to use, but you can never be too small. The overwhelming majority of people who make up the church today are, as always, ordinary. The Lord, however, can use ordinary people to do extraordinary things. In the words of Lesslie Newbigin, "The Church is not an organization of spiritual giants. It is broken men and women who can lead others to the Cross" (Newbigin: 146-147). The Shamgars of the past, not to mention the countless others who do not even have a single verse to preserve their memory, can become the often-unnoticed and perhaps modestly equipped servants who faithfully carry out the work of God's kingdom today.

A Positive Portrait: Deborah's Adventures

Judges 4:1—5:31

PREVIEW

Men did not hold exclusive rights to the role of judge in ancient Israel. In fact, even a cursory glance at 4:1—5:31 leads the reader to suspect that Deborah, rather than being inferior to the male protagonists in the book of Judges, actually possesses greater influence and authority. She serves as both prophet and judge, and she exercises leadership during the episode that affects the single largest number of tribes *[Localized Accounts]*. Finally, she confronts a formidable opponent equipped with iron chariots. It is of more than passing interest, then, that women (Deborah and Jael) play significant roles in the next incident.

Unlike the other episodes in the book of Judges, the adventures of Deborah are preserved in two distinct and somewhat different accounts. The most striking difference is the literary forms of the accounts themselves: the first is written in narrative, the second in poetry. Such a formal difference, however, must not conceal the fact that there are also significant differences in content. Though viewing the two accounts together helps to fill in various gaps in the overall picture, each account nevertheless has its own area of emphasis, and each seeks to present its own perspective on the events.

OUTLINE

Deborah in Story, 4:1-24
4:1-3	Crisis Introduced
4:4-11	Deborah Prophesies to Barak
4:12-16	Barak Pursues Sisera
4:17-24	Jael Pegs Sisera

Deborah in Song, 5:1-31
5:1	Song Introduced
5:2-3	Israel Praises the Lord
5:4-5	Israel Recalls the Lord's Arrival
5:6-12	The Canaanites Oppress Israel
5:13-18	Various Tribes Arise from Israel
5:19-23	The Lord Fights for Israel
5:24-27	Jael Strikes Sisera
5:28-30	A Worried Mother Awaits Sisera
5:31	Israel Prays to the Lord

EXPLANATORY NOTES

Deborah in Story 4:1-24

The narrative version of Deborah's adventures describes a geographical setting which, in terms of the schematic survey recorded in chapter 1, now moves northward from Judah and Benjamin to the house of Joseph (1:22ff.) *[Map, p. 240]*. Swiftly the text recounts the victory of various Israelite tribes over a major northern coalition (cf. 5:19), a victory that must have significant implications for increasing Israelite control in the region (Mayes: 75). Yet the story itself gives only limited attention to this important battle, placing stress instead on the individual conquest of the opposing general at the hands of an unlikely foe. Throughout, the all-consuming issue focuses not so much on who wins the battle, but on who among the earthly participants receives the credit (4:9). As such, the climax of the story comes not in verse 15 but in verse 21.

4:1-3 Crisis Introduced

The tangible effects of Ehud's escapades, though lengthy (3:30), were nevertheless temporary. With the death of this deceptive deliverer, Israel retraces its steps to unspecified sinfulness and reencounters God's judgment. On this occasion, God's judgment comes from within the general region being settled by the Israelite tribes rather than from without. Hazor was a crucial city situated some ten miles north of the Sea of Galilee.

The fact that Hazor was previously defeated by Joshua (Josh. 11) has raised numerous questions and theories (Gray: 114, 200, 254; Malamat, 1960:12-19). Yet the strategic location of the city along the major trade route between Egypt and Mesopotamia makes it easy to imagine that it could have been resettled within a hundred-year span. That Jabin appears in both the Joshua and Judges accounts, however, is more difficult. While most commentators dismiss him here as an unexplainable editorial addition (Soggin: 70; Yadin: 132), the possibility remains that Jabin was a throne name used by successive leaders (Cundall: 81).

Although the ultimate position of authority within enemy ranks is assigned to Jabin, the king appears as nothing more than an afterthought in the story itself. While Eglon was obese and easily deceived, Jabin is absolutely motionless and mute. With the apparent exception of Cushan-Rishathaim (3:8), the success of Israel's oppressors up to this point can hardly be attributed, at least in the writer's mind, to the prowess of the opposing monarchs.

Instead, the dominant enemy character here and throughout chapters 4 and 5 is the commander of the army, Sisera. His non-Semitic name only raises what are for now unanswerable questions about his ethnic background; the location of his home is equally uncertain (Soggin: 63). Of more importance is the technological advantage that he enjoys over his current foe. Although ironworking was first introduced in the region by the Philistines ca. 1,200 B.C., the Israelites never mastered the trade until after the reign of Saul (Hobbs: 33, 56) *[Archaeological Periods]*.

Sisera, however, employs chariots equipped with iron nails and fittings, and he *oppressed the Israelites cruelly*; he inflicted upon them a form of oppression more severe than his predecessors. So great was Sisera's reputation that Jewish legend describes him as follows:

> When he was thirty years old, he had conquered the whole world. At the sound of his voice the strongest of walls fell in a heap, and the wild animals in the woods were chained to the spot by fear. The proportions of his body were vast beyond description. If he took a bath in the river, and dived beneath the surface, enough fish were caught in his beard to feed a multitude, and it required no less than nine hundred horses to draw the chariot in which he rode. (Ginzberg: 35)

As a direct result of their suffering, then, and not because of guilt concerning their sin, the Israelites cry to the Lord for assistance.

4:4-11 Deborah Prophesies to Barak

In previous episodes, such an Israelite gesture brought an immediate and favorable response. Here, for the first time, ambiguity is introduced, an ambiguity that will in subsequent accounts give way to even greater reluctance on the Lord's part. Similarly, we are left with uncertainty concerning the identity of the deliverer. While the narrative suggests that Barak is the deliverer and Deborah the mouthpiece through which he receives his call, the actual sequence of events is hardly smooth or convincing. In fact, Deborah, Barak, and eventually Jael all play active roles in saving Israel (Amit, 1987:89). From all indications, delay replaces immediacy.

According to the narrative description, Deborah lives in the hill country of Ephraim. Perhaps uniquely, she has functioned in a dual capacity at the time. First, she is a prophetess, placing her in the good company of such women in the OT as Miriam (Exod. 15:20) and Huldah (2 Kings 22:14). Second, she serves as a judge in the more traditional or judicial sense of the word *[Role of Judges]*. In this second role, Deborah hears grievances brought to her by surrounding

Israelites, and then renders decisions to settle the disputes.

It is probably in her position as judge that the latest commotion under Sisera first comes to Deborah's attention, for her home is located some fifty miles from the battle scene (4:6-7). It is certainly in her position as prophetess, however, that she sends for Barak; her message to him takes the form of a prophetic oracle. By God's command, Barak is to engage in holy war and free the Israelites from their current oppressors [*Violence and War in Judges*]. It is, without a doubt, a task he prefers to avoid.

Barak's reluctance to accept his assignment, in stark contrast to Deborah's apparent confidence, is clearly envisioned here as some distrust in the prophetic word. Yet this distrust results, at least in part, from what is surely an honest, albeit faithless, appraisal of the situation. Various geographical elements in the account, for example, underline the magnitude of the confrontation depicted here.

For one thing, the leadership connection between Deborah the Ephraimite and Barak the Naphtalite links the central and northern regions into a stylized whole. For another, although only the two northern tribes of Naphtali and Zebulun are assigned the task of serving under Barak, 5:13-18 connects every tribe but Judah and Simeon to the struggle [*Map, p. 240*]. On that basis, the present conflict between Israel and the Canaanite coalition affects and involves more Israelite tribes than any other in the book of Judges [*Localized Accounts*]. It is a confrontation of considerable proportions.

Barak's reluctance, therefore, might be somewhat understandable, but it receives no sympathy here. To gain Deborah's assistance—assistance that is in no way alluded to when Barak actually enters the battle (4:14-16)!—Barak forfeits the honor normally associated with such an important leadership position. But who will receive the honor in his place? Apparently Deborah, *for the Lord will sell Sisera into the hand of a woman* (4:9). The indeterminate reference to a woman, however, leaves the matter wide open. Even the ensuing battle itself fails to recapture the attention that has now shifted to an unknown hero.

With the leading characters in place, notice is lastly given concerning Kenites living near Kedesh in Naphtali (cf. 4:6; Josh. 19:37). The nomadic Kenites were typically much further south, coming as far north as the wilderness of Judah in Judges 1:16. While at first glance such a notice appears to be woefully out of place here, it importantly anticipates and explains the presence of Jael's clan in the region (4:17-22). The stage is now set for both the battle and the ensuing chase scene.

4:12-16   Barak Pursues Sisera

The battle itself, once again, is far more significant and complicated than the present story's level of interest *[Historicity and Truth]*. As such, many of the details remain forever obscure. Concerning Israelite strategy, Barak was earlier told in Deborah's oracle to assemble his troops on Mt. Tabor, situated along the northern edge of the plain of Esdraelon (4:6). God would then lure Sisera's troops to the Kishon River in the valley below. If what is implied here is an ambush of sorts, a possibility seemingly precluded by the nearly ten miles between the two sites, Sisera is somehow informed of Barak's whereabouts (4:12). Nevertheless, he and his considerable army gathered as planned.

What follows is an Israelite attack, but the total victory is credited to the Lord himself. From all indications, the Israelite army appears unnecessary *[Violence and War in Judges]*. Precisely where and how the victory was actually won remains uncertain. The present account suggests a location immediately adjoining Mt. Tabor (4:14), whereas the poem refers to a setting farther away at Megiddo (5:19). Possibly the battle involved two separate phases, as various scholars have suggested.

As to the "how" of the victory, the poem implies that a major thunderstorm occurred, flooding the otherwise trickling Kishon and thereby rendering Sisera's chariots useless (5:20-21). Giving a commander of Sisera's stature a bit of credit, it is hard to imagine that he assembled his forces, so dependent upon chariot maneuverability, in a potential floodplain during the rainy season! Rather, what is surely envisioned here is a sudden and unexpected downpour following the close of the latter rains. Miraculously, the same God who turned water into dry land (Exod. 14:21-22; Josh. 3:14-17) now turns dry land into a sea of mud! As elsewhere, the Lord (not Baal!) controls the weather (cf. Josh. 10:11; 1 Sam. 7:10; Job 38:1; Ps. 18:9-15) *[Baal]*.

4:17-24   Jael Pegs Sisera

Although his army is thoroughly defeated, Sisera somehow manages to escape the carnage. As he flees, attention once again focuses on the unnamed woman referred to in verse 9. Certainly Deborah has done nothing during the battle to distinguish herself in any way, so the mystery remains. In his efforts to get away, Sisera arrives at the tent of Jael, the wife of a Kenite. Verse 17 informs us that *peace (šalom)* exists between Jabin and the Kenites, an alliance of no small benefit to a nomadic group living far away from their original home. On the basis of this alliance, Sisera has every right to expect sanctuary. In addition, he must be assuming that no one will dare search the tent of a woman—although he himself did!—an unthinkable violation of cultural norms. What better place could there be for this runaway commander to hide?

Jael initially and inappropriately offers Sisera hospitality; her husband, the male head, could alone make such an offer (Matthews, 1991:16). Yet she soon denies hospitality in the most graphic way. Likely Jael found herself in a situation of conflicting interests and commitments. While the Kenites do in fact have an alliance with Jabin, they apparently have one with the Israelites as well (1:16; 4:11; Fensham, 1964:51-54). Such multiple alliances present no major problems so long as the participating parties avoid conflict. Once they are at odds, however, choices may well need to be made. Perhaps the Kenite alliance with the Israelites is more firmly established than that with Jabin. Furthermore, the Israelites clearly hold the upper hand at the moment, as Sisera's pathetic condition must indicate. Therefore, Jael sides with them and turns on her guest.

Having served Sisera a drink—5:25 suggests that she gave him milk rather than the requested water, an indication of generosity that probably gives him a sense of false security—Jael proceeds to drive (*taqa'*) a tent peg through the skull of the unsuspecting and sleeping commander in a manner strangely reminiscent of Ehud's thrusting (*taqa'*) his sword through Eglon's enormous belly. With this single swing of a hammer, the enemy is permanently removed and the identity of the mysterious woman revealed. Not only is she a woman, but a foreigner at that!

As for Barak, the latecomer is reduced from a deliverer to a discoverer, or as Webb observes, to the same status as the embarrassed Moabite courtiers who stumble upon the corpse of Eglon, their assassinated king (Webb: 136). The standard reference to the land having peace, however, is reserved until 5:31. Thus the following poem is neatly included within the overall account.

THE TEXT IN BIBLICAL CONTEXT
Women in Leadership Positions

In functioning as both prophetess and judge, Deborah stands out among the majority of biblical characters; few others serve in this type of dual capacity. Even more surprising for some, then, is the fact that such an elevated position belongs to a woman. This narrative, however, represents only one of several in which women function in influential positions.

In the OT, women other than Deborah serve in various ways. Miriam, for example, occupies a position of sufficient importance that later tradition links her with Moses and Aaron as the leaders of the Exodus (Mic. 6:4). Furthermore, both Huldah and possibly Noadiah after her serve as prophetesses, and so does Isaiah's wife. Importantly, in no case does the fact that they are women receive any particular attention (2 Kings 22:14-20; Neh. 6:14; Isa. 8:3). Women likewise appear among the "wise," even to the extent that royal officials seek out their advice (2 Sam. 14:2-3; 20:16-22). Finally, women formally participate in Israel's worship experiences, serving at least as singers during corporate gatherings (2 Chron. 35:25; Neh. 7:67).

In the NT, women clearly play an important role among the followers of Jesus (Luke 8:1-3; 23:55-56; 24:10). Such a role is sustained in the early church, where the likes of Prisca, Phoebe, and Mary serve in significant ways (Rom. 16:1, 3, 6; 1 Cor. 16:19). Even Paul, who apparently forbids women to speak during public services (1 Cor. 14:34-35) and who alludes to a subordinate role for women (1 Cor. 11:2-16), affirms their religious equality, expects them to pray and prophesy, and gladly credits them for their work in promoting the gospel (Gal. 3:28; Phil. 4:3). Clearly, women in the NT do more than stand along the sidelines. Indeed, they participate in the work of the church throughout.

In addition to merely depicting women in important positions, the Bible also presents an ever-expanding development that all too often goes unnoticed. The various instances cited from the OT, for example, apparently anticipate a day envisioned by Joel when men and women will serve side by side and receive equal anointing (2:28-29). Similarly, Peter himself associates the fulfillment of Joel's prophecy with the events of Pentecost (Acts 2:16-21). While it is true, therefore, that the societal structures of the biblical world assign far more authority and privilege to men, the Bible itself progressively attempts to "even the slate."

Reluctant Responses and the Plan of God

Barak's reluctance to accept his God-given commission stands in contrast to the compliance of both Othniel and Ehud before him. Yet it is merely a prelude to an even-greater hesitancy on Gideon's part in the account that follows. Therefore, reluctance alone is not the key issue here. Of greater importance in the Deborah and Barak story, given the emphasis placed upon the mysterious woman, are other matters: God's plans cannot be thwarted, and there are potential risks in responding reluctantly to his call.

To begin with, Barak's experiences make it clear that negative reactions to a divine call do not stifle or obstruct God's plans. In such situations, the Lord may, as with Moses (Exod. 3–4), Gideon (Judg. 6–7), and Jeremiah (Jer. 1:4-10), patiently groom his questioners until they stand prepared for their tasks. On other occasions, however, he may disregard the disinclined and seek suitable replacements, as when he tired of Israel's constant moaning in the wilderness. At that time, he even contemplated destroying his chosen people and making Moses into a great nation (Num. 14:12). God's plans ultimately cannot be thwarted, and reluctant responses cannot change that. So irresistible is God's ability to carry out his plans in spite of human reluctance that, as Luke describes it, even stones might accomplish what people refuse to do (Luke 19:40).

In addition, God's readiness to adopt alternate means suggests that reluctant responses involve great risks. Such risks need not result in dire physical consequences, as was the case with Jonah (Jon. 1) and nearly the case with Israel (Num. 14). With Barak, for instance, the risk results not so much in physical harm as in unfulfilled potential: he lives forever under the shadow of a partial replacement. Barak's original assignment involves him in directing the entire campaign from beginning to end. His reluctance, however, leaves him a spectator during the closing scene. As a spectator, he forfeits the credit for the victory, credit that now goes, he no doubt regrets, to the least likely of all people. Here, as with the intended guests in Jesus' parable of the wedding banquet (Matt. 22:1-14), reluctant responses may well lead to wasted opportunities and a significant loss of blessing.

THE TEXT IN THE LIFE OF THE CHURCH

If Only . . .

Two of the strongest and most heartbreaking words in the English language are "If only. . . ." These words speak of painful regret, wasted opportunities, and an adversely affected future. Surely the builder who constructed a house upon the sand, only to watch it collapse during the first major storm (Matt. 7:26-27), later groaned "If only. . . ." So also sighed the criticized servant who buried his single talent rather than invest it (Matt. 25:24-30). To these could be added countless contemporary examples in which individuals, perhaps even we ourselves, ignored good advice, wasted important opportunities, or responded reluctantly—and lived to regret it.

While sound judgment and wise counsel from the community of faith enable one to say "No" on appropriate occasions, dragging one's feet with God leads frequently to forfeited blessings and deep sorrow. In the words of Jürgen Moltmann,

God has exalted man and given him the prospect of a life that is wide and free, but man hangs back and lets himself down. God promises a new creation of all things in righteousness and peace, but man acts as if everything were as before and remained as before. God honours him with promises, but man does not believe himself capable of what is required of him. This is the sin which most profoundly threatens the believer. It is not the evil he does, but the good he does not do, not his misdeeds, but his omissions, that accuse him. (Moltmann: 1967:22-23)

As many have learned, frequently with considerable pain, saying "Yes" today far surpasses saying "If only . . . " tomorrow.

EXPLANATORY NOTES

Deborah in Song 5:1-31

The poem preserved here is frequently considered to be the oldest text in all of the OT, perhaps reaching its present form as early as the twelfth century B.C. (Globe: 508-512). Variously referred to as a heroic poem (Soggin: 96), war ballad (Lindars: 165), or victory hymn (Boling: 117; Lind: 66), the poem has in fact suffered linguistically during the lengthy process of transmission. Indeed, while the general sense of the poem is sufficiently clear, at least twenty of its verses contain a word or words that present translational difficulties. As a result, some ambiguity in detail must be expected, as the many marginal notes in most translations indicate.

In contrast to the narrative account of chapter 4, which focuses primarily on the individual conquest of Sisera and the honor given to Jael, the poem emphasizes Israelite tribal participation—or the lack thereof—and the marvelous nature of God's victory. Therefore, the climax of the poem comes not in the murder of Sisera, as in chapter 4, but in the battle itself (5:19-23). This battle brings to a close the longer and more general section dealing with God's victory (5:2-23). Final attention then shifts again, as it did in the narrative account, to a particularized description of Sisera's destruction (5:24-30).

5:1 Song Introduced

The setting for the song is clearly the Israelite victory over Jabin, as shown by the connecting phrase *on that day*, here and in 4:23. Although no apparent title is present, the opening verse (5:2) indicates that this is a song of praise. Deborah and Barak, representing the entire community, celebrate their divine deliverance.

5:2-3 Israel Praises the Lord

The opening words of praise cite the people in general and, perhaps, the leaders in particular for their willingness to freely participate in the just-ended struggle. The phrase *When locks are long in Israel*, however, is perplexing and much-discussed. The reference to leaders, evident in the alternate reading *When the princes in Israel take the lead* (NIV), is based on the LXX. The Hebrew has been variously translated as *Because in Israel the people have regained their freedom* (Soggin: 81) or *When the flowing hair was let loose* (Gray: 262-263) *[Septuagint]*. In the latter case, the idea involves the growing of one's hair for either war (Deut. 32:42) or the fulfillment of a solemn vow (Num. 6:5; Ezek. 44:20; Judg. 13:5).

In light of Israel's praise to the Lord, all the kings and influential people throughout the surrounding nations are instructed to pay attention (cf. Ps. 68:32; Isa. 52:15). Just as God's previous deeds in freeing Israel from Egypt stirred all who heard (Exod. 18:8-11; Josh. 2:10-11), so too will the present proclamation of praise create allusions of the Lord's power and might.

5:4-5 *Israel Recalls the Lord's Arrival*

Using imagery of the Sinai theophany (cf. Deut. 33:2; Ps. 68:8; Hab. 3:3), emphasis is now placed upon the fact that God's presence has brought victory rather than either Israel's own capabilities or Deborah's personal leadership skills *[Theophany; Violence and War in Judges]*. In addition, such imagery anticipates the actual storm that plays so important a role in the battle itself (5:20-21). By linking the Sinai experience to the present events, Israel testifies that the Lord marches out on their behalf not merely in a recollection of the past, but also as a remarkable ongoing occurrence.

5:6-12 *The Canaanites Oppress Israel*

For the first time in the song, Deborah makes an appearance. Yet the activities associated with her in 4:4-9 go unexpressed—no settling of disputes, no oracle, and certainly no reference to an unnamed woman. What is important in the song, once again, is not the mysterious woman recipient of honor, but the glory attributed to God.

What is here, however, supplements the narrative account by describing something of the situation during the oppression. Apparently, the Canaanites' exploitation of Israel has resulted in severe economic hardships *[Canaanites]*. Trading has become virtually impossible, and everyday travel is curtailed or diverted, no doubt by the threat of thievery. Even the least-significant and secluded of villages has failed to escape the crisis. People no longer feel safe to leave their homes. As a result of such oppression—oppression rooted in

Israelite idolatry, cautiously assuming the correctness of the reading *When new gods were chosen* (5:8)—Israel has been reduced to a state of utter defenselessness.

In the context of this otherwise dismal situation, Deborah seeks to inspire a renewed appreciation for the Lord's previous acts on Israel's behalf (5:11). All members of the community, from the highest ranking officials (*you who ride on white donkeys,* 5:10) to the common laborers, are summoned to the task of reciting and thereby affirming Israel's sacred traditions in which God delivers his people. In addition to replacing despair with hope, such an act of remembering also places new responsibilities upon the community. As a result, volunteers are sought to join in the struggle (5:9), and Deborah and Barak are themselves encouraged in their leadership capacities (5:12).

5:13-18 Various Tribes Arise from Israel

Such a call for participation brings a mixed response, as evident here, and the refusal of certain tribes to participate is viewed dimly. Those tribes who accepted the call include Ephraim, Benjamin, Machir (western Manasseh), Issachar, and the two featured tribes of the narrative account, Zebulun and Naphtali. Those tribes criticized for not participating include Reuben, Gilead (the region of Gad), Dan, and Asher. Of all the tribes, only Judah and Simeon, situated well off to the south, fail to appear on either list *[Map, p. 240]*.

Even casual reflection upon these lists suggests that those tribes who take active part in the struggle are those concentrated within the central and north-central regions of the land. Clearly, they are the ones most affected by such an "internal" Canaanite coalition, not to mention the ones least affected by surrounding forces causing problems elsewhere.

By way of contrast, the nonparticipating tribes are all situated along the fringes and are typically occupied with other concerns. Reuben and Gad in particular are under almost constant attack from desert marauders, and Dan, who has apparently not yet migrated to their eventual northern destination (18:1ff.), is no doubt dealing with pressure from the Amorites to the southwest (1:34-36). As for the Asherites, their location along the northern Mediterranean coast leaves them in a rather isolated position; 1:32 implies that they have actually forged amenable relationships with the Canaanites there! For these and perhaps other reasons, the criticism leveled against the nonparticipants appears varied and in some cases restrained.

5:19-23 The Lord Fights for Israel

The battle is, once again, the high point of the song (on the battle itself, see notes on 4:12-16). From the theophany onward (5:4-5), anticipation rises for God to actually intervene *[Theophany]*. Even the call for participants and the varying responses rest on the awareness of God's saving deeds and the hope for their renewal in the present. Such anticipation finds fulfillment when, with stirring imagery drawn from the celestial and natural worlds, God rather than Israel destroys the opposing coalition (Lind: 71). Appropriately enough, he does so by manipulating the stars, considered to be the source of rain in Canaanite mythology *[Baal]*. In so doing, the Lord defeats not only the Canaanites, but also their gods (cf. 1 Kings 18:16-46)!

God's victory, accompanied by willing human participation, comes also in spite of human deficiencies, as the following reference to Meroz indicates. About Meroz, which fails to appear in the earlier lists focusing on human participation, nothing much can be said; both its character or makeup as well as its location are unknown. However, the scathing condemnation directed against it, condemnation that far exceeds in severity the earlier criticism of various tribes, implies that it was in a superior position to be of help. Of importance here is the fact that Meroz's failure to assist in the cause is not so much an affront to the people of Israel as a rejection of God himself and the responsibilities that he assigns. Such rejection, even in threatening situations involving holy war, is despised and condemned (cf. Jer. 48:10).

5:24-27 Jael Strikes Sisera

In stark contrast to the failure of Meroz, Jael stands as someone who is ready to join in, even if in so gruesome a way (see notes on 4:17-24). It is important to remember that the song's extreme celebration of Jael's accomplishments reflects the community's response and not necessarily God's (Hamlin: 87-88); yet it is equally important to place the deed carefully within its context. If the song celebrates God's victory, then it must by implication celebrate the removal of his adversaries. The song, in other words, rejoices in the triumph of God more so than in the hideous attack upon an individual.

5:28-30 A Worried Mother Awaits Sisera

In a moving but seemingly vindictive closing scene that is lacking in the narrative account, attention shifts to Sisera's mother at home. What is envisioned here is the common scene in which women, left at home for lengthy periods of time, wait for the men to return from war.

Such a wait may end in joyous reunion, as in 1 Samuel 18:6, but other times it may not. In this case, although the singer knows perfectly well what the outcome will be, no indications of remorse or sympathy are present. Instead, the mother's rising anxiety is expressed in a series of unanswered questions. With each passing question, the possibility of what for her would be an encouraging answer diminishes. As Deborah, the *mother in Israel* (5:7), arises in victory, so the mother of Sisera sinks deeper into despair.

5:31 Israel Prays to the Lord

Although often considered to be a later addition to the poem (Gray: 282), these closing lines provide a suitable thematic conclusion. Previously, Israel has recalled God's saving deeds of the past so as to invite his intervention in the present (5:4-5, 11). Now, given his intervention in the present, similar hopes are projected into the future. In this way, God's saving deeds become a continual source of renewal, encouragement, and hope.

With the final lines of the song, the period of Deborah comes to an end. All that remains is the standard closing, which appears here in verse 31, thereby weaving the story and song into a composite whole. As a result of Deborah's activities, tribal participation, and the Lord's intervention, the land experiences peace for forty years.

THE TEXT IN BIBLICAL CONTEXT

Liberation and Singing

Songs play a significant role in the life of God's redeemed people. In celebration of the Exodus, an event alluded to elsewhere in Judges (2:1—3:6) and throughout the OT, liberated Israel sang a song (Exod. 15:1-18). Similar responses burst forth from Hannah (1 Sam. 2:1-10) and David (2 Sam. 22:1-51), two of many who experienced the Lord's gracious and protective blessings. From the earliest pages of the OT onward, serving the Lord and singing go together.

Perhaps the importance of songs in the Scriptures is most clearly depicted in the Psalter, Israel's "worship book." Here one finds songs of all types and for all occasions: songs of deliverance (Ps. 18), dedication (30), and love (45), songs for the Sabbath (92), and songs for traveling to Jerusalem (120–134). Likewise, Israel is repeatedly encouraged to *sing to the Lord a new song*, a song celebrating the Lord's marvelous deeds (96:1; 98:1). So closely is singing associated with worship that, when reaching for metaphors to capture the severity of impending doom, Amos suggests that the Lord will turn Israel's singing into weeping (Amos 8:3, 10).

Songs, to be sure, are no less important in the NT. Mary sang a song after hearing of her pregnancy (Luke 1:46-55). Furthermore, Paul echoes the exhortations of the Psalter by advising his congregations to sing psalms, hymns, and spiritual songs (Col. 3:16). *Singing and making melody to the Lord in your hearts* (Eph. 5:19), Paul continues, is an appropriate way of giving thanks to God. In fact, singing is such an appropriate way of giving thanks and expressing praise that all of the redeemed gathered around the throne continually do just that (Rev. 5:9-14; 14:3).

THE TEXT IN THE LIFE OF THE CHURCH
Songs from the Liberated Soul

Following the lead of Scripture and the unmistakable impulse of the human heart, the church has through the centuries cultivated and been nourished by a diverse repertoire of inspiring songs. Without undermining the importance of other significant worship activities, Christians of varying traditions have continued to express their deepest religious thoughts and feelings through singing. While one church might emphasize preaching, another communion, and still another Bible reading, all seem to share singing in common.

The songs of the church have been born in a wide variety of contexts and under differing circumstances. Like the Song of Deborah, many of them are responses to a God who sustains his people through adversity and provides a way out of captivity. Negro Spirituals, for example, strengthened our physically enslaved brothers and sisters in nineteenth-century America prior to and following emancipation. Similarly, songs like (former slave-trader) John Newton's "Amazing Grace" and Fanny Crosby's "Blessed Assurance" have nurtured the souls of many spiritually liberated individuals. What these and countless other songs share in common with Deborah's Song is the considerable emphasis typically placed upon three elements:

• *Communal Involvement.* While Deborah and the other singers make mention of various groups who should have participated in this victory over the Canaanites but refused (5:15b-17, 23), their attention focuses on the many who gladly played their part: *When the people offer themselves willingly, praise the Lord!* (5:2, 9). Oppression and adversity often bring with them a sense of isolation and overwhelming discouragement. Reminders that people are neither alone nor working alone tend to lift broken spirits and stimulate hope. In his hymn "Prayer in the Hour of Affliction," a physically afflicted Menno Simons alludes to this very thing:

> I beg my brethren all,
> Who've heard the Master's call,
> My grief and pain now to recall,
> And then, before God's eyes
> Lay pleasant sacrifice;
> Let pleasing prayer as incense rise; . . .
> This in my song I pray
> With brethren everywhere,
> In Word-borne prayer. (1068)

• *Liberation from Evil.* Because the OT generally lacks the more extensive examination of principalities, powers, and demonic forces found later in the NT, the people of Israel tended to see evil embodied in the here-and-now. In winning the battle over Sisera and the Canaanites, therefore, Deborah and her forces marching for the Lord are not simply accumulating real estate or removing a foreign foe. They are cooperating with the Lord's victory over evil and extending the boundaries of God's influence. So it is with the liberating gospel of Jesus Christ, the purpose of which is to procure not simply freedom from sickness, but freedom from sin. Charles Wesley describes this liberty in his hymn "And Can It Be":

> Long my imprisoned spirit lay fast bound in sin and nature's night;
> thine eye diffused a quick'ning ray, I woke, the dungeon flamed with light.
> My chains fell off, my heart was free; I rose, went forth and followed thee.

• *God's Incomprehensible Acts.* According to Deborah's Song, Israel's own capabilities have virtually nothing to do with the outcome of the battle. God's wonderful acts—flooding the plains of Jezreel during the dry season! (5:20-21)—bring victory over the opposition. When the people of God are numbed by their surrounding circumstances, they need to be reminded again of what Brother Andrew refers to as "the excitement of having caught such a spectacular glimpse of God at work" (153). Accordingly, Joachim Neander resembles Deborah in exhorting seventeenth-century singers:

> Praise to the Lord, the Almighty, the King of creation!
> O my soul, praise him, for he is thy health and salvation!
> All ye who hear, now to God's temple draw near.
> Join me in glad adoration! (*Hymnal,* 37)

Judges 6:1—10:5

The Pattern Threatened: Gideon and Abimelech

OVERVIEW

With the narrative concerning Gideon and his son, Abimelech, a narrative that comprises roughly one quarter of the entire book, the writer now moves into a new phase in his overall depiction of the period of the judges. While the accounts of both Ehud and Deborah, once again, generally affirm Othniel's pattern, the present narrative raises serious doubts. All of the major steps in the Judges Cycle remain intact: Israel does evil, God sends an oppressor, Israel cries out, God raises a judge, the judge frees Israel, and the land experiences peace. Yet these steps are increasingly blurred by the surrounding events and conversations.

Likewise, various points of erosion become apparent. The precision and swiftness of Othniel is in the case of Gideon and his son Abimelech replaced by worsening conditions, frequent interruptions, and long delays. During the lifetime of Gideon, therefore, the model of judgeship established by Othniel is severely threatened. Accordingly, Jewish tradition evaluated Gideon, along with Jephthah and Samson, as the three least worthy of all the judges (Sarna: 558).

OUTLINE

An Ambiguous Portrait (Scene 1): Gideon's Quests, 6:1—8:32

An Ambiguous Portrait (Scene 2): Abimelech's Atrocities, 8:33—10:5

An Ambiguous Portrait (Scene 1): Gideon's Quests

Judges 6:1—8:32

PREVIEW

In the account of Gideon and the Midianites, a frightened and initially timid leading character finds himself in the middle of a terrifying crisis. Through the ensuing series of events, Gideon sheds his fear and timidity, only to replace them with an uncontrollable thirst for vengeance. Along the way, much is said about handling difficult situations and the complexities of human nature.

The stories told here concerning Gideon actually comprise two somewhat distinct and contrasting narratives. Following the standard but now longer introduction (6:1-10), the opening narrative focuses primarily on Israel's confrontation with the Midianites (6:11—8:3). In this case, the movement flows from Gideon's call and the establishment of his forces to the climactic defeat of the Midianite oppressors. Throughout, Gideon appears as an insecure deliverer who remains in constant conversation with the ultimate Deliverer, the Lord himself. With the victory over the Midianites secure, we rightfully anticipate the typical concluding comments concerning the land enjoying peace.

Where one expects such comments, however, a second narrative suddenly emerges (8:4-27). In this episode, attention shifts from Israel's corporate struggle with the Midianites to Gideon's personal quest for revenge. Similarly, the seemingly insecure deliverer of the previous narrative gives way to a vindictive headhunter who only mentions the Lord as a casual afterthought. Rather than emphasizing Israel's liberation from the Midianites, this second narrative reaches its climax with Gideon's rejection of kingship and his subsequent construction of an ephod. Ultimately, Gideon, himself on a downward spiral, takes the entire community along with him.

OUTLINE

Crisis and Criticism, 6:1-10
    6:1-6   Crisis Introduced
    6:7-10   A Prophet Rebukes Israel

Gideon Prepared for Leadership, 6:11-40
    6:11-24   The Lord Calls Gideon
    6:25-32   Gideon Demolishes Baal's Altar

6:33-35   Gideon Summons the Israelites
6:36-40   Gideon Tests the Lord

Gideon Triumphant in Combat, 7:1—8:3
7:1-8a   The Lord Reduces Gideon's Troops
7:8b-15   The Lord Encourages Gideon
7:16-25   Israel Conquers the Midianites
8:1-3   Gideon Consoles the Ephraimites

Gideon Revengeful in Victory, 8:4-21
8:4-9   Succoth and Peniel Rebuff Gideon
8:10-12   Gideon Pursues Zebah and Zalmunna
8:13-17   Gideon Repays Succoth and Peniel
8:18-21   Gideon Slays Zebah and Zalmunna

Gideon Corruptive in the Spotlight, 8:22-32
8:22-27   Gideon Constructs an Ephod
8:28-32   Gideon Fathers Abimelech

EXPLANATORY NOTES
Crisis and Criticism 6:1-10
6:1-6 Crisis Introduced

Although the NIV and some other translations read *Again* at the beginning of 6:1, no such connecting term occurs in the Hebrew text. By implication, what follows is in some ways distinct from the preceding accounts; a new stage in the developing story of the judges emerges.

In this case, the unspecified evil committed by the Israelites results in their oppression at the hands of the Midianites. The Midianites were seminomadic people typically associated with northern Arabia, although their wandering lifestyle is reflected in biblical passages showing them throughout Transjordan and in Sinai. The Midianites' vigorous attempts to gain control over portions of Palestine at this time probably reflect a plan to monopolize trade along the region's roadways (Gottwald: 431-432, 463).

In terms of reputation, the OT's depiction of the Midianites is mixed. On one hand, they are genealogically linked to Abraham (Gen. 25:2), and Moses' father-in-law was one of their number (Exod. 18:1). On the other hand, Midian was included among Isaac's rivals banished by Abraham (Gen. 25:6). The Midianites joined forces with Moab in opposing the Israelites on their way to Canaan (Num. 22:4-7). In fact, the Midianites specifically earned the Lord's wrath for leading Israel astray, apparently by seducing them into idolatry and sexual immorality (Num. 25:1-18; 31:1-12). As such, conflict between the Midianites and Israelites began well before the time of Gideon.

Of exceptional importance in these introductory comments is the severity of the oppression. To convey this, the writer carefully and elaborately describes various aspects of the frightful dilemma engulfing the Israelites:

• The Midianite oppressors, along with their allies, are excessive in number, analogous to swarms of locusts. While the individual members of such a swarm are impossible to count, serious estimates suggest that a locust cloud can include over one billion insects and darken the entire sky (Brodsky: 33). As to the Midianites, *neither they nor their camels could be counted.*

• The oppressors are advanced in terms of equipment. Although the Israelites apparently did not have ready access to camels until the time of David (1 Chron. 12:40), their Midianite adversaries use them to great advantage. In addition to their ability to travel considerable distances without water and to do so with considerable speed, camels are naturally imposing in appearance.

• The oppressors are ruthless in character and intent. Rather than a single attack followed by a period of foreign control, all indications suggest that the Midianites are raiding repeatedly. As such, the threat of invasion never subsides. Each day carries with it the fear of recurring attacks and debilitating losses.

Beyond the simple frequency of these attacks, however, is their severity. The Midianites come with total devastation on their minds—they spare nothing (6:4). Once again, the locust imagery intensifies the setting, for it implies not only the great number of locusts, but also the results of their arrival (cf. Joel 1–2). During a six-week locust plague that ravaged Ethiopia in 1959, for example, conservative estimates concluded that enough food was destroyed to feed one million people for one year (Baron: 10-15). In Israel's case, the Midianites *wasted the land as they came in.*

• The oppressors are comprehensive in their outlook and ambitions. Later verses suggest that the northern tribes of Manasseh, Asher, Zebulun, Naphtali, and Ephraim (6:35; 7:24; 8:1) are greatly affected during this time, yet 6:4 indicates that the Midianites destroy Israelite crops as far south as Gaza on the Mediterranean Coast! *[Maps, pp. 241-242].* The geographical scope of the carnage, therefore, includes a sizeable portion of Israel's territory.

Due to the exceptional cruelty of the Midianites, the Israelites are forced to take certain precautions. In a manner that suggests contemporary bomb shelters, they prepare caves and quarters in which to hide whenever attacked. Such precautions spare human lives, at least temporarily, but they do little to protect Israel's more-vulnerable crops and belongings. Therefore, the ongoing conditions are worsening, leaving the Israelites in a state of economic turmoil.

Finally, as Israel's situation grows increasingly catastrophic, then and only then do the people cry out to the Lord for help (6:6). In short, the agony of the immediate situation, not regret over their own evil deeds, leads Israel to seek divine assistance. There is no hint of any lasting change of heart.

6:7-10 A Prophet Rebukes Israel

Rather than an immediate, positive response to Israel's cries, the Lord sends a prophet to confront them. Only here and in the Deborah narrative is prophecy mentioned in Judges. Otherwise, similar speeches come either from the mouths of angelic messengers or from the Lord himself (2:1-5; 5:23; 10:11-14). In the case of Deborah, she too prophesied after Israel cried out, but it was a prophetic summons for Barak to take action (4:4-9). In the present instance, however, the prophetic speech takes the form of a stern rebuke. In that sense, it closely resembles that of the messenger in 2:1-5.

Also similar to the messenger's speech is the content of this prophetic word. Reference is made once again to the Lord's saving deeds in the past, deeds in which God not only delivered Israel from oppression, but also provided a land for them to inhabit. In return, he sought their allegiance and prohibited them from worshiping foreign gods. Israel, however, has repeatedly ignored this prohibition, thereby bringing upon themselves such oppressive situations. Disobedience, therefore, is the ultimate cause of Israel's ongoing troubles. Furthermore, the Lord delays in delivering them this time, thus implying that he is tiring of their behavior. Hence, the prophetic speech interrupts the sequence and postpones the hoped-for response of the Lord.

Gideon Prepared for Leadership 6:11-40

In addition to the prophetic speech, the Lord's deliverance is now further delayed by a lengthy period of preparation for the chosen deliverer.

6:11-24 The Lord Calls Gideon

At the conclusion of the prophet's rebuke, the angel of the Lord (cf. 2:1-5) visits Ophrah, the location of which remains uncertain. It belongs to Manasseh's holdings and is thus distinguished from a similarly named Benjaminite town, four miles north of Bethel (Josh. 18:23; 1 Sam. 13:17). The oak, reminiscent of Deborah's palm (4:5), suggests a place where God's oracles are given. However, such a place by this time is dominated by Baal worship, as 6:25-32 clearly indicates [Asherah; Ashtoreth; Baal].

The unsuspecting benefactor of the angel's visit is Gideon, the son of an Abiezrite and therefore a descendant of Manasseh (Josh. 17:2). His activities indicate the harshness of Israel's situation—he is *beating out wheat in the wine press, to hide it from the Midianites* (6:11).

A winepress, typically a large vat carved out of the rock and connected to a lower, smaller vat by a channel, could be located almost anyplace grapes were available. The grapes were simply placed in the large vat and trampled under foot until the juice flowed into the lower vat. In this way, no additional implements were needed. Threshing wheat, however, normally involved either beating the stalks or crushing them on a stone floor with a heavy, ox-drawn sledge. In either case, the work was performed in an exposed place so that, when the threshed material was tossed up, the wind could carry away the lighter, unwanted chaff (Ps. 1:4).

Gideon, therefore, is improvising by threshing wheat in a less noticeable winepress. That he can do so also indicates that only limited amounts of wheat are available. Most of the grain stalk has already been confiscated by the Midianites.

In beginning the conversation, the angel surprisingly addresses Gideon, who is working under cover, as *mighty warrior* (*gibbor hehayil*). Precisely the same Hebrew term elsewhere describes both Jephthah (11:1) and Boaz (Ruth 2:1), and David himself is similarly characterized (1 Sam. 16:18). Some have suggested, with only limited evidence, that the designation actually places Gideon within a specific social class (Gray: 285; Soggin: 115); it is at least a title of significant respect. As the resulting dialogue indicates, however, Gideon hardly shares the angel's perspective.

The angel's affirmation of the Lord's presence is reminiscent of similar promises to Moses (Exod. 3:12) and Joshua (Josh. 1:5). Still, Gideon raises two serious objections: (1) Israel's oppression scarcely indicates the presence of the Lord; and (2) such oppression is in stark contrast to salvation stories told to Gideon and his contemporaries by their fathers.

To answer Gideon's initial objection, the Lord himself responds rather than the angel. However, too much significance should not be attached to such a distinction between "Lord" and "angel" (contra Boling: 131). Most likely, the terms are used interchangeably: in these cases the angel is a representation of God himself. Significantly, the Lord's reply essentially ignores Gideon's concerns and instead directs a command to the deliverer-to-be: *Go. . . . I hereby commission you* (6:14). Nevertheless, Gideon, still unaware of his visitor's identity, is not yet ready to comply. Whether out of humility or simple lack of self-confidence, he refers to his own unimpressive credentials. Moses' apparent inferiority complex (Exod. 3:11) has become Gideon's insignificant family heritage. To both, God's answer is the same: *I will be with you*. Neither, however, is so easily convinced.

In an attempt to determine ultimately the validity of this experience—to prove to himself that he is not hallucinating—Gideon politely requests a sign (6:17). That he desires to present an offering (*minḥah*, 6:18) indicates that Gideon is slowly realizing the importance of the occasion and perhaps even the identity of his visitor. The term *minḥah* refers in the OT to both gifts presented to special people or superiors (Gen. 32:13; 1 Sam. 10:27; 1 Kings 4:21; 2 Kings 8:8; 2 Chron. 17:5) as well as to sacrificial offerings (Exod. 29:41; Lev. 2:1). It is impossible to determine precisely how Gideon initially intends the present, though it finally becomes the sacrificial variety.

In any case, the magnitude of the offering further underscores Gideon's escalating excitement. An ephah of flour, equivalent to nearly forty-five pounds, is on another occasion enough to accompany the giving of a three-year-old bull (1 Sam. 1:24)! It is noteworthy that Gideon takes the time to prepare such a feast, particularly when grain is in short supply. The visitor shows graciousness in leisurely waiting for Gideon to prepare the offering.

In accordance with his visitor's instructions, Gideon places the entire offering on a nearby rock, perhaps even the winepress where he has been working. What follows is a theophany that recalls Moses' experience at the burning bush (Exod. 3:2) *[Theophany]*. In a burst of flames, Gideon's previous uncertainty vanishes as the fire illumines the visitor's identity (6:21). Gideon has received the verification he has longed for, but with it the fear that seeing a pure and holy God face to face means certain death (Gen. 16:13; 32:30; Judg. 13:22; Isa. 6:5; cf. Exod. 20:19).

Nevertheless, Gideon is immediately assured that he will not die. *Peace* (*šalom*), the Lord replies. *Šalom*, a term with a broad semantical range, captures virtually every aspect of a positive and healthy relationship: wholeness, prosperity, harmony. As such, rather than merely preserving Gideon's life, the Lord establishes a new relationship with his chosen instrument. In order to forever remember this experience, Gideon, like others before him, builds an altar with a commemorative name (Gen. 33:20; 35:7; cf. Gen. 12:7).

6:25-32 Gideon Demolishes Baal's Altar

Without delay, Gideon's initial task is specified. Appropriately enough, this task has not so much to do with the Midianites as it does with the disastrous religious situation in Gideon's own backyard. The ultimate problem, as elsewhere in Judges, is not the oppressor, but the evil in which Israel is so thoroughly entangled. Gideon, therefore, must put his own house in order before carrying out the more extensive work awaiting him. As such, the assignment has the potential to alienate him from both his family as well as his clan.

Completing this task involves destroying the altar to Baal and cutting down the associated pole (*'ašerah*), both of which are apparently under the supervision of Gideon's father. In addition to the standard altar, Canaanite shrines typically include a standing stone symbolizing the male deity as well as a pole symbolizing the female deity *[Asherah; Baal]*. The law of Moses specifically commanded that the Israelites should destroy these things (Exod. 34:13; Deut. 7:5), although they repeatedly failed to comply (Judg. 2:2-3) *[Prohibition Against Images]*.

In their place, Gideon is instructed to erect yet another altar to the Lord and, using the wood from the razed pole, to offer one of his father's bulls as a sacrifice. Since he can summon ten servants to assist him with the work, he is not as insignificant as he has insinuated (6:15). Yet why he would solicit the help of so many others to accomplish a terrifying and potentially threatening task remains a rather humorous enigma. Gideon, who threshes in secret, now attempts to destroy the altar in secret, an attempt no doubt thwarted by one of his own accomplices.

Upon the completion of this assignment, the community immediately reacts to take on Baal's cause; this stands in direct contrast to Gideon's initial reluctance to take on God's cause. Likewise, it fully justifies Gideon's previous fears and further underscores the importance of Baal worship among the people. In the face of death threats, Joash, Gideon's father, comes to his defense with sensible words that Gideon himself might utter if he were not so afraid: *Will you contend for Baal? . . . If he is a god, let him contend for himself.* Yet, the community is doing precisely what is expected in the face of blatant, sacrilegious behavior. Israelite law itself instructs the people to deal with blasphemers (not to mention selected other lawbreakers) in a similar way (Lev. 24:14-16). Nevertheless, the would-be executioners apparently disperse, leaving Gideon alive.

With the atmosphere somewhat more relaxed, Joash memorializes the occasion, not by building a new altar, but by giving Gideon a new name. *Jerub-Baal*, often understood to mean "let Baal contend" (*rib*), more likely means "let Baal show himself great" (*rbb*). In either case, the name is an invitation, no doubt sarcastic in tone, for Baal to right the wrong committed by Gideon. Such an invitation, which seemingly implies a subtle shift in Joash's own religious convictions, is one that Baal chooses not to accept.

6:33-35 Gideon Summons the Israelites

In the midst of Gideon's ongoing preparation, notice is given that the opposing forces have crossed the Jordan and assembled in the Jezreel Valley. This valley, separating the central region of Samaria from the northern tribal territories, provides both fertile soil and great maneuverability for travel and assaults *[Map, p. 242]*. As a result, the Jezreel Valley is an area upon which nearly everyone tried to stake a claim. The Israelites, however, were rarely capable of controlling it, and only recently under Deborah and Barak have they established their authority there (Judg. 4–5). That authority, however, had since dissipated at the hands of their oppressors.

In the face of this latest Midianite threat, Gideon is in no position to act alone; only a short time earlier, he was working in secret, requesting a special sign, and benefiting from his father's defense. Instead, he receives assistance from both divine and human sources.

First, *the Spirit of the Lord came upon* him (6:34, NIV) *[Holy Spirit in the OT]*. The rather familiar translation *came upon*, however, fails to do justice to the Hebrew *labaš* ("to put on clothing"), a term used only rarely in relation to God's Spirit (1 Chron. 12:18; 2 Chron. 24:20). Typically, *labaš* refers to the everyday act of putting on a garment. At times, however, it assumes a metaphorical usage, denoting the putting on of such things as "righteousness" (Job 29:14, Isa. 59:17), "vengeance" (Isa. 59:17), and "cursing" (Ps. 109:18). In Gideon's case, the Spirit of God has "put him on" as one would put on clothing. Clearly, the Spirit is the driving force and Gideon the more passive respondent (cf. NRSV: *took possession of*).

Second, Gideon, the freshly endowed charismatic deliverer, summons human assistance. Those called first are Gideon's fellow Abiezrites—would most of them have been Baal worshipers at

Ophrah just days ago? Next, messengers solicit the support of Manasseh, Asher, Zebulun, and Naphtali, those northern tribes surrounding the Jezreel Valley and therefore at greatest risk [Maps, pp. 240, 242]. While no specific indication is given here concerning the extent of their response, 7:3 suggests that 32,000 men assemble. No one wants to forfeit any of the advantages gained through Deborah's and Barak's efforts in the region, if indeed those advantages still remain.

6:36-40 Gideon Tests the Lord

With the granting of Gideon's previous request (6:17-24), the assembling of the enemy, and the gathering of Israelite forces, the stage is set for the anticipated battle. It comes as somewhat of a surprise, then, to find Gideon reopening negotiations with God. In spite of all that has just transpired, Gideon remains most apprehensive concerning God's plans and his own role in them. Regardless of whatever progress has been made, he as yet cannot affirm the *mighty warrior* title given him by the angel of the Lord (6:12). Gideon, in other words, needs additional preparation.

In this case, he devises a test. Testing (*nasah*) God in the OT is prohibited (Deut. 6:16), both because it calls into question God's faithfulness and because it reflects great disdain on the part of the one testing; it is normally an attempt to force God to do something (Exod. 17:7; Num. 14:22; Ps. 78:18; Brensinger: 111-112). Here, however, the Lord accepts the idea, no doubt because it grows out of Gideon's fluctuating sense of security and his continuing need for assurance. God's patience and mercy, therefore, pierce legal expectations and allow for honest searching.

As for the test itself, the stipulations are actually quite simple. Gideon intends to place a woolen fleece upon a nearby threshing floor. Given the terms, this first test is positive—a wet fleece, but a dry floor.

Even with that, Gideon remains apprehensive. While no doubt anticipating the outcome of the test during the night, Gideon recognizes a serious flaw in his proposal. Given the fact that wool absorbs considerably more dew than stone, one would expect the fleece to remain wet far longer than the floor. The test is therefore no test at all! To remedy the problem, Gideon merely reverses the arrangement, asking that the fleece be dry but the floor wet. Such a shift in details, however, has no effect on the outcome—a dry fleece, but a wet floor.

THE TEXT IN BIBLICAL CONTEXT

Desperate Situations

In the story of Gideon, the writer deliberately uses considerable detail to depict an apparently hopeless situation. Israel faces a ruthless, sizeable and well-equipped opponent. On the surface, then, the Israelites stand virtually no chance of emerging alive, let alone victorious. Indeed, only an act of God will do.

Elsewhere, various biblical writers similarly highlight certain details as a way of emphasizing the absolute desperation of situations in which God will eventually intervene. The youthful and diminutive David, himself unable to maneuver while wearing the king's armor, is matched against a giant of a man who can direct a fifteen-pound spear with great accuracy (1 Sam. 17:4-7, 39, 42). Hezekiah and his people remain huddled within the walls of Jerusalem while the entire Assyrian army prepares to march upon them (2 Kings 18–19; Isa. 36–37). Even Sennacherib, the Assyrian ruler, recognizes an insurmountable situation when he sees one; his own annals record that he had Hezekiah bottled up "like a bird in a cage" (Pritchard: 288).

Finally, certain desperate people approach Jesus, their hopelessness expressed in unambiguous details—crippled "for thirty-eight years," blind "from birth," and dead for "four days" (John 5:5; 9:1; 11:39). In these and other instances, the critical situations confronting human beings offer no resolution short of divine intervention. Rather than simply stating that "with God all things are possible," the biblical writers persuasively and artistically demonstrate it (Matt. 19:26; Mark 10:27; Luke 1:37; 18:27).

Requesting Signs

With rattling knees, Gideon asks for three successive signs (6:17, 36-37, 39). Incredibly, not only does the Lord provide each of these, but he also adds a fourth for good measure (7:10-11)! Gideon, therefore, takes his place alongside other biblical characters who ask for and subsequently receive signs from God. These include:

Text	Person	Situation	Sign
Gen. 15:8-21	Abraham	Assurance of possessing a new land	Smoke and fire
Exod. 4:1-9	Moses	Confidence in leading the Israelites	Staff/serpent and leprous hand
2 Kings 20:8-11	Hezekiah	Assurance of promised healing	Retreating shadow
Luke 1:8-25	Zechariah	Confirmation of his wife's pregnancy	Inability to speak

Others, such as Jeroboam, receive signs without even asking for them (1 Kings 13:1-5). Still others, including Ahaz, are offered signs but refuse them (Isa. 7:10-17). Finally, many desire signs without obtaining them (Matt. 12:38-39; 16:1-4; Mark 8:11-12; cf. John 4:48).

On the basis of such examples, it appears that signs are primarily given to two types of people: (1) those who are sincere but needy, and (2) those who are corrupt but uninterested. At the same time, signs are withheld from those who blatantly and defiantly put God to the test for no suitable reason. In other words, the Lord rarely gives signs solely to satisfy the daring challenges of his antagonists. Instead, God provides signs to encourage and strengthen his people or to confirm the dependability of his word.

THE TEXT IN THE LIFE OF THE CHURCH

The journey of faith is not the same for all travelers. Some, often through no fault of their own, encounter more bends and ditches than others. Similarly, some experience greater pain and have far more miles to cover. Whether it be the result of poor parenting, sad personal decisions, varying personality types, inferior natural abilities, or simply fate—life treats people differently. Within this wide spectrum of spiritual participants, the opening events of the Gideon narrative speak at least two special words to the weary and fainthearted:

God's Presence During Difficult Moments

"Help! I'm going round the bend!" a tattered minister cried out to God. "Don't worry," came the reply, "I'm coming round there with you!" (Horsman: 91). In much the same way, God responds to both Israel and Gideon during the Midianite crisis. On the national level, the hideous oppression meted out by the Midianites might cause the Israelites to hide in caves, but it fails to scare the Lord away. In answer to Israel's plea for mercy, God draws near. On a more personal level, the Lord similarly demonstrates his continuing presence to Gideon, his chosen but intimidated vessel of deliverance. Rather than leaving him alone, God steps right up beside Gideon during the most difficult and challenging moments of his life. The Lord, in other words, does not abandon his people when circumstances turn sour, even if the turmoil results from their own doing (Ps. 46:1).

God's Patience During Weaker Moments

In addition to meeting Gideon's repeated requests, the Lord later offers unsolicited reassurance. In the same way that Job presents sacrifices "just in case" his children have sinned, so too does God provide an encouraging dream "just in case" Gideon's doubts and fears linger (Job 1:5; Judg. 7:10-11, 13-14). Rather than insisting that Gideon immediately rise to the desired level of commitment, the Lord nurtures him through his moments of weakness. While not condoning evasiveness or prolonged excuse-making, God deals graciously and patiently with all of the Gideons of the world who genuinely need help and reassurance. "God does not require us to have arrived," writes Sarah Horsman, "only to be moving in the right direction" (41). Apparently, people in need of assistance are more usable in the long run than those who charge out and insistently go to work on their own.

EXPLANATORY NOTES

Gideon Triumphant in Combat 7:1—8:3

7:1-8a The Lord Reduces Gideon's Troops

If by this point Gideon is satisfied to move ahead, the Lord is not. Quite simply, the troops amassed by Gideon are too large in number, for the victory might then be attributed to their own resourcefulness. To prevent such a diversion of praise rightfully directed to God himself, a reduction of troops is necessary.

To bring about such a reduction, two steps are taken. First, in accord with Deuteronomy 20:8, everyone—apparently excluding Gideon!—who suffers great fear is sent home. Fear, after all, is contagious and can therefore paralyze an entire army. On the basis of this criterion, 22,000 of the 32,000 men leave Mount Gilboa (7:3, reading Gilboa for the problematic Gilead, which is located on the eastern side of the Jordan River). Only 10,000 men remain to fight the enormous Midianite army.

Yet 10,000 still exceed the Lord's envisioned limit, so a second step is taken involving drinking postures. The test itself remains a bit unclear. As it now stands in most translations, the text appears slightly distorted; it suggests that those who lap the water with their tongues, as a dog laps (7:5), do so with their hands to their mouths (7:6)! In reality, one would expect the kneelers to use their hands rather than the lappers. Generally, the difficulty is either overlooked or ignored, and the resulting assumption is that God chooses those who drink hand to mouth. Such drinkers, after all, are more alert and probably more competent.

The NRSV, however, follows a helpful alternative reading for verses 5b-6a that appears in one of the major manuscripts of the LXX [Septuagint]. There, the phrase *with their hands to their mouths* actually appears, not in verse 6 but in verse 5. Accordingly, the passage reads:

> "All those who lap the water with their tongues, as a dog laps, you shall put to one side; all those who kneel down to drink, putting their hands to their mouths, you shall put to the other side." The number of those that lapped was three hundred; but all the rest of the troops knelt down to drink water.

In this case, the test is clear and consistent. The alert individuals kneel down and raise the water to their mouths. The others put their faces directly above the water, and are therefore less aware of impending dangers. Any knowledgeable military commander would of course choose his forces from among the kneelers. By way of contrast, the Lord selects only the lappers! Not only does he reduce the number to an insignificant 300, but even to the 300 least competent! With such an army, the Israelites can hardly help but recognize that God, and not they themselves, secures the victory *[Violence and War in Judges]*.

7:8b-15 The Lord Encourages Gideon

With Gideon presumably prepared and the troops in order, surely the battle is imminent. In fact, even the command to *attack* is forcefully issued (7:9). Once again, however, the battle is not quite imminent. One final preparatory item remains. Apparently the Lord detects a final trace of fear in Gideon. Since it is impossible to dismiss the leader with the other 22,000 nervous soldiers, other provisions need to be made. As such, God offers Gideon one additional, unrequested confidence-building measure.

In this final event before the anticipated battle, Gideon and his servant Purah descend to the fringes of the Midianite camp, apparently where the perimeter guards are stationed. Precisely why Purah, who is otherwise unknown, accompanies Gideon is unclear. The term *na'ar*, literally "young boy," refers in similar contexts to a shield-bearer (9:54; 1 Sam. 14:1, 6), but perhaps his role here is to verify the message and to lend support. After all, nothing about Gideon up to this point suggests that he would want to make such a venture alone. By reemphasizing the enormity of Midian's forces (cf. 6:1-6), the writer further heightens this sense of Gideon's continuing anxiety and the magnitude of his task.

Upon arriving at their destination, Gideon is privileged to hear a conversation about a dream between two Midianite soldiers. In the ancient world, dreams were viewed with the utmost seriousness; they were considered channels through which the gods communicated their wishes and intentions. Furthermore, the importance attributed to dreams often increased according to the status of the dreamer. Pharaoh's dreams, for example, were for some a matter of life and death (Gen. 41). So in Gideon's case, the dream of a Midianite soldier carries great significance.

As to the dream's interpretation, the barley loaf seems to represent the people of Israel, an agricultural community known for growing such crops. Likewise, the tent is an appropriate image for the raiding Midianites, seminomads associated with tent-dwelling. Clearly, the dream poses no interpretative difficulties for the second soldier, who immediately sees in it Midian's impending destruction at the hands of the Israelites. Neither is the significance of the dream lost on Gideon; upon hearing both the dream and its interpretation, he returns to camp with renewed excitement and confidence.

As he arrives, Gideon exhorts his troops with essentially the same command given to him by the Lord only a short time ago: *Get up; for the Lord has given the army of Midian into your hand* (7:15). After a long and protracted sequence of events—events that clearly contrast the readiness of Othniel, Ehud, Deborah, and even Barak with the extreme hesitation of Gideon—Gideon now stands ready for battle.

7:16-25 Israel Conquers the Midianites

With the completion of Gideon's preparation, the long-awaited battle finally arrives. The Israelite strategy is once again simple enough. Gideon divides his meager forces into three groups of one hundred men each. Every soldier then receives, of all things, a horn and a large clay jar containing only a torch. These are hardly the sort of fear-inducing weapons typically employed in serious combat. That they are used here, however, suits the overall context exceptionally well. Given the prior concern over a possible misappropriation of credit (7:2), such unusual weaponry complements the massive reduction of Israelite troops. The Lord can deliver his people with limited numbers and even with inferior equipment.

After distributing the supplies, the three Israelite companies situate themselves at various points on the perimeter of the Midianite camp by *the beginning of the middle watch*. In ancient Israel, the night was divided into three watches, each four hours in duration (Exod. 14:24; 1 Sam. 11:11; Jub. 49:10, 12; Mark 13:35, likely due to Roman influence, implies a later division into four watches). By the beginning of the middle watch, around ten o'clock, a sizeable portion of the Midianite army no doubt lies fast asleep. Furthermore, insofar as new guards are posted between watches, the recently positioned replacements need to adjust to nighttime duty. As a result, such transition periods are marked by increased vulnerability, regardless of the precision with which such changes are made.

Under such circumstances, the Israelite forces follow Gideon's lead, blowing their horns and smashing their jars. Instantly, the otherwise dark night becomes one of glaring lights, blaring trumpets, and shouting: *A sword for the Lord and for Gideon!* (7:20). Then, as Gideon's forces stand watching, the startled Midianites panic and lose all sanity.

The Midianites are not lacking aggression and immediately go on the attack, but they desperately need perspective. Rather than confronting their assailants, they start turning on each other. From all indications, the Israelite army is actually superfluous! To assure, however, that such self-destructive behavior is not attributed to any psychological deficiencies on the Midianites' part, the writer makes clear that all of this is due to the Lord's intervention. Now Gideon, who earlier confronted the angel of the Lord about divine "inactivity" (6:13), can see God's wondrous works for himself.

With the initial phase of the battle completed, the remaining Midianites, demoralized and terrified, flee the scene. Although none of the particular sites referred to here can be identified with certainty (Martin: 99), the general direction seems clear enough. The Midianites take the only serious option open to them, heading southeast, back across the Jordan to the region from which they have come (6:33).

While in pursuit, Gideon sends for recruits from among the various northern tribes. He has done so earlier, before the battle began (6:35). Considerable assistance has come from Manasseh, Asher, Zebulun, and Naphtali. The resulting army, however, proving too large for the Lord's plans, has been drastically reduced. Now those same tribes—minus Zebulun—are summoned, and surely many of the original troops are recalled [Map, p. 240].

That they have time to respond suggests a complexity in the events themselves that goes beyond the apparent swiftness of the narrative. That they respond so quickly implies that the initial success of the three hundred gives added confidence to those who previously succumbed to fear. However, it is not clear why additional forces are apparently deemed appropriate at this stage of the conflict when they were dismissed earlier. Perhaps the Lord's opening demonstration at the Midianite camp was sufficient to prevent any misappropriation of credit.

Beyond the support of the original northern tribes, additional assistance is now requested from the tribe of Ephraim. In particular,

Ephraim, given its more southerly location, is assigned the task of blocking the fleeing Midianites near one of the tributaries emptying into the Jordan (the precise location of Beth Barah remains unknown). This they do, but apparently with only limited success (see 8:1-3). In the process, however, the Ephraimites manage to capture Oreb and Zeeb, two of the Midianite leaders (cf. Ps. 83:11; Isa. 10:26). Their capture is a major accomplishment for Ephraim, as shown by their stature and imposing names ("raven," "wolf"), which no doubt reflect the way previous opposition forces viewed them. As such, after killing them at now unidentifiable locations, the Ephraimites present the heads of Oreb and Zeeb as war trophies to Gideon (7:25; cf. 1 Sam. 17:54).

8:1-3 Gideon Consoles the Ephraimites

Following the capture of Oreb and Zeeb, the Ephraimites express anything but the kind of celebratory enthusiasm that one might expect. Instead, they vigorously criticize Gideon for his failure to include them sooner in his plans. Such criticism grows, in part, out of the fact that Ephraim was unable to prevent the escape of a number of Midianites. If they had been summoned earlier, they could have more thoroughly cut off the enemy and thus avoided the need for ongoing pursuits.

The grounds for their unanticipated reaction, however, go far deeper than mere misgivings over military strategy. Ephraim, for a variety of reasons, was from the start one of Israel's more prominent tribes. First, situated primarily in the central hills, Ephraim was among the more successful northern tribes at gaining control of and protecting its territory (1:22-26). The extent of settlements in their region receives further corroboration in the archaeological record, which reveals no less than one hundred sites dating from this general period (Mazar: 335).

Second, the important worship centers of Bethel and Shiloh were both located within its borders. Third, such dominant figures as Joshua (Num. 13:8) and later Samuel (1 Sam. 1:1) and Jeroboam (1 Kings 11:26) claimed Ephraimite descent. Not surprisingly, then, by the time of Isaiah and Hosea, Ephraim came to represent the entire Northern Kingdom (Isa. 7:1-17; Hos. 5).

The Ephraimites, in other words, are accustomed to having a major role in Israel's undertakings. Now, however, seemingly less significant and less able tribes are admirably functioning together—without them. Resentment ensues. Ephraim similarly resents losing the predominant position during Jephthah's activities, though the consequences in that instance prove far more severe (12:1-6).

In this case, Gideon handles the Ephraimites' criticism by employing proverbial wisdom. By asking *Is not the gleaning of the grapes of Ephraim better than the vintage of Abiezer?* he emphasizes the Ephraimites' accomplishments without drawing attention to what he and the others have done. In fact, Gideon actually downplays the significance of his own achievements (v. 8:3). By extending a grateful "pat on the back," Gideon wisely silences criticism with praise.

THE TEXT IN BIBLICAL CONTEXT

Divine Works and Human Downsizing

Quite typically, Gideon begins his military activities by establishing as sizeable an army as he possibly can. Incredibly, the Lord then methodically whittles away at his troops until only a few remain. Though already outnumbered at the start, the final Israelite force is just a fraction of the opposing Midianites. Only following this reduction, however, is Gideon's army suitable for divine use.

As surprising and even amusing as this notion may seem, similar though less obvious acts of reduction appear throughout Scripture. Abraham, for instance, is called to abandon the security and prosperity of his homeland, traveling instead to an unknown land situated precisely between the two major metropolitan areas of the day— Mesopotamia and Egypt (Gen. 12:1). These ancient industrial powerhouses, it would seem, offered too many attractions that conflicted with Abraham's developing faith. An act of downsizing, therefore, was required. Solomon provides another example, yet in reverse! Though initially suitable in God's hands, his unending accumulation of political power and economic resources eventually render him useless (1 Kings 10:26-29; 11:1). Clearly, nothing less than a massive act of reduction could change the course of Solomon's unraveling life.

This concept of downsizing also occurs frequently in the NT. Indeed, it lies at the very heart of the gospel. Jesus himself sets the stage; he "emptied himself, taking the form of a slave" (Phil. 2:7). On the basis of his own example, he then summons his disciples to a life of self-denial and even instructs the rich young ruler to sell all that he has (Matt. 19:16-22; Mark 10:17-22; Luke 18:18-23). Furthermore, in response to a question about eternal prestige, Jesus suggests that childlike humility is the sign of heavenly greatness (Matt. 18:4; cf. Phil. 2:3).

Unmistakably, acts of reduction and self-denial repeatedly prepare people for spiritual service. The Bible makes plain that power, pride, and possessions often obstruct divine activity. Yet genuine human weakness provides God with fertile soil in which to perform his mighty works (2 Cor. 12:9). In all divine-human partnerships, God alone brings victory.

Compassionate Responses

When confronted by the disgruntled Ephraimites, Gideon faces a potentially explosive situation. Unlike the later Jephthah, Gideon wisely opts for gentle diplomacy rather than brute force (Judg. 12:1-6). As a result, the commotion subsides without further adverse developments. Saul and Elisha do much the same thing later. Saul has every reason to respond vindictively and put nonsupporters of his regime to death, but he instead offers grace (1 Sam. 10:27; 11:12-13). Likewise, Elisha surprisingly treats the apprehended Arameans with unanticipated hospitality (2 Kings 6:8-23). Because of this treatment, the enemy *no longer came raiding into the land of Israel* (6:23). In these and other instances in the OT, "a soft answer turns away wrath, but a harsh word stirs up anger" (Prov. 15:1; for an opposite response, nearly resulting in his death, cf. Nabal's answer to David's messengers, 1 Sam. 25:10-13).

Clearly, the wisdom of this somewhat simple but demanding principle also left indelible impressions within the hearts and minds of Jesus and his followers. Jesus, in fact, raises peacemaking to lofty heights (Matt. 5:9). Among other things, he envisions a process through which individuals actively and graciously calm otherwise hostile situations (Luke 9:54). Later writers likewise encourage this gentle mode of dealing with others (1 Thess. 2:7; 2 Tim. 2:24; Titus 3:2; Heb. 12:14; James 3:17-18). Without sanctioning either unhealthy compromise or superficiality, the Scriptures repeatedly assert that gentleness serves the purposes of Christ far better than hostile aggression.

THE TEXT IN THE LIFE OF THE CHURCH

Self-Emptying for Faithful Service

Size, speed, and productivity are considered important—even in the church. These reflections, in the nature of corrections, emerge from Israel's victory over the Midianites:

• *Size.* The church, as a living organism, longs to grow and reproduce. However, great size is no prerequisite for effective and faithful service. Small churches may even have an advantage, for they have "much less of a vested interest in the continuance of the world and thus a better chance of getting a focus on the end of the world" (Eller: 103).

• *Quality.* God works effectively with ordinary people. The three hundred lappers are but a few who join other ordinary but effective people: Samuel, a boy; David, a young and unassuming shepherd; Amos, a common laborer; and Peter and Andrew, fishermen (1 Sam. 3:1; 16:11; Amos 7:14; Matt. 4:18). To these can be added the farmers, tax collectors, prostitutes, and slaves who dot the pages of both Scripture and the history of the church. Even Conrad Grebel, so influential a figure among the early Swiss Anabaptists, was a college dropout who knew a former life of violence, immorality, and drunkenness (Estep: 23-30). To be sure, the work of Christ welcomes also the most gifted; to leave one's talents undeveloped is a pitiable thing indeed. Nevertheless, no one is too unlearned or too incompetent to find a meaningful niche within God's family (1 Cor. 1:26-31).

• *Caliber of the Equipment.* Frustrated by the failure of conventional missionary strategies to bring people closer to God, Vincent Donovan began to work among the Masai of East Africa. Without the aid of schools, buildings, and sizeable resources, Donovan simply decided to take the message of Christ to the Masai. "I have no theory, no plan, no strategy, no gimmicks—no idea of what will come" (Donovan: 16). What "came" was a reception of the gospel among the Masai well beyond anything previously seen. Frequently today, Christians are enticed into believing that sophisticated equipment and elaborate facilities are essential in proclaiming the gospel of Jesus Christ. Yet Gideon's potsherds and Donovan's gimmick-free approach remind us that equipment is far less important than the divine Supplier.

• *Importance of Reduction.* While God can do tremendous things with ordinary and poorly equipped people, he frequently has greater difficulty using the strong and mighty. Drastic reduction and self-emptying are fundamentally important in the Christian life. While facing the threat of imprisonment in Nazi Germany, Dietrich Bonhoeffer reflected upon the opening petition of the Lord's Prayer: "Thy kingdom come. Thy will be done." Based on these reflections, he advised his friends and fellow dissenters that "by these we learn to forget ourselves and our personal condition and to hold them as of little account."

Then, with force that reverberates to this very day, Bonhoeffer asked a penetrating question: "How are we to remain steadfast as long as we remain so important to ourselves?" (Bethge: 487). For John Wesley, the answer would have been self-evident. The people of God, he maintained, must demonstrate "a willingness to be as the 'filth and offscouring of the world'" (1989:381; cf. 1 Cor. 4:13).

Gideon Revengeful in Victory 8:4-21

Virtually all commentators note a major shift in the narrative at this point. With the capture of Oreb and Zeeb (7:25) and the tribal unity resulting from Gideon's skillful handling of the Ephraimites, Israel's conflict with Midian has apparently ended. Somewhat unexpectedly, however, Gideon now resumes the chase. He is once again accompanied in his pursuit by only the three hundred men. Where are the most-recent recruits? Are they pursuing the Midianites on a separate course? Have they returned home?

Of even greater importance than issues such as these, however, is the apparent shift within Gideon himself and the Lord's absolute silence. The Gideon who repeatedly needs reassurance and who graciously deals with vigorous criticism no longer exists. In his place appears a new Gideon, one who ruthlessly seeks revenge on all who cross him. Likewise, the dialogue between Gideon and God, so characteristic of the previous section, is totally lacking here. Indeed, the only references to the Lord at all come in the form of two formalized statements from Gideon's own mouth (8:19, 23). God never speaks, nor is there any clear indication that he acts. On the contrary, everything suggests that Gideon himself has taken control.

8:4-9 Succoth and Peniel Rebuff Gideon

In continuing to pursue the oppressors, Gideon and his three hundred men now chase two previously unmentioned Midianite kings, Zebah and Zalmunna. Rather than being their actual names, Zebah ("sacrifice") and Zalmunna ("shelter refused") may be comical titles given by the now-confident Israelites in anticipation of the final outcome. While en route, Gideon's thoroughly exhausted troops arrive at what is probably a temporary settlement at Succoth ("booths"). Typically associated with Tell Deir Alla, just east of the Jordan and some two miles north of the Jabbok, Succoth appears in Joshua 13:27 as part of the territory allotted to the tribe of Gad *[Map, p. 240]*. If the as yet unverifiable association with Tell Deir Alla is correct, then the archaeological data similarly implies that Succoth has come under Israelite control by the time of the Judges (Mazar: 358). Apparently, when Gideon approaches the people of Succoth, he is actually soliciting provisions from fellow, though remotely connected, Israelites.

Regardless of any such tribal connections, the men of Succoth flatly deny Gideon's request, perhaps for two reasons. First, Succoth no doubt fears reprisal from the Midianites, a fear implied in their question about Zebah and Zalmunna. In spite of the initial Israelite victory in the Jezreel Valley (7:16-25), the news of which may not have reached Succoth, the Midianites maintain a sizeable numerical advantage over their pursuers (8:10). Furthermore, the Midianite retreat most likely appears as nothing more than the typical return after another successful raid. To most onlookers, then, the ultimate outcome of the conflict is far from certain. By regrouping, the Midianites can return with a vengeance.

Second, the true nature of Gideon's quest perhaps came to the attention of the people of Succoth. What at first appears to be the culmination of a divinely supported battle turns out, in reality, to be a crusade for personal revenge (8:19). Rather than freeing his people from oppression, Gideon seeks to punish those who have killed his brothers. As a result, Succoth wants no part of it.

Whatever the reason, Gideon is rebuffed. In contrast to his earlier response to the Ephraimites (8:1-3), Gideon here promises a vicious reprisal after he concludes his quest (8:7). Precisely what he has in mind, however, remains somewhat unclear. The verb *dwš*, translated *tear* in the NIV, actually means to "trample" (Isa. 41:15) or "thresh" (Deut. 25:4; Hos. 10:11). Hence, Gideon threatens to thresh the people of Succoth with thorns and briars, much like he has threshed wheat at the beginning of the narrative (6:11). In both instances, what is threshed ends up crushed and dismembered.

Following his experience at Succoth, Gideon makes a similar request for food to the people of Peniel. Peniel, otherwise known as the site where Jacob struggled with an angel (Gen. 32:22-32; Hos. 12:4), is usually identified with Tulul edh-Dhahab, just east of Tell Deir Alla ("Succoth"). Here, after receiving the same negative response, Gideon again promises severe retribution. After returning "safe and sound" (*šalom*), he will *tear down this tower* (*migdal*), a reference to an unknown structure. As in the cases of Shechem (9:46-49) and Thebez (9:50-53), such a tower probably serves as a fortress in the event of an attack.

8:10-12 Gideon Pursues Zebah and Zalmunna

In spite of these rejections, Gideon and his weary warriors continue their quest, finally confronting the Midianite forces at Karkor. The locations of both Karkor and Nobah remain unknown. Jogbehah is usually identified with Khirbet Jubeihat, some seven miles northwest of Amman or Rabbath-ammon *[Map, p. 242]*. Gideon continues east, past Jogbehah; perhaps the Midianites have retreated deep into Transjordan, as far as their home bases. To reach this distant place, Gideon's forces travel along *a caravan route* that must be familiar and commonly used by tent-dwellers; its mention here serves as a reference point. Still grossly outnumbered, the Israelites pull yet another surprise attack; no doubt the distance has left the Midianites feeling relatively secure. Once again, the outcome is an overwhelming victory for Gideon and his troops. With the capture of the two Midianite kings, any remaining cohesion on the part of the disheartened oppressors disintegrates, and the conflict finally comes to a close.

8:13-17 Gideon Repays Succoth and Peniel

Following this final encounter with the Midianite army, Gideon and his forces, along with the two vanquished kings, begin their northwesterly return along the unidentifiable *Ascent of Heres*. Just prior to reaching Succoth, Gideon commandeers and interrogates a young man (*na'ar*) from the town. This young man listed *for him* the requested information, thus showing the spread of literacy in the area. Whether he is a common young man or a trained servant, however, is unclear. Some of the earliest examples of alphabetic script found in Palestine predate this time and were scratched on mine walls by ordinary slaves in Sinai; hence, either identification is possible. What he writes down, however, is clear enough: the names of Succoth's princes and elders.

The numbers *seventy* and *seven*, frequently signifying completeness (8:30; 9:2; notes on 10:6; Gen. 46:27; 2 Kings 10:1), suggest that all of the officials have been accounted for. With the list in hand and the Midianite kings in public display, Gideon "threshes" the men of Succoth (supplying *wayyadoš* from versions of 8:16, *and he threshed;* instead of the Hebrew *wayyoda', and he taught;* cf. 8:7). This is a torturous act that surely results in countless casualties.

Likewise, Gideon destroys the tower at Peniel, just as he promised (8:8-9). In addition to Peniel's tower, however, he goes beyond his original threat and slays all the men of the town. Rather than providing a punishment in some way commensurate with the offense, Gideon acts ruthlessly. In fact, his atrocities approach those of Damascus, who drew the Lord's wrath because they *have threshed Gilead with threshing sledges of iron* (Amos 1:3). Gideon clearly stands unwaveringly true to his word, even when his word appears faulty and self-serving.

8:18-21 Gideon Slays Zebah and Zalmunna

With his other responsibilities cared for, Gideon must yet deal with the conquered Midianite kings. Since Jether plays a role in the narrative (8:20), the scene has apparently reverted back to Ophrah. Thus Gideon has returned to his home and clan with Zebah and Zalmunna in his custody.

The event that forms the background for this entire encounter, however, remains a mystery. No mention has been made of the fate of Gideon's full-brothers (as distinguished from half-brothers in a polygamous society), nor could their deaths have occurred during the initial Israelite rout of the Midianites near the hill of Moreh (7:1, 16-25). Instead, the story refers to an otherwise unknown episode, perhaps during an earlier Midianite raid. Zebah and Zalmunna recall the event, however, and they further note the physical similarities between their previous victims (Gideon's half-brothers) and their present kingly conqueror. Recognizing all this and Gideon's tenacity in tracking them down, they consider their fate a foregone conclusion.

As for Gideon, the killing of his brothers apparently has constituted a crime worthy of exact retribution (Lev. 24:17; Deut. 19:21). As a result, he plans for nothing less than the destruction of their slayers. If he would have been fulfilling a special divine mandate to totally destroy Israel's oppressors, he would not even have suggested the possibility of sparing the prisoners (8:19). Gideon, once again, is clearly on a personal mission to avenge the deaths of his brothers.

Gideon's ambitions, however, do not fit convincingly into the normal framework of the blood avenger, a practice whereby the nearest relative of the victim sought and punished the guilty party (Num. 35:6-34). In such a framework, the context for the avenger seems to be crimes *within* a given society lacking alternative governmental structures and controls. Zebah and Zalmunna were non-Israelites. Furthermore, whatever the precise act that they have committed, it apparently occurred during a military raid. Such an assumption appears more reasonable, at least, than imagining that these two Midianite kings themselves functioned as sole perpetrators in otherwise isolated homicides.

By way of comparison, Joab's killing of Abner for slaying his brother in wartime is considered an illegitimate act (2 Sam. 3:27, 30; 1 Kings 2:5; cf. 2 Sam. 2:17-23). Similarly, David refused to hold Joab accountable for the death of his revolutionary son, Absalom, even though the victim hung helplessly in a tree (2 Sam. 18:1—19:8). Even in the case of the Gibeonites, the writer carefully points out that they were not Israelites; and the vengeance they requested was not for Saul's ruthlessness itself, but because he disregarded an earlier Israelite-Gibeonite treaty (2 Sam. 21:2-6).

In the present case, then, while Gideon's response might be humanly, emotionally, and even culturally understandable, its legitimacy raises serious questions. Clearly, given the despised state of the Midianite forces, the oppression facing the Israelites has ended.

Gideon, therefore, has nothing else to gain but the completion of a personal vendetta against his captives. In his vindictiveness and self-inspired zeal, Gideon eventually usurps the administrative authority reserved for the Lord himself (Deut. 32:35; cf. Rom. 12:19).

To carry out this final act, Gideon turns to his eldest son, Jether. The killing of two prestigious opponents by such a young and unproven executioner would normally be both an honor for Jether as well as an embarrassment for Zebah and Zalmunna. Jether's youthful apprehension, however, prevents him from completing the assignment. As a result, the Midianite kings courageously and defiantly taunt Gideon to perform the task himself. Bolstered further, no doubt, by this apparent challenge, Gideon does precisely that. In so doing, he not only achieves the revenge for which he longs, but valuable booty along with it.

Gideon Corruptive in the Spotlight 8:22-32

Along with Gideon's successful exploits comes increased popularity. In the face of such recently found fame, Gideon's downward slide worsens.

8:22-27 Gideon Constructs an Ephod

Before the afterglow of recent events subsides, the Israelites offer Gideon a promotion into a more-permanent position. Just who constitutes *the Israelites* goes unspecified, though we must surely imagine a relatively localized area at this point in time (cf. 9:6) *[Localized Accounts]*. Their proposal is unambiguous—hereditary kingship involving Gideon and his descendants. A similar plea will of course be made later during Samuel's lifetime, but with different results (1 Sam. 8).

In this case, the request clearly grows out of admiration for Gideon's involvement in freeing the people from Midianite oppression. Importantly, Gideon is credited with the victory. Throughout the earlier portions of the Gideon narrative, the verb "to deliver" (yš') has appeared six times, each time with the Lord as the driving force (6:14, 15, 36, 37; 7:2, 7). In addition, the Israelite troops were intentionally reduced to safeguard against the misappropriation of credit—God alone saves Israel (7:2) *[Violence and War in Judges]*. Yet, even before the dust from the battle settles, such a misappropriation does take place. Rather than the Lord, Gideon *delivered* (yš') *us out of the hand of Midian,* the Israelites say (8:22).

In spite of the Israelites' glaring failure to understand the true source of their victory, however, such a request should come as no great surprise. Gideon has tended to take matters into his own hands

(8:4-21). So it seems a rather natural outgrowth that his followers might overestimate his role. Furthermore, by his handling of Succoth, Peniel, and the Midianite leaders, Gideon in fact has modeled much of what ancient kingship encompassed. In a sense, then, Gideon has brought on the request by acting the part.

Nevertheless, Gideon declines the invitation to be king, and in the process makes an apparent attempt to correct the Israelites' faulty thinking. *The Lord will rule over you* reflects the notion that Israel was to be a theocracy, with God serving as king. While Gideon's response is therefore commendable, one must wonder to what extent he himself has fully embraced such a position. Later Gideon names his son Abimelech ("My father is king") and perhaps subtly betrays his deeper sentiments and aspirations concerning personal rule.

After rejecting this significant proposal, Gideon offers a proposition of his own. Out of what must have been an exceptionally sizeable booty collected from the defeated Midianites—the terms *Midian* and *Ishmael* are similarly alternated in Genesis 37:25-28, 36; 39:1— Gideon requests each soldier to give him one earring (*nezem*). While *nezem* can refer to either an earring or a nose-ring, such nose-rings are a part of a woman's apparel in the OT (Gen. 24:47; Isa. 3:21; Ezek. 16:12). The total collected equal just over forty pounds of gold! To this are added a variety of other items taken from the two kings and their camels. But such a significant amount represents only the beginning of all that has been gathered from the devastated Midianites.

When Gideon initially makes his request, he apparently offers no explanation for their use. The soldiers no doubt assume that he simply wants greater compensation for his extensive achievements. Gideon, however, upon receiving the gold rings, fashions them into an ephod, which he then places in his hometown of Ophrah. An ephod was an important priestly garment used when making inquiry of the Lord (Exod. 28:6-8; 1 Sam. 14:3; 23:9-12; 30:7-8), perhaps in connection with the Urim and Thummim (Exod. 28:30; 1 Sam. 28:6). Precisely what form Gideon's ephod took, however, is unclear. Apparently he makes either a linen garment ornamented with gold, or a solid gold facsimile. In either case, the ephod soon becomes more than a symbol, serving instead as an object of worship. As happened later with Jeroboam's golden calves (1 Kings 12:28-30), now Israel stumbles over a golden figure.

Exactly what Gideon has in mind with this ephod is unclear. It must be recalled, however, that he has earlier destroyed the altar of Baal located in Ophrah, and subsequently has built an altar to the Lord in its place (6:25-27). Furthermore, Gideon has offered a sacrifice to God there, and he has successfully sought a word from the Lord before going into battle (6:36-40). In other words, Gideon has previously performed priestly functions; now he seemingly consecrates himself as a priest (Halpern, 1983:227). While Gideon admirably turns down the offer of kingship, he creates, knowingly or not, a new religion instead. In a sense, Gideon has come full circle. He began his ministry in Ophrah by destroying the altar of Baal and the associated Asherah pole. By the end of his ministry, Ophrah has a golden ephod to take their place.

8:28-32 Gideon Fathers Abimelech

Significantly, an additional qualifying phrase appears for the first time in connection with the land experiencing peace. By specifying that such peace is limited to *the days of Gideon*, the writer intimates that the effects of Gideon's activities are tenuous and temporary. In fact, his own son Abimelech, here introduced, will create sufficient havoc to make peace nothing but a distant memory.

Gideon fathered many sons, the number seventy serving here and elsewhere in the OT to symbolize a large amount (Fensham, 1977:113-115). Abimelech, however, is the only one born of a (non-Israelite) concubine from Shechem (notes on 9:1-6). Given Abimelech's later influence among the leaders of that city, however, the designation "concubine" may be somewhat misleading. The relationship envisioned here is a legitimate though secondary one, probably similar to the so-called ṣadiqa marriages of ancient Arab society (de Vaux: 29). In such marriages, the woman remains with her parents rather than moving in with her husband, who then visits her from time to time. Furthermore, any offspring resulting from their union remain with and belong to the mother's family, not the father's.

In Abimelech's case, such an arrangement helps clarify the predominance of his mother's clan in the events that follow, and it greatly heightens his own isolation from his other brothers. They are the rightful heirs of their father, both in terms of possessions and position. Abimelech, as a result, is on the outside looking in.

THE TEXT IN BIBLICAL CONTEXT
Seeking Revenge

Methodically and ruthlessly, the Gideon of chapter 8 goes about removing one personal foe after another. Gideon so desperately wants personal revenge that he drags the forces of Israel along with him.

How different these revengeful deeds are from his gentle restoration of the Ephraimites just a short time before.

In spite of the magnitude of Gideon's ambitions as well as the apparent illegitimacy surrounding them, he at least acted during a time when blood vengeance constituted a known and accepted societal procedure. While acknowledging such a procedure, however, the Bible increasingly strives to limit and actually remove personal acts of revenge. The *lex talionis* ("an eye for an eye"), first of all, served not to encourage retribution, but to limit it (Exod. 21:23-25; Lev. 24:20; Deut. 19:21; cf. Gen. 4:23-24; Boecker: 171-175). Similarly, the cities of refuge provided some safety for the accused (Num. 35:9-28). Finally, the OT itself already affirms a higher ideal when it encourages the Israelites to "not seek revenge or bear a grudge against one of your people," but rather to "love your neighbor as yourself" (Lev. 19:18; cf. Prov. 25:21). Ideally, exercising vengeance is the prerogative of God alone (Deut. 32:35).

Building upon this foundation, the NT takes the development to its logical conclusion. Rather than extracting an eye for an eye, Jesus instructs his followers to turn the other cheek (Matt. 5:38-42). Likewise, when James and John suggest calling down fire upon the Samaritans, an echo of the Gideon of Judges 8, Jesus rebukes them (Luke 9:51-56). Paul encourages the believers in Rome not to "repay anyone evil for evil" (Rom. 12:17). Clearly, neither Jesus nor Paul view the exercising of personal vengeance as appropriate human behavior. In echoing Deuteronomy 32:35, Paul holds that a far more suitable alternative is to live humbly and peaceably, leaving vengeance in God's hands (Rom. 12:18-19).

Dealing with Public Affirmation

In the excitement surrounding the demise of the Midianites, Gideon receives a glorious reception and an offer of a kingly throne. Although Gideon apparently refuses the offer, the glowing public response eventually wears him down. While basking in the spotlight, Gideon self-destructs, and he takes his supporters along with him.

As a means of safeguarding against this type of development, the sages of ancient Israel repeatedly highlight the destructive capabilities of pride (Prov. 11:2; 16:18; 18:12; 29:23). Similar warnings appear in the teachings of both Jesus and Paul, who encourage balanced personal evaluations as well as loftier views of God. Jesus, for example, warned against loving "human glory more than the glory that comes from God" (John 12:43). Paul went so far as to prohibit new converts from holding certain church offices for fear that conceit might result

(1 Tim. 3:6). Clearly, while public affirmation of a proper sort is desirable and welcome (e.g., Gen. 49:8; Deut. 26:19; Prov. 31:28; Rom. 13:3; 1 Pet. 2:14), enthusiastic responses often bring out the worst in people (e.g., Matt. 6:2; Gal. 1:10; 1 Thess. 2:4-6).

THE TEXT IN THE LIFE OF THE CHURCH
Taming Anger

Lactantius, a church father living in the third and fourth centuries, described the appearance of a person overcome by anger:

> When it falls upon the mind of anyone, as a violent tempest it excites such waves that it changes the condition of the mind, the eyes gleam, the countenance trembles, the tongue stammers, the teeth chatter, the countenance is alternately stained now with redness spread over it, now with white paleness. (7)

For all we know, Lactantius may have had Gideon's reaction to Succoth and Peniel in mind. Yet, while many believers like to see themselves as the peacemakers of Judges 8:1-3, they similarly know the emotional struggle associated with anger, bitterness, and the desire for revenge. To deny such feelings is in effect to deny our humanity.

Anger alone, however, does not necessarily constitute wrongdoing; it needs to be promptly processed and not nursed into ongoing hatred (Ps. 4:4; Matt. 5:22; Eph. 4:26-27). Indeed, anger operating within an appropriate context can lead to the performance of significant and even threatening tasks (1 Sam. 11:6; Matt. 21:12-13; Mark 11:15-18; Luke 19:45-46). Rather, as Gideon so clearly illustrates, the problem with anger is that it frequently leads to hatred and the longing for revenge (Ps. 37:8; James 1:19-20). The key, therefore, is neither denying our anger nor venting it uncontrollably, but freeing it from its injurious and self-seeking impulse.

As Alastair Campbell so aptly states, Christians must seek to

> sever the link between anger and destructiveness and to find ways in which people's powerful reactions to life's dangers around them may be put to the service of human wholeness. (31)

Such a task can best be undertaken with the support, encouragement, and loving correction of the body of Christ.

An Ambiguous Portrait (Scene 2): Abimelech's Atrocities

Judges 8:33—10:5

PREVIEW

History does repeat itself. With the death of Gideon and the Israelites' renewed sinfulness, the stage is once again set for a divinely appointed oppressor. Now, however, most of the standard introductory comments are omitted, and the reader's attention is directed to one of Gideon's sons, Abimelech. In place of some external aggressor, Abimelech himself causes enough turmoil to throw the Israelites into yet another oppressive state. By this stage in the book of Judges, then, serious internal corruption at least temporarily overshadows external conflict.

The dominant theme in the Abimelech narrative unmistakably centers on the notion of divine retribution for a power-hungry character (9:23-24, 56-57). Accordingly, the story develops through a major turning point in 9:23-24. Prior to this turning point, Abimelech successfully solidifies his position over the city of Shechem and its immediate environs, but at the expense of the rest of Gideon's family. Following the turning point, everything unravels.

Such unraveling, however, does not result from Abimelech's political incompetence, but from the Lord's retributive intervention. In this way, Abimelech eventually falls and, like the previous external oppressors, his reign of terror ends. All that remains is for Tola, his successor, to calmly pick up the pieces (10:1-2).

OUTLINE

Crisis Introduced, 8:33-35

Abimelech Becomes King, 9:1-6

Jotham Shouts a Fable, 9:7-21

Shechem Betrays Abimelech, 9:22-33

Abimelech Destroys Shechem, 9:34-49

A Woman Stones Abimelech, 9:50-57

Tola and Jair Lead Israel, 10:1-5

EXPLANATORY NOTES
Crisis Introduced 8:33-35

As anticipated earlier by the phrase *in the days of Gideon* (8:28), the
death of this latest deliverer immediately gives way to renewed corruption. In this case, the Israelites pay homage to Baal-Berith ("Lord
of the covenant"), the Canaanite god worshiped in Shechem *[Baal;
Canaanites]*. Possibly, the term "covenant" in the deity's name refers
to an agreement worked out between the native inhabitants of the city
and the Israelites moving in. After all, there are other indications that
the Canaanites and Israelites constitute two segments of Shechem's
overall population (notes on 9:1-6).

In addition to worshiping Baal-Berith, the Israelites are here
accused of a second offense. Just as they have forgotten the Lord and
his marvelous deeds, so too have they forgotten Gideon and his works
on their behalf. In other words, the people of Israel are guilty of both
religious and political harlotry—they abandon the Lord as well as
Gideon's family. Forgetting the Lord and his deeds has become characteristic of Israel's behavior, and it was a major theme of the previous narrative (7:2-3; 8:22-23). The failure to remain faithful to
Gideon's family, however, is a new idea that awaits development in
the narrative that follows. In this way, 8:33-35 links the two narratives
by recalling the story of Gideon and anticipating that of Abimelech
(Webb: 156-157).

Abimelech Becomes King 9:1-6

It is important to note, once again, that although Israel is in the midst
of yet another rebellious episode, no explicit mention is made here of
the divinely ordained oppression, cry for mercy, or the raising up of a
deliverer—the elements so characteristic of previous episodes.
Instead, the story shifts inward and focuses further attention on Israel's
declining fortunes under Gideon's own son. Accordingly, the people's
misery in this case grows up from within.

In contrast to his father, Gideon (8:23), Abimelech looks longing-
ly on the position of kingship. Based on his scheme, Abimelech
assumes that, following his father's refusal, a similar offer will be forthcoming to one of the sons. The very nature of Abimelech's question
(9:2) even implies that Gideon's other sons are already exercising
some corporate control over the area. Furthermore, given his own
marginal status in his father's family (notes on 8:31), Abimelech realizes that his own chances for royal power are virtually nonexistent. As
a result, he takes matters into his own hands and actively campaigns
for the position.

The position sought by Abimelech is even more limited in scope than that offered to Gideon. Unlike many of the surrounding nations, Canaan lacked a centralized political system before the development of Israel's monarchy. Instead, the region was controlled by independently governed city-states *[Canaanites]*. Following this deeply engrained system, then, Abimelech seeks an elevated position in Shechem.

Shechem, contemporary Tell Balata, is located some forty miles north of Jerusalem. In a fertile valley between Mount Ebal and Mount Gerazim, the city controlled significant trade routes that converged there, already centuries before Abimelech *[Map, p. 242]*. Mentioned with some frequency in the patriarchal narratives, including a venerated connection with God's call of Abraham (Gen. 12:6; 33:18; 35:4; 37:12), Shechem's early prominence receives further corroboration from various Egyptian texts dating to the nineteenth century B.C. Likewise, the Amarna Letters of the fourteenth century B.C. indicate that the city was perhaps the most important one in central Palestine at that time *[Ancient Near Eastern Texts]*. Later, Shechem was the site for the renewal of the covenant under Joshua (Josh. 24) as well as the northern coronation of Rehoboam (1 Kings 12:1). Indeed, the city even functioned temporarily as the capital of the newly established Northern Kingdom of Israel (1 Kings 12:25).

The sources, however, do not reveal precisely how Shechem came under Israelite control. For example, no reference is made to the city's capture during the conquest under Joshua. Yet, as mentioned above, Shechem served as the site for the renewal of the covenant. Likely the process of incorporating Shechem into the Israelite holdings was relatively peaceful—the city came to terms with the invaders (Ruiv: 256). As a result, a large percentage of the original Canaanite population has remained, although they seemingly allow for Israelite involvement in the governance of their affairs.

To gain his desired position, Abimelech solicits the support of his mother's relatives, who apparently exercise at least some influence in Shechem. By implication, Abimelech lacks the personal prominence needed to approach the city's leaders himself. Notice, similarly, that in gathering the backing of his *mother's kinsfolk*, Abimelech never alludes to any personal qualifications other than parentage. In other words, the very genealogical consideration that separates him from his other brothers is here set forth as an advantage. In his attempts to secure power, Abimelech appeals to deep-rooted feelings concerning ethnic differences—prejudice. He does so because he has no other support for his cause.

As a result of the strong lobbying of Abimelech's maternal relatives, the leaders of Shechem reject the rule by Gideon's other sons and indeed select Abimelech. Bolstered by a sizeable donation that these same leaders take from the temple treasury (1 Kings 15:18; 2 Kings 18:15-16), Abimelech immediately hires a group of reckless and undisciplined men—a bunch of thugs!—to do his dirty work. That he does so perhaps gives some indication of the intended nature of his reign; yet it receives no immediate response from his supporters. No doubt they now share some of the animosity toward Gideon's other sons that Abimelech himself feels, particularly in light of Gideon's escalating popularity and wealth following the Midianite affair. They assume that Abimelech will remove his political rivals, an assumption firmly rooted in common practice of the day. Therefore this entire episode presents certain segments of Shechem's population with an opportunity to express actively their discontentment with Gideon and his other sons.

Removing his political rivals is what Abimelech does next. It is difficult to say precisely what lies behind the reference to a single *stone* (9:5). If 1 Samuel 14:33-35 is a parallel, then perhaps Abimelech deliberately desecrates a sacred Israelite ritual by offering his brothers as sacrifices (Boling: 171). McKenzie suggests, however, that Abimelech is "motivated by a superstitious observance of the ancient belief that the blood of the murdered man cries from the ground for vengeance" (140). The stone, in other words, is employed as a means of gathering the blood and thereby preventing its absorption into the soil (Gen. 4:10-12).

The official ceremony to finalize Abimelech's kingship takes place by the great oak tree in Shechem, a site with sacred connections to both Jacob (Gen. 35:4) and Joshua (Josh. 24:26). While the name *Beth-millo* remains somewhat obscure, it likely refers to an upper area of the city built upon large, man-made platforms. Such platforms result from the construction of retaining walls on the slopes of the hill; the enclosed area is then filled in (Heb.: *ml'*) to form a level building surface.

Excavations at Shechem indicate that the temple there (of Baal-Berith?) stood on a platform of this type (Wright: 80-102). Furthermore, the OT refers to the Millo in Jerusalem, where similar structures have likewise been uncovered (2 Sam. 5:9; 1 Kings 9:15; 11:27; 2 Kings 12:20; 1 Chron. 11:8; 2 Chron. 32:5; see Kenyon: 100-103). Since the priests and other influential people surely reside on the Millo, its mention here underlines the importance of the occasion.

Abimelech does not function as a king in the traditional sense of the word. Residing outside the city (9:41), Abimelech appears more as a hired defense minister in charge of protecting the city in times of crisis. Included among the responsibilities of Shechem's leaders is apparently the authority to select kings and also to depose those who fall out of their liking (9:22-23). In that event, however, the strength of the soon-to-be deposed king deserves careful consideration. In the case of Abimelech, as the story clearly illustrates, the leaders of Shechem regrettably neglect the important point.

Jotham Shouts a Fable 9:7-21

Word of Abimelech's coronation soon reaches Jotham, Gideon's youngest and now only-surviving son, who has escaped from the carnage at Ophrah (9:5). Jotham's subsequent address from a mountain is clearly reminiscent of the tribal ceremony announcing blessings and cursings (Deut. 27:12-13; Josh. 8:30-35), an event which likewise involved Mount Gerazim. In that instance, however, the people's response was one of strong affirmation, a response nowhere hinted at here.

Jotham's oration includes two distinct parts. First, he makes use of what is probably a familiar fable to many in his audience (9:8-15). Fables, parable-like stories involving plants and animals that are told and retold to convey simple truths, appear throughout the ancient Near East and indeed elsewhere in the OT (2 Kings 14:9). Here, Jotham employs one in much the same way that Nathan used a parable when confronting David (2 Sam. 12:1-7). Rather than merely reasoning with the people of Shechem, he adapts the fable in the hope that his listeners will see themselves among the characters. Second, Jotham makes his own application to ensure that the people understand the intended point (9:16-20).

The fable itself reports that an assembly of trees longs for the security and stability that they suppose a king can provide. As a result, they diligently search for a suitable candidate to assume the position. In each of three cases, however, the respective candidates consider their present responsibilities to be more important and more useful than serving as king. Their common expression *to sway over the trees* seems to convey a note of contempt: "Why should we merely nod to our subjects when we have more pressing things to do?"

Out of desperation resulting from these rejections, the trees finally turn their attention to the *bramble* or thornbush, a nuisance to virtually everyone. The bramble responds to the invitation with a disbelieving threat. Implied in the threat is of course the potentially disas-

trous results of choosing a thoroughly inept leader, results that can ultimately destroy even the strongest among the subjects (*cedars of
Lebanon*).

As one might expect, the details of Jotham's fable do not fit precisely within the context of Abimelech's anointing, since Abimelech
actively sought royal power. Yet the point seems clear enough. By
selecting their new king, the leaders of Shechem have come under the
control of the least-competent candidate (as compared to Gideon's
other sons, including Jotham himself?). They have, in reality, crawled
under a thornbush. Rather than providing the desired strength and
security, Abimelech will be the kindling with which Shechem is con-
sumed.

Despite the fable's self-evident meaning, Jotham offers an application that actually shifts the focus from Abimelech to the people who
anointed him. Although Jotham couches his words in an "if . . . then"
style, there is no question as to his personal conclusions. By choosing
Abimelech, *the son of* Gideon's *slave woman* (9:18), the leaders of
Shechem have demonstrated total disdain for Gideon and his family.
Further, in supporting their new monarch, these people have served
as accomplices in the murderous removal of Gideon's sons.

This same Gideon, Jotham reminds them, has shown no regard
for his own life; he *risked his life* when ridding them of the Midianite
threat (9:17). To ignore or forget him now is an unthinkable breach
of honorable conduct, a breach that will, Jotham predicts, result in
their eventual destruction. In its present context, the fable is not so
much a critique of the institution of kingship, as some have suggested, but of those who select and follow unworthy and incompetent
kings.

No mention is made of the listeners' response. One can only sur-
mise from the context that they either remained unmoved or else considered the selection of Abimelech a completed and unalterable act. In
any case, Jotham, concerned for his life, returns to hiding (9:5, 21).
The location of *Beer* ("well") remains unknown, although it may be
connected in some way with modern el-Bireh, some ten miles south
of the Sea of Galilee.

Shechem Betrays Abimelech 9:22-33

The somewhat tenuous relationship between Abimelech and the leaders of Shechem, rooted in prejudice and sustained by aggression, has
seemed destined to fail from the start. Accordingly, Jotham's pronouncement only serves to heighten already existing suspicions to this
effect. Yet somehow the arrangement holds for three years, during

which Abimelech exercises control over Shechem and its immediate surroundings. At that point, however, everything begins to unravel. Rather than merely resulting from human tension and conflict, this unraveling is an act of retribution on the Lord's part. It is intended to repay Abimelech and the people of Shechem for their shockingly unfair treatment of Gideon's family (9:24). The turning point itself occurs when the Lord *sent an evil spirit between Abimelech and the lords of Shechem* (cf. 1 Sam. 16:14; 18:10). In other words, God stirs up negative and divisive feelings among the various parties, to inspire a confrontation.

On the surface, what ignites the conflict is a practice instituted by the leaders of Shechem involving the local trade routes. At the instigation of these local leaders, men have been positioned at various places along the hills, to ambush seemingly well-to-do caravans. Recalling the location of Shechem at the juncture of several significant trade routes, such a procedure no doubt results in lucrative profits for *the lords of Shechem*.

Apparently, however, these profits are at Abimelech's expense. Likely he and his wandering thugs consider the control of these routes part of their domain. In exchange for promised protection, for example, Abimelech might well collect sizeable sums from such journeying merchants. By robbing the caravans, Shechem's leaders are taking money right out of Abimelech's pocket. Yet we read of no immediate reaction on his part once word reaches him of these events (9:25). His later activities, however, suggest that these and other occurrences eventually lead to deeply engrained hostilities.

In an adversarial atmosphere such as this, one additional provocation tends to produce utter chaos. In this instance, the provocation comes in the form of *Gaal son of Ebed*, a man unknown elsewhere in Scripture. From all indications, Gaal takes advantage of an extremely volatile situation and, during a joyous festival applauding an abundant harvest of grapes, presents himself as a desirable alternative to Abimelech. Given the unusual circumstances—the tension of conflict coupled with the drunkenness of celebration—the leaders of Shechem are poised to make yet another dreadful decision.

Gaal's line of reasoning with the people of Shechem is indeed an interesting one. In an earlier quest for power, Abimelech has used his mother's family to his advantage, relegating his brothers to the status of *Jerub-Baal's* sons (9:1-2). Now, Gaal bypasses Abimelech's maternal connections and therefore his ties to Shechem, emphasizing that Abimelech too is *Jerub-Baal's son* (9:28). Abimelech, in other words, is not a full-fledged Shechemite.

Continuing his genealogical arguments, Gaal suggests that, rather than following a half-breed like Abimelech, the people of Shechem ought to show their allegiance to *the men of Hamor*. Hamor was the father of Shechem, the ancient ancestor of the city itself (Gen. 34). An element of Shechem's population traces their lineage back to Hamor, making them the "purest" of all the Shechemites. However, it is impossible to say precisely who they are, what role they play in the city, and what possible connections Gaal has to them. What is clear is that Gaal takes Abimelech's earlier genealogical approach one step further in an attempt to shift the people's allegiances. If such an attempt proves successful, he stands ready and willing, not only to remove the fallen Abimelech, but also to fill the resulting leadership void.

Upon hearing Gaal's boastful claims and defiant challenges, Zebul, Abimelech's right-hand man in Shechem, sends to inform Abimelech of the impending insurrection. Zebul's proposal lacks originality and offers no ingenious military strategy: he simply encourages Abimelech to bring his forces into the fields surrounding Shechem during the coming night and attack the city at daybreak (9:32-33). Of great importance, however, is Zebul's recommendation for Abimelech to promptly go on the offensive. In essence, Zebul suggests that Abimelech immediately stop the insurrection rather than waiting to see how it develops. In this way, Gaal and his followers will be deprived of the opportunity to organize their efforts.

Abimelech Destroys Shechem 9:34-49

Upon receiving the message, Abimelech quickly moves into action. That Zebul, his chief officer, still associates freely with Gaal indicates that the insurrection has not yet passed the infancy stage. Zebul alertly aids Abimelech's efforts in two major ways. To begin with, he temporarily postpones Gaal's own operations by suggesting that the oncoming troops are merely a figment of his imagination. In so doing, Zebul not only enables Abimelech to advance unhindered, but he also prevents Gaal from notifying and organizing his own forces.

Second, Zebul offers a stiff and irresistible challenge (9:38) after Gaal ultimately realizes that what he sees is indeed not a figment of his imagination. He clearly sees the enemy coming *from the direction of Elon-meonenim*, an unidentifiable tree where divination is practiced (a link to the bramble in Jotham's parable?). Now, Gaal has no choice but to fight, regardless of how ill-prepared he and his supporters may be.

Following a decisive victory, Abimelech temporarily retires to his residence in *Arumah*. While the location of Arumah remains uncertain, a likely possibility is Khirbet el-Ormeh, situated five miles southeast of Shechem. In Abimelech's absence, the task of cleaning up the city falls on Zebul, whose first order of business involves banishing Gaal and his brothers from Shechem. This apparent act of leniency, coupled with the surprising fact that no fatalities whatsoever are mentioned in connection with the battle, suggests that Abimelech and his forces act in this instance with some restraint. Nevertheless, the following verses only too clearly demonstrate that lying behind such restraint are devious and destructive intentions. Abimelech wants more than the motley crew fighting alongside Gaal, and he knows how to get them.

With the defeat of Gaal and his forces and their subsequent expulsion from Shechem, the situation seemingly returns to normal. The Shechemites' renewed activity could involve banditry or even a counterattack against Abimelech, but the context strongly suggests otherwise. Far more likely, the people *went out into the fields* to resume their usual agricultural responsibilities. That they do so with fear and apprehension must be assumed; the events of the recent past linger in everyone's mind. Yet, even if the threat of further violence remains, the possibility of losing their crops poses too great a risk for the area's inhabitants to take.

Since Abimelech has intimate familiarity with the customs and procedures of the people, this is no doubt just what he has anticipated. Rather than confronting a fortified city, he simply waits for its citizens to expose themselves in the field. His supposed restraint in the earlier stage of the battle, therefore, turns out to have been nothing more than an intentional military maneuver.

Upon receiving word of the Shechemites' activities, probably from a watchman deliberately stationed near the fields for this purpose, Abimelech sets his plan in motion. Without offering any noteworthy resistance, Shechem and its remaining inhabitants are utterly destroyed. The severity of Abimelech's treatment of Shechem finds probable corroboration in the city's archaeological record, where a sizeable destruction layer dating to this period was uncovered (Wright: 101-122).

The precise significance of scattering salt, however, is somewhat unclear—the practice appears nowhere else in the OT. Some suggest that the act constitutes an attempt to offset the effects of the blood, thereby preventing revengeful attacks from the spirits of the slaughtered Shechemites (Honeyman: 195). Others see here a ritual intended to purify the site for its placement under a divinely ordained "no rebuilding" policy (Gevirtz: 60-62). Given the symbolic associations between salt and absolute desolation in the OT, however, Abimelech is most likely cursing Shechem, condemning it to a future of total barrenness (Deut. 29:23; Ps. 107:34; Jer. 17:6; 48:9). Such curses involving the throwing of salt do appear in various ancient texts outside of the Bible (Gaster: 428).

With the destruction of Shechem a completed act, what follows now in 9:46-49 comes as a surprise. *The tower of Shechem* appears as a separate compound situated outside the city proper. As a result, some see here an incident subsequent to the destruction of Shechem, and have attempted to locate a suitable site for the tower somewhere along the archaeological landscape (Soggin: 192-193). Up to this point, such attempts have met with little success.

The present episode, however, may in reality be an elaboration of an event that occurred *during* the destruction of the city itself. Accordingly, *when . . . heard of it* (9:46) refers to the people within the city receiving word of the carnage going on in the fields (9:44). Similarly, the tower constitutes a distinct section of Shechem, perhaps being an alternate name for Beth-millo (9:6; Wright: 126). If so, the events recounted here transpire in the following manner.

As Abimelech and his forces turn their efforts from the fields to the city proper, those (influential) people living in the upper portion of Shechem seek refuge somewhere in the temple of El-Berith ("God of the covenant"), the same structure from which they had earlier taken money to finance Abimelech's campaign (9:4)! *The stronghold* (ṣeriaḥ) apparently is a fortified section of the temple itself—no secret vaults or underground chambers have been found to suggest otherwise (cf. 1 Sam. 13:6, where ṣeriaḥ refers to a cave).

Mount Zalmon is perhaps another name for Ebal. With wood from there, Abimelech scorches both the stronghold and all the people in it. This burning of the stronghold unmistakably connects the event with Jotham's fiery pronouncement from Mount Gerazim (9:20, 56-57). Shechem, to say the least, has paid a brutal price for its ungrateful behavior and its selection of an unworthy king.

A Woman Stones Abimelech 9:50-57

In a final episode strongly resembling the previous account, Abimelech captures the city of Thebez. Once again, the exact location of this site remains uncertain, although the typically suggested places are all situated at least ten miles northeast of Shechem (Boling: 182). The reasons for Abimelech's attack on Thebez are similarly unclear. One can only imagine that its inhabitants took part in the recent rebellion, hoping with Shechem to rid themselves of his control.

The residents of Thebez seek refuge in still another tower, climbing even onto the roof. Here, Abimelech employs precisely the same strategy used in Shechem. While he is trying to set the tower on fire, however, an unnamed woman drops *an upper millstone on Abimelech's head*, cracking his skull. Milling is not done on the roof of the tower! Instead, this woman has carried the stone with her as a defensive precaution, showing foresight that paid off far better than even she could have imagined.

In ordering his armor-bearer to kill him with his sword, Abimelech seeks to avoid the great embarrassment, particularly for a soldier of his stature, of dying at the hands of a woman (cf. 4:17-21; 5:24-27). Nevertheless, the embarrassment eventually becomes his legacy (2 Sam. 11:21). Ironically, the same man who killed his seventy brothers on a single stone (9:5) now dies under the weight of a single stone.

With Abimelech dead and the conflict over, the writer finally reflects on the underlying causes of such a strange sequence of events (9:56-57). On the surface, one can simply attribute the fate of Abimelech to his own revengeful disposition, in which case he differs from his father only by degree (8:4-28). Likewise, the absolute devastation of the people of Shechem stems from their own political naïveté, so clearly reflected in their ill-conceived selection of Abimelech as their king. The writer, however, flatly rejects such notions, at least in their simplest forms. Instead, what happened to both Abimelech and the Shechemites constitutes nothing less than divine retribution. With great precision, God has dealt with these culprits according to the way they had dealt with Gideon's family. Accordingly, we are left with a rather penetrating summation, and an eerie reminder: and *on them came the curse of Jotham son of Jerub-Baal.*

Tola and Jair Lead Israel 10:1-5

With the close of the Abimelech narrative, notices are given concerning two of the so-called "minor" judges (cf. 3:31; 12:8-15). Considerable energy has been devoted in recent years to understanding the roles of these figures in the life of ancient Israel. Sadly, too little information remains with which to construct firm conclusions. Whether the likes of Tola, Jair, and the other minor judges served Israel in the typical judicial sense, rendering legal decisions, remains impossible to say. It is significant that no heroic exploits are attributed to them here, at least in the ongoing development of the book of Judges. Given Israel's bleak internal condition, a condition depicted with grim vividness in the preceding narrative, what is needed at this point is stable and dependable leadership, not dynamic demonstrations. On such a stage, then, Tola and Jair quietly and uneventfully appear.

Concerning the actual form of these accounts, the presentation of the minor judges differs from that of the major judges. The standard stages of the cycle are conspicuously absent. In addition, both the specification of administrative time periods as well as the designation of burial places constitute details uniquely characteristic of the minor judges. With the major judges, by way of contrast, the periods of service are typically depicted with the round figure of forty years (or a multiple thereof). Here such details as an odd count of years indicate greater specificity and therefore less stylistic refashioning, as though these brief notices are taken directly from an earlier list or register. In any case, it is clear that the writer strategically situates the accounts of the minor judges. In the present instance, Tola uneventfully calms the smoldering crisis under Abimelech, while Jair lavishly illustrates the peace that follows (Webb: 160-161).

The typical transitional phrase introducing the minor judges is simply "After him" (10:3; 12:8, 11, 13). Likewise, Jair, Ibzan, Elon, and Abdon all "judged" (šapaṭ) Israel (NIV "led"). In the cases of both Shamgar and Tola, however, these standard formulas are slightly varied (3:31; 10:1). In place of "after him," Shamgar and Tola are chronologically linked to their specific predecessors, either through the use of the verb "came" (hayah; not in Heb. of 10:3) or the name Abimelech (10:1). Furthermore, rather than simply "judging" Israel, both save/deliver (yaša‘) the local constituency of Israelites through their endeavors.

Shamgar's saving activity clearly comes at the expense of the Philistines. With Tola, however, no such explicit opponent appears. Instead, Tola's responsibility likely involves saving the Israelites, not from an external adversary, but from the dreadful effects of Abimelech's butchery. Israel now requires deliverance and rebuilding following internal oppression.

As for Tola himself, genealogical lists in the OT associate him and Puah with the tribe of Issachar (Gen. 46:13; Num. 26:23; 1 Chron. 7:1). As such, he appears here residing outside his own tribal territory. The location of Shamir remains uncertain, although the hill country of Ephraim indicates an area south of Shechem [Map, p. 242].

Some, however, see the name Shamir as a variant of "Samaria" and associate the two. This identification is questionable for at least two reasons. Samaria was first established by Omri in the ninth century B.C., well after the time of Tola (1 Kings 16:24). Furthermore, archaeological evidence at Samaria dating earlier than Omri's reign is limited to some Early Bronze pottery (3000-2000 B.C.), well before the time in question *[Archaeological Periods]*. Therefore, to associate Shamir with Samaria would lead one to date the account of Tola no earlier than the time of Omri, when Samaria came into existence. Second, Samaria is too far north to fit the description *hill country of Ephraim;* it actually lies within the territory allotted to Manasseh.

With stability restored, Jair leads Israel during a time free of noteworthy conflict. Jair himself is connected to the tribe of Manasseh, part of which has conquered and controlled the area of Gilead on the eastern side of the Jordan River (Num. 32:39-42; Deut. 3:14). The name *Havvoth Jair* stems from Manasseh's earliest efforts in the region (Num. 32:41; cf. 1 Kings 4:13; 1 Chron. 2:22-23). That the sons of Jair rode *thirty donkeys* and supervised *thirty towns* serves to illustrate the relative peace and prosperity of the period. Donkeys, especially those used specifically for riding, were greatly respected and often associated with nobility (Judg. 5:10; 1 Kings 1:33; Zech. 9:9).

After leading Israel for twenty-two years, Jair dies and is buried in *Kamon.* Kamon is usually identified with present-day Qamm, located a few miles west of Irbid in northern Transjordan.

THE TEXT IN BIBLICAL CONTEXT
Speaking in Parables
Finding himself in what must have been the most desperate situation in his life, Jotham feels compelled to offer an all-important response. Included among his listeners are the perpetrators of the crime, so great persuasive skill is needed. Rather than presenting an analytical confrontation, therefore, Jotham tells a parable.

Parables and other stories appear throughout Scripture in a host of contexts and with varying purposes. Among these, parables at times serve to convince the listener of wrongdoing, particularly in situations when the speaker is either of lower standing or in danger. In addition to Jotham's parable (Judg. 9), OT examples include these:

Text	Recipient	Speaker	Purpose
2 Sam. 12:1-14	David	Nathan	Leads David to see his sin with Uriah and Bathsheba
2 Sam. 14:4-24	David	Woman of Tekoa	Encourages David to bring estranged son Absalom back to Jerusalem
1 Kings 20:39-42	Ahab	Unnamed prophet	Condemns Ahab for releasing opposing king
2 Kings 14:9-10	Amaziah	Jehoash	Deters Amaziah from challenging Israel

Related but less-similar parallels appear also in the prophetic literature (as in Isa. 5:1-7; Ezek. 15; 17; 19; 23; 24:3-14).

Jesus uses parables for similar purposes. In the so-called "parable of the tenants" (Matt. 21:33-46; Mark 12:1-12; Luke 20:9-19), for instance, Jesus emphasizes how the chief priests and Pharisees have rejected him as well as the preceding prophets. Rather than acknowledging the truth of the parable as David had done, these recipients seek to destroy the storyteller. The parable delivered the message with resounding clarity!

Grasping for Power

Although his father Gideon turned down the invitation to reign, Abimelech leaves no stones uncovered in his own quest for kingship. In so doing, he takes his place among the many biblical characters who thirst for power and authority. Already in the creation account, the act of reaching for the fruit constitutes nothing less than a grasping for independence and power (Gen. 3:5). Since then, human beings have all too often "gone and done likewise." The people of Babel, for example, erect a tower to make a name for themselves (Gen. 11:4). Aspiring leaders jockey for power and kill without reservation to either attain it or preserve it (e.g., 1 Sam. 19; 1 Kings 2:13-46; 15:27; 16:10, 15-19). Prophets forfeit their integrity, proclaiming unreliable "good news" for the sake of position (e.g., 1 Kings 22; 2 Chron. 18:1-27; Jer. 5:31; 14:14-16; 28; Ezek. 13). Even the disciples walking side by side with Jesus argue about who is the greatest (Mark 9:34; Luke 22:24). Consistently, the Scriptures depict a consuming urge within human beings to reach for power.

In addition to depicting this urge, however, the Scriptures invariably stand in judgment upon those who yield to it. Typically, the quest for power reflects an arrogant sense of self-sufficiency. As a result, dependence upon the power of God increasingly fades away (e.g., Deut. 8:17-18; 32:15; 2 Chron. 26:14-21). The quest for power also results in a disregard for other human beings, particularly those who either stand in the way or are in need of assistance (e.g., Job 35:9; Ps. 10:10; Eccles. 4:1). Finally, the quest for power blurs priorities and leads people to neglect more important things, including the fear of God, patience, self-control, and wisdom (e.g., Ps. 147:10-11; Eccles. 9:16; Jer. 9:23-24). No wonder, then, that Jesus informs his disciples that "whoever wants to be first must be last of all and servant of all" (Mark 9:35; cf. Matt. 20:27; 23:11; Mark 10:44; Luke 22:26).

Stable Administrators

Absalom, King David's son, was incomparably good-looking (2 Sam. 14:25). Likewise, he was shrewd, ambitious, and unusually dynamic (2 Sam. 13:23-29; 15:1-6, 10-12). Absalom, therefore, possessed many of the characteristics frequently associated with popular leaders. It comes as no surprise, then, that he *stole the hearts of the people of Israel* (2 Sam. 15:6, 13). He did so, of course, in spite of the fact that he apparently lacked balance and stability in equally noteworthy proportions. While Absalom offered dynamism and charisma, he provided little if any substance.

In the chaotic aftermath of Abimelech's reign here in Judges 9, the people's confidence in their dynamic leaders no longer exists. With morale at its lowest point, internal stability desperately needs to be restored. Quietly and deliberately, Tola and Jair go about doing just that.

In the Bible's various depictions of leadership, there is a significant place for forceful proclamation and dynamic demonstration. These more visible and charismatic expressions, however, are no substitutes for stable and dependable administrators who oversee the daily and sometimes mundane operations of the community. Indeed, the root word Paul uses when mentioning the gift of "administration" (*kubernē-*) appears elsewhere in both the LXX and the NT with reference to steering a ship (1 Cor. 12:28; cf. Ezek. 27:8; Acts 27:11; Rev. 18:17) *[Septuagint]*. A ship wanders off course without a capable pilot; so do the people of God in the absence of wise and steady supervision (Prov. 11:14; Rom. 12:8).

THE TEXT IN THE LIFE OF THE CHURCH

Power in Serving

"Power, whether vested in many or few, is ever grasping, and like the grave, cries 'Give, give.'" So wrote Abigail Adams to John Adams on November 27, 1775 (Walsh: ix). Of similar mind, T. S. Eliot somewhat scornfully concluded that "most of the troubles in the world are caused by people wanting to be important." The truth of these evaluations has in no way diminished in recent years, even among Christians. If anything, the flood of horror stories arising from all parts of the globe adds further credibility to such claims.

In such a context, the drastically opposing approaches to power demonstrated by Abimelech and Jesus challenge the community of faith to rethink the nature of its mission. In contrast to Abimelech, who seeks power at all costs, Jesus *already possessed* power:

Jesus knew that the Father had put all things under his power, and that he had come from God and was returning to God. (John 13:3)

Rather than using that power destructively or craving for more, Jesus

got up from the meal, took off his outer clothing, and wrapped a towel around his waist. After that, he poured water into a basin and began to wash his disciples' feet, drying them with the towel that was wrapped around him.
(John 13:4-5)

Like their master, the followers of Jesus already possess far more power than they can possibly imagine (Luke 24:49; Acts 1:8). As a result, they can discard any self-centered quest for human power, choosing instead to wash the world's feet through confident and courageous service.

Balanced Leadership

During a visit to Africa a few years ago, I learned from various Zambian and Zimbabwean church leaders that they regularly lose members to more "demonstrative" churches. People, they told me, seem to prefer personal magnetism, lofty promises, and exotic mani- festations in place of stable and sound teaching. In Zambia and Zimbabwe, like most places, people often search for the kind of dynamic demonstrations pictured elsewhere in Judges (cf. John 4:48; 1 Cor. 1:22).

In reality, such searches frequently end in either an ecstatic but temporary experience, or else an unhealthy and unquestioning attach- ment to those performing the demonstration. Balanced leadership, therefore, must encompass more than charisma, as desirable and important as that may be. Balanced leadership, both within the church and beyond, includes the steady and dependable instruction and administration provided by the Tolas and Jairs of the world.

Judges 10:6—16:31

The Pattern Ignored: Jephthah and Samson

OVERVIEW

In spite of the noticeable deterioration in Israel's condition during the lifetimes of Gideon and particularly Abimelech, the descending journey envisioned by the writer has by no means reached its lowest point. In fact, a considerable distance still lies ahead. The spotlight now shifts to Jephthah and Samson, during whose ventures the model established by Othniel dwindles nearly out of sight. Entire stages of the cycle outlined in 2:6—3:6 are now missing, and remaining stages grow increasingly difficult to discern [Breakdown of the Judges Cycle]. Jephthah, for one thing, does not receive a divine call, and Samson shows no significant points of contact with the esteemed judges portrayed earlier. By this time, the earlier-established pattern has been largely lost.

OUTLINE

A Negative Portrait: Jephthah's Undertakings, 10:6—12:7

Negative Portraits: Ibzan's, Elon's, and Abdon's Operations, 12:8-15

A Negative Portrait: Samson's Stunts, 13:1—16:31

A Negative Portrait: Jephthah's Undertakings

Judges 10:6—12:7

PREVIEW

Bargaining can be a hazardous activity, for a person who bargains always runs the risk of being shortchanged. In the account of Jephthah, a series of five distinct but at times overlapping bargaining sessions occur; the final four directly involve Jephthah himself. Each session results in some form of death or destruction. The outcome grows increasingly more severe as the narrative proceeds:

Bargaining Parties	Outcome
Israelites and the Lord, 10:6-16	Foreign gods destroyed
Israelites and Jephthah, 10:17—11:11	Ammonites eventually destroyed
Jephthah and Ammonite King, 11:12-28	Diplomacy fails
Jephthah and the Lord, 11:29-40	Jephthah's daughter destroyed
Jephthah and Ephraim, 12:1-7	Ephraimites destroyed

What begins with the positive removal of unwanted deities and the triumph over enemies concludes with a civil war and the annihilation of a multitude of Israelites (Ephraimite forces). As the catalyst, an otherwise competent and shrewd Jephthah bargains once too often, causing his entire world, as well as that of the Israelites, to come crashing down. Unmistakably, Israel's worsening internal condition outshines any pressures exerted from without.

OUTLINE

Israel Bargains with God, 10:6-16
    10:6-10   Crisis Introduced
    10:11-16   The Lord Rebukes Israel

Jephthah Bargains with Israel, 10:17—11:11
    10:17-18   Israel Seeks a Leader
    11:1-11   Jephthah Recruited as Leader

Jephthah Bargains with Ammon, 11:12-28

Jephthah Bargains with God, 11:29-40
    11:29-31   Jephthah Makes a Vow

11:32-33   Jephthah Subdues the Ammonites
11:34-40   Jephthah Fulfills His Vow

Jephthah Bargains No More: Ephraim Destroyed, 12:1-7

EXPLANATORY NOTES
Israel Bargains with God 10:6-16
10:6-10 Crisis Introduced

In spite of whatever stability Tola offered following the debacle under Abimelech, the Israelites soon return to their anticipated evil ways. Now, in addition to the Canaanite Baals and Astartes, Israel's religious waywardness expands to include the gods of many of the surrounding peoples [Ashtoreth; Baal]. The accompanying list of deities, however, is somewhat imprecise, its importance lying more in the impressions it creates than in the distinctiveness of the gods themselves. In fact, the Arameans who settled in Syria, the Sidonians residing on the northern Mediterranean coast, and the Philistines—all worshiped gods who were themselves a part of the standard Canaanite pantheon. As such, by worshiping these deities, along with Chemosh of the Moabites and Milcom of the Ammonites (1 Kings 11:5, 7, 33; 2 Kings 23:13), the Israelites are not so much seduced by new and distant gods as they are increasingly dominated by the religious practices of the people *immediately* around them [Map, p. 242].

To further emphasize the extent of Israel's spiritual harlotry by this time, the writer here employs a swift and subtle brush stroke that too often escapes the modern reader. Of more importance than the foreign deities themselves is the number of them—seven. The symbolic significance of the number *seven* in the Bible has long been noted, for it frequently denotes the idea of completeness or perfection (notes on 8:14; Gen. 1:1—2:4; 29:15-30; 41:1-36; Lev. 25:2-7; Ps. 12:6; Matt. 18:21-22; Rev. 2–3). In this case, then, the Israelites have totally and unreservedly abandoned the Lord in favor of counterfeit gods. Their unfaithfulness constitutes complete defection to the opposing side.

In response to this latest episode of Israelite disloyalty, *the anger of the Lord was kindled against Israel* (10:7). Typically, as with Ehud, Deborah, Gideon, and Samson, divine anger goes unmentioned—the Lord simply hands over his rebellious people to various oppressors. Both here and in the account of Othniel (3:8), however, the Lord's fury burns brightly *(wayyihar-'ap yhwh)*. Significantly, the introductory materials (2:6—3:6) twice anticipated the fiery wrath of

God, and associated the expected outbreaking of his anger with two distinct stages of the story (Stone: 306-307).

First, the Lord's anger (*wayyiḥar-'ap yhwh*) finds expression when he casts Israel into the hands of their enemies (2:14). In so doing, God clearly hoped to rid his people of their unfaithful tendencies. When such efforts repeatedly failed, the Lord grew angry again (*wayyiḥar-'ap yhwh*) and refused to participate further in the removal of the Canaanites from the land (2:20). In the case of Othniel, then, the Lord's anger initiates the first stage, the redemptive and transforming process involving oppression and deliverance (3:8-9). Now, in 10:7, the Lord's fiery anger apparently signals divine exasperation and with it the beginning of the end.

On this second occasion, the anger of the Lord results in domination at the hands of the Philistines and the Ammonites. In the following account of Jephthah, however, the Ammonites alone function as the oppressors; the task of dealing with the Philistines falls on Samson's shoulders. The Ammonites, who inhabit a region east of the Jordan River and Jericho, also come into conflict with the Israelites later, during the reigns of Saul (1 Sam. 11) and David (2 Sam. 12:26-31). Of these two subsequent confrontations, both resulting in Israelite victories, the first perhaps indicates a particularly gruesome streak in Ammonite war strategies (1 Sam. 11:2; cf. Amos 1:13-15).

Here in Judges 10, such cruelty affects primarily the Israelites living in Gilead, also east of the Jordan, between the Jordan and Ammon. Eventually, however, the Ammonites expand their vision, causing trouble also in the western territories of Judah, Benjamin, and Ephraim (10:9) [Maps, pp. 240, 242]. Following eighteen years of domination and this recent wave of expanded violence, the Israelites once again find themselves on their knees. In this case, however, their cries specifically include an acknowledgment of sin (10:10; cf. 3:9, 15; 4:3; 6:6). Whether this constitutes a genuine and lasting act of repentance remains an open question.

10:11-16 The Lord Rebukes Israel

Rather than sending a prophet, as God did in the previous account (6:7-10), the Lord himself responds to Israel's plea. The content of his response, however, bears some similarity to that of the prophet, although it is expanded and includes an explicit denial of further aid. In a form parallel to the earlier list of seven foreign gods (10:6), the Lord now refers to seven former oppressive experiences from which he has delivered his people. By implication, the Lord's mercy and compassion have previously known no limits. Indeed, his desire and ability to deliver his people have more than matched their tendency to go astray.

With respect to the various episodes mentioned in the list, an allusion to the *Egyptians* calls to mind the exodus itself. Other events that provide the appropriate frame of reference for the Lord's reply include Israel's victory over Sihon and the *Amorites* (Num. 21:21-35), the *Ammonites* (Judg. 3:13), the *Philistines* (3:31), and the *Amalekites* (3:13; 6:3). No mention appears elsewhere of a confrontation with the *Sidonians*, although one can easily imagine them as part of the northern coalition defeated by Deborah and Barak (5:19). Finally, the *Maonites* may refer to the Meunites, who later come into conflict with the people of Judah (1 Chron. 4:41; 2 Chron. 26:7). The LXX, however, reads *Midianites* for *Maonites*, recalling Israel's liberation under Gideon (Judg. 6–8) *[Septuagint]*.

In spite of these past merciful acts by a patient Deity, the Israelites' habitual sinfulness has gone unabated. At this point, then, the Lord's patience wears frighteningly thin. Rather than following this look at the past with the call of yet another deliverer, as he did in the case of Gideon, God flatly refuses to intervene. Furthermore, God mocks the Israelites' own tiresome behavior by encouraging the people to *cry to the gods whom you have chosen* (10:14). How different is this characterization of the Lord from what was depicted in 3:9-10!

Such a forceful rebuke notwithstanding, the Israelites continue their urgent appeal for divine assistance. Now, in addition to repeating their initial confession, they throw their fate in the Lord's hands and remove the foreign gods they have accumulated. Yet their plea, *"Do to us whatever seems good to you; but deliver us this day,"* appears somewhat self-centered. Once again, the cry for help turns out to be just that, and the confession of sin a mere bargaining chip that only masks the deeper pain of oppression. Israel, as Polzin rightly points out, attempts "once more to use Yahweh to insure their peace and tranquillity" (178).

The Lord, however, will have nothing more to do with these wearisome gimmicks. Frequently commentators see in 10:16b a major shift in God's response. Given the Israelites' renewed plea and the removal of their counterfeit gods, the Lord relents and mercifully intervenes on their behalf (Boling: 193; Cundall: 140; Martin: 135). Such an interpretation, however, fails to do justice to both the context and the specific Hebrew verb employed here. Elsewhere, as in Jeremiah 26:13 and Jonah 3:10, the Lord's relenting is captured by either the verb *šub* ("to return, go back") or *naham* ("to regret, be sorry"), neither of which appears here. Instead, the verb is *qaṣar*, which involves the element of growing weary or impatient.

The Israelites, for example, grow impatient (*qaṣar*) in the wilderness when lacking food and water (Num. 21:4). Similarly, Job feels increasingly weary (*qaṣar*) under the weight of his affliction (Job 21:4). The most-illustrative occurrence is in the story of Samson, when he grows sick and tired (*qaṣar*) of Delilah's nagging (Judg. 16:16).

Rather than merciful compassion, the Lord here experiences total aggravation! (Stone: 320-325). Like the shepherd with the tiresome sheep (Zech. 11:8-9), God now wants nothing more to do with Israel's perpetual whining. Importantly, then, the following narrative makes absolutely no reference to the Lord calling a deliverer. Such a summons comes solely from the Gileadites themselves.

THE TEXT IN BIBLICAL CONTEXT

Wearying God

Through their constant flings with idolatry and their empty petitions, the Israelites increasingly exhaust the Lord's patience and mercy. Just as he previously grew weary with the whole of his rebellious creation, so now does he express unmistakable irritation with his wayward community (Gen. 6:1-7). Clearly, while human beings have the capacity to bring great joy and satisfaction to the heart of God, so too can they weary him (cf. Gen. 6:6; 1 Kings 3:10; Job 1:8; 2:3; Eph. 5:10; Col. 1:10).

God's frustration with his people appears with considerable frequency in both narrative accounts as well as prophetic speeches. With respect to the accounts, the Israelites' journey through the wilderness provides perhaps the best example. Time after time, they try God's patience by grumbling and complaining (Exod. 33:1-6; Num. 11:1; 12:9). In fact, God's irritation reaches such sizeable proportions that he proposes discarding them and establishing a new nation with Moses (Num. 14:11-12). While such a substitution never materialized, a substitute later replaced Saul, whose disobedience led directly to his divine rejection (1 Sam. 15:11, 22-26).

In the preaching of the prophets, the notion of wearying God constitutes a recurring theme. Isaiah, for example, chastises the community for burdening God by associating righteousness with the mere performance of external rituals (1:10-14). Jeremiah attributes God's irritation to constant rejection and backsliding on Israel's part (15:6). Finally, Malachi accuses the community of wearying God through empty and indeed inflammatory words (2:17). Generally speaking, then, the prophets repeatedly link the Lord's profound frustration to the various expressions of Israel's chronic sinfulness (cf. Isa. 7:13; 43:24; Ezek. 6:9).

Sadly but perhaps not unexpectedly, the NT amply illustrates that moments of frustration continued to plague God well after the last of ancient Israel's prophets. No passage more graphically portrays this than the letter to the church in Laodicea: "I am about to spit you out of my mouth" (Rev. 3:16). Jesus himself expresses similar sentiments on more than one occasion.

The remarkable disbelief of the very cities in which Jesus had performed most of his miracles, for example, drives him to conclude that even Sodom stands a better chance on the day of judgment than they do (Matt. 11:20-24). Likewise, his reaction to his disciples' inability to heal a demon-possessed child betrays an unmistakable and painful sense of futility: "How long shall I stay with you? How long shall I put up with you?" (Matt. 17:17; Luke 9:41). Although God's involvement in redeeming the world ultimately brings him deep satisfaction and lasting joy, the pages of Scripture all too often reveal moments of intense frustration along the way.

THE TEXT IN THE LIFE OF THE CHURCH

A God in Pain

Due largely to the influence of such Greek philosophers as Plato and Aristotle, many people in the ancient world, including most of the early church fathers, believed that God was incapable of feeling a wide range of common emotions (Ngien: 38). Similarly, the lingering effects of Enlightenment thinking lead many today to envision God primarily as a rational and intellectual being, void of genuine feeling. Because God is perfect, he knows nothing about anger and hate, or love and compassion, according to such views.

How different this perspective is from the one found throughout much of the Bible. As Jewish theologian Abraham Heschel has noted,

> To the biblical mind the denial of man's relevance to God is as inconceivable as the denial of God's relevance to man. This principle leads to the basic affirmation of God's participation in human history, to the certainty that the events in the world concern Him and arouse His reaction. It finds its deepest expression in the fact that God can actually suffer. (259)

Rather than encountering an abstract idea or an unemotional brute, we find in Judges 10:11-16 what Meyer Levin calls a "compassionate, torn, and sorrowing God who gave us free will out of love, and having forbidden Himself to interfere, must behold in agony what we do with our freedom" (28). We find, in other words, a humbling glimpse of the pain and frustration brought upon God by none other than his own people (Moltmann, 1981:21-57).

An awareness of the misery one often causes, however, need not end with guilt and despair. Indeed, such insight has the potential to spark genuine transformation. Seeing a parent weep, for example, may well lead an otherwise uncaring child to reach out in greater affection. In the same way, realizing that *we humans actually do cause God pain* can soften our hardened hearts and encourage us to love the Lord with ever-deepening devotion. Like the formerly rebellious and ungrateful teenager who finally reaches out to his hurt but now delighted parents, so too can the community of faith caringly turn God's sorrow into joy.

Jephthah Bargains with Israel 10:17—11:11

10:17-18 Israel Seeks a Leader

As the impending battle draws closer, the Israelites and Ammonites gather at their respective bases in Gilead and Mizpah. The location of Mizpah remains uncertain, although the general setting east of the Jordan distinguishes it from the Mizpah situated in Benjamin (Josh. 18:26). That the Ammonites *were called to arms* in typical military fashion reflects precision, order, and competent leadership. The Israelites, in contrast, simply *assembled*. Even in this simple act of gathering, then, Israel's lack of direction stands out (Webb: 49).

There is now an immediate and urgent need for a military commander. The question about leadership is strangely reminiscent of one asked earlier by the whole community (1:1), although the context has changed immeasurably. Now, in place of a unified offensive, the Israelites appear desperate and disoriented. As a result, they attach a reward of sorts to the job description: the new military commander will also be *head over all the inhabitants of Gilead*. In the tribal structure of the day, no higher position exists. Accompanying the offer is perhaps the expectation that one of them will function in the designated role, an expectation that never materializes. Instead, the eventually agreed-upon candidate will surprisingly come from the fringes of society.

11:1-11 Jephthah Recruited as Leader

Jephthah, like Gideon before him, is a man of notable military competence (11:1). Yet the similarities between Jephthah and Abimelech are even more striking. Both, for example, have been conceived through secondary relationships: Abimelech's mother was a concubine (8:31), and Jephthah's a prostitute. Both therefore are outcasts from their fathers' families, living either with the mother's clan

(9:1) or, as with Jephthah, in forced exile (11:2-3). Finally, both sur-round themselves with a group of undisciplined adventurers (9:4). Given Abimelech's unforgettable atrocities, one can only hope that the similarities stop here.

The land of Tob, the place of Jephthah's exile, is normally asso-ciated with modern et-Taiyibeh, situated some twelve miles northeast of Ramoth-gilead. From there, the Ammonites later recruited merce-naries in their renewed struggles with Israel (2 Sam. 10:6-13). In the present case, however, such mercenaries rally around Jephthah him-self, giving him a personal band of raiders similar to the one that accompanied David following his flight from Saul (1 Sam. 22:2; 27:1-4). Even as David's raiders enabled him to solidify his position before he became king, Jephthah's supporters will soon become instrumen-tal in his own military and political advancement.

In preparation for the upcoming battle, the candidate of choice is none other than the banished Jephthah. The choice of Jephthah, in spite of his prior treatment at the hands of the people of Gilead, is actually not as shocking as it might at first appear. During his time in the land of Tob, he and his fellow guerrillas no doubt live off the booty gained through mercenary activities. As a result, they have become experienced and seasoned fighters. In seeking out Jephthah, then, the elders hope to enlist the assistance of "professionals," even if it means swallowing their pride. Whereas Abimelech took the initiative and employed his thugs to forcibly solidify his position, Jephthah's thugs are precisely the reason why he is approached in the first place.

In consulting with Jephthah about his services, the elders initially make no offer concerning his functioning as head over all the Gileadites, an offer they previously agreed upon (10:18). Instead, they simply ask him to function as commander of their forces (11:6). Realizing that Jephthah knows nothing about their earlier conversa-tions, they attempt to secure his involvement without paying so great a reward. When Jephthah responds unenthusiastically, questioning their motives and ambitions, they immediately sweeten the prize by placing the original offer on the table.

Still unconvinced, Jephthah bargains further, constructing a model of the upcoming battle with the Ammonites. In his model, Jephthah alludes to the Lord's ultimate role as Israel's Deliverer. Whether his doing so constitutes a personal statement of faith, however, is anoth-er matter (Cundall: 142). By equating a victory with the work of the Lord, Jephthah may just as well hope to solidify his own position. After all, who among the Gileadites will dare rescind an offer made to the human architect of a divinely ordained triumph? Throughout the entire encounter, then, Jephthah shrewdly capitalizes on the elders' obvious desperation, even extracting an oath so as to guarantee the validity of their proposal.

At home, Jephthah receives the overwhelming support of the Gileadites, who affirm his selection during a sacred ceremony at Mizpah (11:11; cf. 10:17). Such a ceremony is intended to ratify the agreement in the Lord's presence; yet it must be remembered that the choice of Jephthah reflects no divine initiative. The Lord has had nothing to say since his castigation of the Israelites in 10:11-14. Nevertheless, Jephthah now assumes both of the posts, commander and head over the Gileadites, although the latter position depends upon triumph over the Ammonites (10:18; 11:8). That will happen soon enough.

Jephthah Bargains with Ammon   11:12-28

Jephthah's first act as military commander involves simple diplomacy: he sends messengers to the king of the Ammonites in an attempt to ascertain the reasons behind their assault (11:12). The king responds to these efforts and thereby recognizes Jephthah's newly established role; Jephthah is indeed the leader of the Israelites. Furthermore, the content of the Ammonite response indicates that the ongoing struggle grew out of a border dispute, the type of dispute so prevalent in the region throughout much of history. According to the king, the Israelites illegally confiscated some Ammonite territory during their earlier travels from Egypt. The area in question is due east of the Jordan River, bordered on the north by the Jabbok River and on the south by the Arnon [Map, p. 242]. Now, by simply returning the disputed terrain peacefully, Jephthah can avoid additional confrontation.

In this second message (11:15-27), which is by no means conciliatory in nature, Jephthah rather forcefully and determinedly supports Israel's occupation by appealing to three distinct elements. First, Jephthah draws upon the traditions of the wilderness wanderings and specifically cites the Israelites' nonaggressive tactics during their journey to Canaan (11:15-22). In accord with such tactics, Israel peaceably contacted the Edomite, Moabite, and Amorite leaders in attempts to gain right of passage through their territories. When these rights were denied, the Israelites deliberately went around Edom and Moab, even though doing so greatly lengthened the distance of their journey (Num. 20:14-21; 21:4, 10-13, 21-31; Deut. 2:2-18). In the process, no foreign territory was confiscated.

Only after bypassing Moab, then, did Israel arrive at the territory now being claimed by the Ammonites. Significantly, however, this territory apparently never belonged to the Ammonites, who were situated further east (cf. 2 Sam. 11:1; 12:26-31). Instead, the land between the Arnon and the Jabbok generally fell under Moabite control, as indicated by its inclusion elsewhere under the name of Moab (Num. 35:1; Deut. 1:5). Similarly, the Moabite Stone informs us that during the later reign of Omri (1 Kings 16:21-28), the capital of Moab was in Dhiban, located in just this region *[Map, p. 242]*.

The Moabites, however, were occasionally unable to maintain control of the area, and they actually lost the land at the hands of the invading Amorites just before Israel's arrival (Num. 21:26). The Israelites then captured the disputed territory from the belligerent Amorites, *not* the Ammonites or Moabites, although they first sought a peaceful crossing (11:19-22; Num. 21:21-31).

If this region between the Arnon and the Jabbok originally belonged to Moab, only to be conquered by the Amorites and still later by the Israelites, one might wonder why the king of the Ammonites laid such a claim to it in the first place. Some commentators simply conclude that he probably never did. Rather, given the obvious Moabite orientation of Jephthah's message (even *your god Chemosh* in 11:24 is a Moabite deity), later Israelite diplomacy with the Moabites is merely placed here in an Ammonite context. Others suggest that Jephthah, knowingly or unknowingly, confused and distorted many of the facts (Klein: 89; Cundall: 144-145). Yet, as Boling rightly points out, Jephthah's reconstruction of the events actually reflects a relatively high historicity (205; Sternberg: 116).

A far more likely solution, therefore, sees the Ammonite claim resulting from another shift on the political scene of Jephthah's day. By this time, the Ammonites have gained the upper hand over their Moabite neighbors to the south, perhaps in part because of the Moabite defeat alluded to in Judges 3:12-30 (Boling: 202-203; Soggin: 210; Webb: 56). As a result, the Ammonites take upon themselves Moab's former claims, including those to the region in question. In essence, what was once Moab's now belongs to Ammon, at least in the Ammonite view of things.

Following this brief summation, Jephthah secondly argues that, historical claims aside, the Israelite conquest of the territory amounted to nothing less than an act of God (11:21, 23-24). Therefore, the land belongs to Israel for theological reasons. In the ancient Near East, battles between nations similarly involved battles between their gods. When Israel defeated Sihon, then, God likewise defeated the Amorite deities. In short, the God of Israel has given this territory to his people as part of their inheritance. As a result, all other claims to it are invalid.

Such an understanding, Jephthah maintains, ought to be perfect-ly clear to the present king of Ammon, who himself functions with a similar worldview. Land given to him by *Chemosh*, the Moabite deity responsible for providing various territories now included among Ammon's present holdings, is similarly considered by the king to be privileged Ammonite property. Jephthah, in other words, applies a theological principle that the opposing king himself embraces. In so doing, Jephthah does not necessarily place Chemosh and the God of Israel on equal grounds, as some have suggested (Burney: 300; Klein: 89). Instead, he cleverly uses mutually accepted categories that he no doubt considers irrefutable.

Finally, after defending Israel's occupation of the land on historical and theological grounds, Jephthah appeals to simple common sense (11:25-26). In his view, the current debate centers on an event that occurred in the relatively distant past. If the situation needed correct-ing, then Balak, the Moabite king at the time of Israel's journey, was the one to do it. Instead of doing so, however, he merely sought to protect his remaining holdings south of the Arnon, even though the Israelites had already passed by (Num. 22–25).

Insofar as Balak made no effort to regain his former property, why should the king of Ammon now think he has the right to make such an attempt? At least, the Ammonites should have raised their con-cerns earlier. After all, the Israelites have in fact lived in the area *for three hundred years*, a period of time that closely agrees with the 301 total years of oppression and liberation stated up to this point in the book (11:26) *[Chronology]*. Quite simply, too much time has elapsed for any legitimate alteration of the situation.

After rehearsing Israel's claim to the disputed area and disallowing the claim of the Ammonite king, Jephthah concludes his message with what amounts to a declaration of war (11:27). By reaffirming Israelite innocence and subsequently calling upon the Lord to decide the dispute, Jephthah unilaterally rules out any thought of territorial compromise. In his mind, the Ammonites have become unjustifiably militaristic, and apparently nothing short of their retreat will avert war.

Jephthah Bargains with God 11:29-40

11:29-31 Jephthah Makes a Vow

Given Jephthah's inability to persuade the Ammonite monarch to abandon his ambitions, the Israelite commander now moves into posi-tion. In spite of enduring near-total neglect in the preceding narrative, neglect in part hidden by the Gileadites' religious presumption (11:10-11), *the Spirit of the Lord* now comes upon Jephthah (cf. 3:10;

6:34; 13:25; 14:6,19) [Holy Spirit in the OT]. The Lord, in other words, sets aside his utter aggravation and graciously works through an instrument that he himself has not explicitly selected. Once again, divine mercy far surpasses human unfaithfulness. Whether or not Jephthah realizes his fresh endowment of empowerment, however, remains mysteriously obscure, for he immediately makes what will develop into his most devastating mistake.

In approaching Jephthah's notorious vow (neder), various points must be kept in mind. First, in the narrative Jephthah never speaks even a word to the Lord, nor is he the recipient of any divine pronouncement. No prior dialogue serves as an experiential foundation for Jephthah's present behavior. As a result, the vow emerges from a relational vacuum.

Second, while Jephthah already functions as commander of the Israelite forces, the ultimate position of tribal head ultimately hinges on him subduing the Ammonites. Because Jephthah has a great deal to lose in the approaching campaign, he resorts to a vow with high stakes.

Finally, as his prior sessions with the elders of Gilead and the king of Ammon so clearly demonstrate, Jephthah is a negotiator by nature. Uttering a vow is a further extension of his previous tactics. In this case, the stakes are admittedly higher and his counterpart none other than the Lord himself. Nevertheless, the vow, a planned and deliberate bargaining chip, reflects Jephthah at his authentic and unmitigated best.

As to the vow itself, Jephthah's words are simultaneously ambiguous and yet unmistakable. With ambiguity, the text does not distinguish clearly between animal and human sacrifice. As such, the translation *whoever* rather than *whatever* ('ašer means either) removes the tension without justification. In addition, houses of the day have space for domestic animals, including sheep and goats (Mazar: 340-344, 485-489). It is entirely possible, therefore, for an animal to come out of the house. While the phrase *to meet me* (liqra'ti) ordinarily implies human volition (Moore: 299), Jephthah's precise intentions nevertheless remain somewhat out of focus. As a result, a burdensome uneasiness surrounds the event; Jephthah's entire household hangs precariously in the balance.

While the subject of Jephthah's vow remains unclear, the nature of the act is unmistakable. Whatever comes out of his house, Jephthah intends to present to the Lord as a *burnt offering* ('olah). The noun 'olah, whether in OT contexts of celebration or petition, consistently refers to a burnt offering (Gen. 8:20; 22:2; Lev. 1:4; 1 Sam. 7:9; Jer. 14:12).

11:32-33 Jephthah Subdues the Ammonites

With the uttering of Jephthah's vow and the great anticipation surrounding it, the otherwise climactic battle with the Ammonites receives little further literary attention. Much the same thing happened when Deborah turned everyone's attention from the Canaanite coalition to an as-yet-unnamed heroine (4:9). Here, the battle occupies a mere two verses, even though the extent of Jephthah's accomplishments indicates a significant victory indeed. While *Aroer, Minnith,* and *Abel Karamim* all defy certain identification, the region in question is in the vicinity of Rabbath-Ammon, the Ammonite capital (the modern city of Amman) *[Map, p. 242].* Whatever the full benefits of this Israelite victory over the Ammonites might be, however, it was not until the campaigns of David that Israel ultimately brought the Ammonites under control (2 Sam. 10; 12:26-31; 1 Chron. 19:1—20:3).

11:34-40 Jephthah Fulfills His Vow

With the victory in hand, Jephthah returns to the place where everyone's attention has nervously remained—his home in Mizpah. Now, without any intervening moments to savor the battle's outcome or his promised elevation to tribal head, Jephthah watches in helpless horror as his daughter—his only child!—comes to greet him. In the traditional role of jubilant women welcoming home their heroes, this unsuspecting child dances in total celebration (Exod. 15:20-21; Judg. 5:28-30; 1 Sam. 18:6-7). Readers, however, can only join in the unfolding suffering.

In seeing his approaching daughter, Jephthah immediately breaks into mourning (11:35). Tearing one's clothes constitutes a common expression of grief and despair throughout the ancient world in general and the OT in particular (Gen. 37:29, 34; 44:13; 2 Sam. 13:19, 31; 2 Kings 2:12; Job 1:20; Isa. 36:22; Jer. 41:5). The conflict with the Ammonites and the promised promotion, both of which gave rise to the vow in the first place, now give way to the harsh and terrifying consequences. These consequences alter Jephthah's perspective as well.

In the midst of his mourning, however, Jephthah adds gross insensitivity to his excessive tendency to bargain: he blames the child for his ill fortune! He does acknowledge his regrettable vow, irrevocable because of the absolute importance of the spoken word. Yet Jephthah "thinks of himself and indicts his daughter for the predicament" (Trible: 102). Similarly, he offers her no comfort or reassurance. The child, without siblings, therefore finds herself with no noticeable parental compassion either. How different is David's response a short time later. Upon learning of the death of his rebellious son, David cries, "O my son Absalom, my son, my son Absalom! Would I had died instead of you, O Absalom, my son, my son!" (2 Sam. 18:33).

Although the terms of Jephthah's vow are nowhere spelled out for his daughter, the manner of his reaction and the subsequent nature of her request suggest a deepening understanding of the situation. At the same time, the child's response reflects a more admirable and godly spirit than any seen elsewhere in the narrative. She, the unmistakable victim, becomes a devout encourager (11:36). Yet, before fulfilling the vow, she requests a two-month grace period during which she and her friends can mourn her virginity and resulting childlessness. Children are nothing less than a blessing from God, a blessing through which the parents' name and identity live on. In this case, not only would the daughter vanish from history, but indeed Jephthah's entire family. She was, after all, an only child.

Following this period of mourning, the daughter returns willingly to her father's house. Upon her arrival, Jephthah *did with her according to the vow he had made* (11:39). Although the writer graciously refrains from including additional details, even to the point of refusing to specify the act, the outcome is clear enough. Unlike Abraham, who himself was about to sacrifice his only child, Jephthah receives no substitute offering (Gen. 22). For Abraham, the entire event was a divinely ordained test. By way of contrast, Jephthah's dilemma has resulted from a self-motivated attempt to counteract his own faithlessness; God has nothing to do with it. He is left, therefore, to face the consequences of his deeds, the OT's consistent abhorrence of human sacrifices notwithstanding (Lev. 18:21; 20:1-5; Deut. 12:31; 18:10; 2 Kings 16:3; Jer. 7:31). Jephthah's bargaining finally catches up with him, and his daughter forfeits her life to pay the price.

This apparent clarity concerning the consequences of Jephthah's vow finds acceptance (not approval!) among most commentators throughout history. Yet occasional attempts have been made to provide an alternate explanation. Largely on the basis of the concluding reference to the girl's virginity (11:39), a reference reiterating the magnitude of her loss, some interpreters suggest that, rather than dying, Jephthah's daughter goes without sexual relations for the duration of her life (Keil and Delitzsch: 388-395). According to this view, she is sentenced to a lifetime of unending virginity, perhaps even in service at a local temple.

The OT, however, considers childlessness a sign of great misfortune, not devotion. Furthermore, no clear support exists for women serving in the above-mentioned position. In Exodus 38:8 and 1 Samuel 2:22, for example, no indication attributes permanence to the women's roles at the Tent of Meeting. As well intended as such views might be, they simply confuse the issue. Jephthah's deed, though unarguably detestable, must be allowed to stand.

The tradition in which the young women of Israel annually commemorate Jephthah's daughter (11:39-40) goes unmentioned elsewhere in the OT. It was no doubt practiced solely in the area of Gilead, and has therefore left no additional mark in Scripture. Significantly, the local women who mourn for and with Jephthah's daughter now corporately counteract at least a portion of her misfortune. While the girl may not live on in her offspring, she does so in the acts of her friends.

Jephthah Bargains No More: Ephraim Destroyed 12:1-7

Even after the crisis at home and the ultimate fulfillment of his costly vow, Jephthah's tragic demise continues. Following his victory over the Ammonites, Israel's beleaguered leader faces a major intertribal conflict, once again at the instigation of the Ephraimites. Insulted by their lack of involvement in the just-completed battle, the Ephraimites cross to the eastern side of the Jordan and confront Jephthah at *Zaphon*. Zaphon apparently lies in the Jordan Valley, about five miles northwest of Succoth (cf. 8:4-9). Precisely why the Ephraimites meet Jephthah there rather than in his hometown of Mizpah (11:34), however, remains unclear. No additional clues are provided about Zaphon's role or significance in the story.

In challenging Jephthah, the Ephraimites essentially repeat a previous episode in which they complained to Gideon about their exclusion from the battle against Midian. Once again Ephraim clearly relishes the type of influential position allotted to it during the judgeship of Ehud (3:27). As a dominant tribe, however, the Ephraimites have responded negatively to perceived slights. Gideon wisely appeased their anger and carefully avoided an outbreak of violence. Jephthah, in contrast, makes no attempt whatsoever at peaceful resolution. No doubt reeling from the consequences of his negotiations with God and the lingering pain of his vow, Jephthah gives up serious bargaining and goes swiftly for the kill.

In his response to the Ephraimites, Jephthah contends that he did in fact solicit their support, but to no avail (12:2). While no such summons to Ephraim appears anywhere in the story, neither it nor the implied refusal are difficult to imagine (cf. 1 Sam. 11:3). On the contrary, a Gileadite appeal to the surrounding tribes, particularly in the midst of such an ongoing oppression, might well be expected. Likewise, the fact the Ephraimites show no significant care for those on the east side of the Jordan ("on the other side of the tracks"; cf. 12:4) implies at least a possible unwillingness on their part to provide assistance. Given the lack of outside support, therefore, Jephthah argues that he had no choice but to fight the Ammonites with local personnel alone.

Jephthah's increasing disdain for the Ephraimites, already apparent in the opening lines of his response, is further expressed in the manner in which he attributes the victory to the Lord (12:3). If the Israelite victory over the Ammonites was in fact a divine initiative, then what right, he asks, does Ephraim have to raise objections? By raising such objections, the Ephraimites are in fact arguing against God himself. From every imaginable perspective, then, the present Ephraimite assault lacks foundation.

Armed conflict appears as inevitable after Jephthah's rebuttal as it did following the final message sent to the Ammonite king (11:14-27). A civil war follows, and Jephthah secures a particularly convincing victory. Jephthah is harsh because the Ephraimites have engaged in prejudicial name-calling. The Ephraimites have accused the Gileadites of being marginalized offshoots, *fugitives* from the larger western tribes (12:4). As a result, the offended people of Gilead have a personal score to settle.

Following the battle itself, the Gileadites circle back and capture *the fords of the Jordan against the Ephraimites* (12:5; cf. 3:28; 7:24). In so doing, they gain control of the passageways through which the surviving Ephraimites will naturally seek to return home. While patrolling these areas, the Gileadites devise a test to determine Ephraimite identity, a test based upon a pronunciational difference between their opponents and themselves. That the word *shibboleth* means either "ear of corn" or "stream of water" is of little consequence in the story; any word beginning with *sh* (š) would have served the same purpose. In a manner similar to contemporary Arabic, the Ephraimite dialect pronounced *sh* as *s*. Such a pronunciational difference has been so deeply ingrained that the Ephraimites find it physically impossible to produce the alien sound *sh*. With the uttering of this single word, therefore, the identity of imposters immediately surfaces and seals their fate (cf. Matt. 26:69-75). Thus Jephthah detects and destroys Ephraimite forces, his fellow Israelites.

While the round number *forty-two thousand* exceeds reasonable

limits for the period in question, its impact in the story is clear enough
[Historicity and Truth]. Once the energy of Israel's judges was directed solely at removing foreign oppressors; now Jephthah's activities
conclude with the mass destruction of Israelites themselves. As a
result, no reference appears concerning the land experiencing peace
(cf. 3:11, 30; 5:31; 8:28). Instead, Jephthah's judgeship, which for
the first time in the book is shorter than the period of oppression that
induced it, simply ends in the shadow of Israel's ever-worsening internal fortunes.

THE TEXT IN BIBLICAL CONTEXT

Making Vows

Vows constituted a common and accepted practice among both the
Israelites as well as their neighbors (cf. Jon. 1:16; Jer. 44:25). Rather
than condemning them, the legislative materials in the OT even provide instructions to ensure that vows are properly carried out.

According to these materials, vows were strictly voluntary in nature
(Deut. 23:21-23). They appear on various occasions in the same context as freewill offerings (Lev. 7:16; 22:18, 21; Num. 15:3; 29:39;
Deut. 12:6). Once made, however, a vow had to be carefully followed
(Num. 30:2; Ps. 50:14). Breaking a vow was in reality far worse than
never making one in the first place (Eccles. 5:4-5; cf. Mal. 1:14).
Therefore, none should be pronounced without careful thought and
consideration (Prov. 20:25). Extensive regulations were laid out for
vows and pledges of women; their husbands or fathers could invalidate
them (Num. 30:1-16).

Judged by content, one can distinguish two kinds of vows.
Occasionally, people took vows in order to renounce something that
was otherwise permitted. Nazirites, for instance, refrained from products of the vine (Num. 6). More frequently, an individual or group typically promised to give something extra (e.g., a sacrifice or service) to
God if God first acted on their behalf. Vows of this second type, therefore, appear regularly in prayers and usually follow the "If . . . then"
format seen here in Judges 11:30-31. Further examples:

1. Jacob's vow when searching for a wife (Gen. 28:20-22)
If God will be with me, watch over me, give me food and clothing, and
    enable me to return safely,
Then the Lord will be my God.
Outcome: Conditions met and vow apparently kept.

2. Israel's vow in the face of a Canaanite threat (Num. 21:1-3)
If God will deliver the enemy into our hands,

Then we will destroy their cities.
Outcome: Conditions met and vow kept.

3. Hannah's vow when grieving over her barrenness (1 Sam. 1:11)
If God will give me a son,
Then I will give him back to the Lord, and no razor will touch his head.
Outcome: Conditions met and vow kept.

4. Absalom's vow during his exile from Jerusalem (2 Sam. 15:8)
If God brings me back to Jerusalem,
Then I will serve/worship the Lord.
Outcome: Conditions met but vow broken.

Most likely the majority of other cases in the OT originally followed this same basic pattern, although the precise components no longer remain clearly specified (e.g., 1 Sam. 1:21; Ps. 22:25; 56:12; 61:5, 8; 65:1; 66:13; 116:14, 18; 132:2-5; Prov. 7:14; Isa. 19:21; Jon. 1:16; 2:9).

In the NT, vows appear infrequently. Paul apparently made a Nazirite-like vow for a certain period of time, as did four young men in Jerusalem (Acts 18:18; 21:23; cf. 23:14). Jesus himself says little on the subject; the few instances suggest significant apprehension on his part. In a debate with the Pharisees, Jesus condemns vows made for the wrong reasons (Matt. 5:33-37; 15:4-6; Mark 7:9-13). For vows to have any validity, they must not be a means of evading more important responsibilities. Elsewhere, Jesus instructs his followers to refrain from swearing and taking oaths (Matt. 5:33-37; cf. James 5:12). Although such activities typically go beyond the pronouncement of vows, Jesus' insistence on simplified responses (saying "Yes" or "No") at least cautions against making casual and/or grandiose promises.

Human Sacrifices

In sacrificing his daughter, Jephthah performs an act that has parallels throughout the ancient Near East. The king of Moab, for example, sacrificed his firstborn son in a moment of military desperation (2 Kings 3:27). Likewise, the Canaanites at least occasionally engaged in the practice (Deut. 12:31; 18:9-10). These few cases in the OT merely confirm extrabiblical sources: human sacrifices were a part of Israel's cultural context (Green: 199; Stager and Wolff).

In spite of their periodic acceptance in the ancient world, human sacrifices find no endorsement in the OT. Even in the case of Abraham and Isaac, God sought to test Abraham, not to kill Isaac (Gen. 22:1-19). Elsewhere, the law clearly prohibits human sacrifices, and the prophets vigorously condemn them (Lev. 18:21; 20:2; Deut. 12:31; 18:9-10; Jer. 7:31; 19:4-6: 32:35; Ezek. 16:20-21; 23:37-39). Such words of denunciation, however, did not prevent human sacrifices from occasionally taking place in Israel (2 Kings 16:3; 17:17; 21:6; Ps. 106:37-38). Indeed, various people even entertained the mistaken notion that God actually desired them (Mic. 6:7-8).

THE TEXT IN THE LIFE OF THE CHURCH

The Longevity of Words

In the ancient world, words possessed the same degree of reality as any tangible object. To speak constituted an act of creation, an act that gave life to identifiable "words." Talking too much or too carelessly, therefore, simply cluttered the world with unwanted and undesirable verbal debris. In today's way of thinking, such debris could simply be swept under the carpet with a casual "I was just kidding" or "I didn't mean it." In the ancient world, however, the reality of words prevented their effortless dismissal. "Three things can never be retrieved," the wise men instructed the unlearned: "a fired arrow, a wasted opportunity, and a spoken word." If we can in part regain the wisdom of this outlook, we will increasingly think before we speak, recognizing that our words may live longer than even we ourselves.

The Impact of Words

"Thanks to words, we have been able to rise above the brutes; and thanks to words, we have often sunk to the level of the demons." So wrote British novelist Aldous Huxley, expressing sentiments shared by many in the ancient world. Once spoken, a word could in fact alter the course of life, both for the good and the bad. *Rash words are like sword thrusts,* according to Proverbs 12:18, *but the tongue of the wise brings healing.* While words of course rarely resulted in the sacrificing of an only child, as did Jephthah's, their capacity to produce weighty results was rarely forgotten. Moderns, caught in an information age, have strong reason to choose words carefully. Life-giving words are far to be preferred over words that debilitate and cause regret and grief for years to come.

Negative Portraits: Ibzan's, Elon's, and Abdon's Operations

Judges 12:8-15

PREVIEW

Decay, though often immediately noticeable, can also be subtle and more difficult to detect. After the death of Jephthah, the final so-called minor judges are examples of this (preview of 10:1-5).

In this case, three such judges appear, thereby completing the sequence in which the number of minor judges in each list exceeds that of the previous list by one (Shamgar in 3:31; Tola and Jair in 10:1-5). Similarly, the nature of these brief notices again approximates the surrounding literary context; the accounts of Ibzan, Elon, and Abdon subtly reflect the eroding situation so clearly depicted with both Jephthah and Samson. To begin with, each of these three judges serves for a noticeably short period of time, as do Jephthah and Samson (cf. 10:2-3). By implication, Israel seemingly experiences little stability and has frequent administrative changes.

Furthermore, none of these individuals "saves/delivers" Israel, an activity so characteristic of the earlier judges. Indeed, nothing remotely resembling the dominant themes of the book appears here. Instead, attention totally swerves to familial concerns, at least when any such details are known. In short, the importance of these brief accounts lies in the fact that they digress from the major themes of the narrative and get lost in secondary concerns. Like the narrative, the situation depicted in the book of Judges continues to unravel.

OUTLINE

Ibzan Leads Israel, 12:8-10

Elon Leads Israel, 12:11-12

Abdon Leads Israel, 12:13-15

EXPLANATORY NOTES
Ibzan Leads Israel 12:8-10

Early writers, such as Josephus, assumed that Ibzan's hometown was *Bethlehem* in Judah. Jewish tradition even equates Ibzan with none other than the Bethlehemite Boaz, the husband of Ruth (Simon and Slotki: *Baba Bathra* 91a). The OT, however, knows of two

Bethlehems. On the basis of the general northern movement of the book of Judges as well as the relative isolation of Judah during this period, Ibzan's hometown should probably be equated with the lesser-known town of Bethlehem, situated within Zebulun's territory (Josh. 19:15) [Map, p. 240].

Ibzan's importance within his community finds expression here in the number of his children. As in most tribal contexts today, numerous children indicate a sizeable harem, and with it considerable influence. That he arranges marriages for his children outside his own clan further underlines Ibzan's authoritative position, recognized by those beyond his immediate circle.

Elon Leads Israel 12:11-12

If the identification of Ibzan's hometown with the northern town of Bethlehem is correct (12:8), then two of these three minor judges are Zebulunites. While the precise location of *Aijalon* remains uncertain, the designation *in the land of Zebulun* clearly distinguishes it from the better-known site of the same name situated some fourteen miles northwest of Jerusalem (Josh. 19:42; 21:24; Judg. 1:35; 1 Chron. 6:69; 2 Chron. 11:10) [Map, p. 240]. Interestingly, the names Elon and Aijalon are, apart from differing vocalizations, exactly the same in Hebrew. The town, therefore, bears the name of the clan that has settled there (Gen. 46:14; Num. 26:26).

Abdon Leads Israel 12:13-15

Abdon, the final minor judge, comes from the town of *Pirathon* (cf. 2 Sam. 23:30; 1 Chron. 11:31; 27:14). The site is typically associated with the modern Arab village of Far'ata, approximately six miles southwest of Nablus (biblical Shechem), in the area of *Ephraim* (12:15) [Maps, pp. 240, 242]. Once again, Abdon enjoys significant influence, although the descending number of sons to grandsons (forty to thirty) seems striking. During the best of days, one expects expansion or at least stability rather than decline.

The reference to the *hill country of the Amalekites*, finally, is puzzling indeed. Perhaps a group of Amalekites, whether associated with the previously mentioned marauders or not (cf. 3:13; 6:3; 7:12; 10:12), has established a settlement in the area (cf. 5:14). Various manuscripts of the LXX, however, read *Sellem* for *Amalekites* [Septuagint]. Yet, the equally unclear *Sellem* is helpful only in that it removes the baffling reference to the Amalekites! As such, the mystery remains.

A Negative Portrait: Samson's Stunts

Judges 13:1—16:31

PREVIEW

Some people never seem to learn from their mistakes. Instead, they repeat them, often with ever-increasing consequences. Samson is just such a person. In spite of his unlimited potential and legendary exploits, Samson gets caught in a downward spiral from which he never escapes [Historicity and Truth].

The account of Samson is noticeably different from the preceding narratives. Such differences center primarily on Samson himself. Samson, unlike the deliverers who went before him, operates totally on his own, lacking even the moral support of the local Israelites. His various activities constitute a series of personal adventures more than a concerted effort to free his people from oppression. Finally, whatever advantages are gained through his involvements, Samson's entire career assumes mediocrity or, at the least, incompleteness. In spite of the great expectations surrounding the announcement of his birth, Samson will only begin the task of confronting the Philistines (13:5) [Sea Peoples].

On a more formal basis, the account of Samson also deviates significantly from the pattern outlined earlier (cf. 2:11-19). Indeed, three of the stages of the Judges Cycle are totally absent: there is no cry for deliverance, no final act of deliverance, and no resulting peace. In addition, a fourth stage, that of the deliverer's call, is limited in scope and stands somewhat overshadowed by the extensive birth narrative in which it appears [Breakdown of the Judges Cycle]. From all indications, Samson's career reveals a near-total unraveling of the pattern, a pattern modeled so forcefully by Othniel (3:7-11). While Samson does fairly much whatever he pleases, the contented Israelites around him sleep soundly in their bed of Philistine domination.

In spite of such variations, the overall Samson narrative reflects a clearly discernible structural pattern. Following the lengthy announcement of Samson's birth (13:1-25), the narrative breaks into two distinct but symmetrical units (14:1—15:20 and 16:1-31; Exum, 1981:3-9). In these two units, Samson's major activities in the first are repeated in the second, though with increased intensity:

Judges 14:1—15:20	**Judges 16:1-31**
Chooses one non-Israelite woman, 14:1-2	Chooses two non-Israelite women, 16:1, 4
Reveals the answer to his riddle, 14:17	Reveals the secret of his strength, 16:17
Loses his non-Israelite wife, 14:20; 15:2, 6	Loses his strength, sight, and the the Lord's presence, 16:19-21
Kills 1,000 Philistines, 15:15	Kills self & countless Philistines, 16:30

Samson, in other words, travels essentially the same road twice, but his actions as well as their consequences are significantly more severe the second time around. This progression ultimately reaches its climax in 16:30, when both Samson and the startled Philistines lie dead among the rubble.

OUTLINE

Samson Predicted and Produced, 13:1-25

13:1	Crisis Introduced
13:2-5	A Messenger Announces Samson's Birth
13:6-14	The Messenger Pays a Second Visit
13:15-23	Manoah Offers a Sacrifice
13:24-25	A Barren Woman Bears Samson

Samson Fancies a Philistine, 14:1—15:20

14:1-9	Samson Selects a Bride
14:10-18	Samson Divulges His Riddle
14:19—15:6	Samson Loses His Wife
15:7-20	Samson Gains His Revenge

Samson Delights in Delilah, 16:1-31

16:1-3	Samson Sleeps with a Prostitute
16:4-17	Samson Divulges His Secret
16:18-22	Samson Loses His Strength
16:23-31	Samson Gains His Revenge

EXPLANATORY NOTES

Samson Predicted and Produced 13:1-25

Following a brief statement about the crisis (13:1), a lengthy narrative announces the coming birth of Israel's next deliverer. With this narrative, the trend of providing increasingly expanded introductions to the various judges continues. The process of raising up deliverers, once again, is not nearly as quick or as smooth as it had been at the start (3:9). In the present case, however, the nature of the announcement raises our hopes that Israel's downward slide will finally be curtailed. This announcement includes the common motif of a barren woman as well as the infant's noteworthy dedication to the Lord. Here is the judge that everyone has been waiting for, a true leader to fill the ever-widening void. Yet time will prove otherwise.

13:1 Crisis Introduced

For the final time in the book, the refrain occurs: *The Israelites did evil in the eyes of the Lord.* No details are provided. With the low point of apostasy reached during Jephthah's lifetime (10:6), the writer apparently runs out of words to adequately describe Israel's continued sinfulness. The Danites and Judahites in the southwestern portion of the country are under the control of the Philistines. Such control, therefore, completes the oppression by the Philistines and Ammonites summarized in 10:7. Whereas Jephthah dealt decisively with the Ammonite invaders east of the Jordan, someone must yet face the Philistines to the southwest *[Sea Peoples]*.

The Philistines, along with other groups, comprise the so-called Sea Peoples, refugees who have fled the upheaval of the Aegean area toward the close of the thirteenth century B.C. In the process of relocating, these people have caused havoc throughout the eastern Mediterranean, engaging in military campaigns as far south as Egypt. Finally settling along the southern coast of Palestine early in the twelfth century B.C., the Philistines have established five major city-states: Gaza, Ashdod, Ashkelon, Gath, and Ekron *[Map, p. 242]*.

However, these fertile but limited holdings have failed to satisfy their thirst for territory; the Philistines turn their attention eastward. In the process, they come into regular conflict with another group settling further inland—the Israelites. Such conflict has already surfaced in Judges 3:31, when the Israelites win temporary relief through Shamgar's exploits. The Philistines were not ultimately brought under control, however, until the time of David (2 Sam. 5:17-25; 8:1). In the interlude, they were nothing less than a constant thorn in Israel's side (1 Sam. 4-6; 13-14; 17; 27-31).

13:2-5 A Messenger Announces Samson's Birth

Zorah was situated some fifteen miles west of Jerusalem in the Valley of Sorek. Zorah and the territory around it was originally allotted to the tribe of Dan, although the Danites proved unsuccessful at controlling it (Josh. 19:40-48, Judg. 1:34). Due in large measure to Amorite and Philistine pressure, a sizeable contingent of Danites eventually migrate northward and settle in Laish (Josh. 19:47; Judg. 18)

[Maps, pp. 240, 242]. In spite of the present ordering of the materials, both Judges 5:17 as well as the overall context of the present narrative (few Danites seem to live where Samson is) suggest that such a migration actually has occurred before the time of Samson. If so, then Manoah and his family are among the Danites who remained behind.

Manoah's unnamed wife is both sterile and childless. Recalling the case of Jephthah's grieving daughter (11:29-40), peoples' memories live on after death in the form of their children. To be childless, therefore, is a tragedy that for many indicates divine disfavor. In spite of the brevity of comment, Manoah's wife finds herself in a most unenviable and socially low position. An a*ngel of the Lord* (cf. 2:1-5) brings word of her impending pregnancy. Only once before has such a messenger brought news of a promised child (Gen. 18:10). Furthermore, Manoah's wife now joins the likes of Sarah, Rachel, Hannah, and Elizabeth, barren women in Scripture who miraculously give birth (Gen. 18:10; 21:1-7; 30:22-24; 1 Sam. 1:19-20; Luke 1:5-25, 57). If their children—Isaac, Joseph, Samuel, and John the Baptist—serve as indications of the type of offspring born in such situations, then expectations surrounding Samson's birth are understandably high (TBC after 13:1-25).

The angel provides Manoah's wife with important instructions, both for herself as well as for the child. Basic to these instructions is the fact that the boy shall *be a nazirite (nazir)*, someone specifically "dedicated" or "consecrated" to God (13:5). The person entering this holy state of service normally took the vows personally and voluntarily, and for a specific period of time (Num. 6:1-4). The vow requires that three primary conditions be carefully followed: (1) abstain from products of the vine, including but not limited to wine, and all intoxicating drinks (cf. Jer. 35); (2) refrain from cutting the hair for the entire period of service (hair was a sign of life in the ancient Near East); and (3) avoid contact with any dead body. If a nazirite violates any of these stipulations and therefore becomes defiled, a formal procedure of reconsecration is to be undertaken, and the term of service reentered from the beginning (Num. 6:9-12).

In the Samson narrative, certain variations clearly appear, probably suggesting that there are in fact two somewhat distinct types of nazirites (cf. Amos 2:11-12). First, the mother takes the vows on behalf of the child. Samson, therefore, does not choose this form of life voluntarily. Second, the envisioned period of service is not restricted, but extended throughout the child's entire lifetime, at least according to the mother's later testimony (13:7). Finally, the responsibility of observing certain aspects of the vow falls upon the mother herself, not just the dedicated child. Such a responsibility most likely serves as preparation for the approaching birth and is simply transferred to the child after he is born. In this case, the nazirite has nothing to do with either the actual making of the vows or the specific terms. Nevertheless, the terms remain with him far into the future, and his conduct will inevitably be evaluated accordingly.

Using the features of the barren mother, the birth announcement, and the seriousness of the nazirite vows, the writer magnifies the apparently impeccable qualifications of the coming deliverer. Expectations, which might reach unreasonable heights, are qualified by the comment that he *shall begin* (rather than "complete") *to deliver Israel from the hand of the Philistines* (13:5).

13:6-14 The Messenger Pays a Second Visit

Typically, the expression *man of God* (13:6) indicates a prophetic figure, such as Moses (Josh. 14:6), Samuel (1 Sam. 9:6), Elijah (1 Kings 17:24; 2 Kings 1:11), and Elisha (2 Kings 4:7; cf. 1 Sam. 2:27; 1 Kings 13:1). The woman has yet to recognize the true identity of the messenger. Not until later will either the woman or Manoah fully grasp the nature of this incident (13:22).

In recounting the experience for Manoah, the woman presents an edited and interpreted version of the messenger's instructions. She specifies the duration of the vows, stating that the child will be a nazirite *from birth until the day of his death* (137). Furthermore, in her excitement, she omits two crucial points: the prohibition against cutting the hair as well as the child's anticipated role in delivering Israel. As a result, Manoah's prayerful plea for additional information seems far less objectionable than at first. While he perhaps lacks some of the confidence so characteristic of his wife, he similarly lacks some of the details.

In response to Manoah's prayer, the messenger returns. In contrast to his wife's rather straightforward acceptance or lack of curiosity (13:6), Manoah swiftly verifies the man's identity and solicits additional information: *What is to be the boy's rule of life; what is he to do?* Intriguingly, however, the messenger's answer is even more abbreviated than the woman's prior report. In fact, he bypasses the question altogether and focuses solely on the woman's responsibilities before she gives birth (13:13-14). Nowhere is there a hint as to the child's intended purpose and function!

Therefore, Manoah still lacks a good deal of the information originally disclosed to his wife. By implication, the messenger has during his initial visit disclosed all the information needed. As with Gideon, subsequent encounters serve to reinforce or encourage rather than to provide additional and unnecessary instruction (6:11-24, 36-40).

13:15-23 Manoah Offers a Sacrifice

In typical Near Eastern fashion, Manoah extends an offer of exceptional hospitality: a meal that takes hours to prepare (cf. Gen. 18:1-15; Judg. 6:17-19). Soon, his inquisitiveness reaches new heights. By asking for the messenger's name, Manoah seeks additional insight and information, for names in the ancient world typically embody the nature and character of the person. That the name is *wonderful* (peli') suggests both the uniqueness of the messenger and the limitations of human understanding (cf. Isa. 9:6).

Undaunted by these cloudy responses and outright refusals, Manoah presses on and prepares both the burnt offering as well as an accompanying grain offering (Num. 15:1-16). In the process of actually offering these on a nearby altar, someone "works a wonder" (mapli'). The ambiguity as to the identity of this someone results from the fact that no clear subject appears in the Hebrew text. As a result, various translations see the messenger as the wonder-worker, much as with Gideon's offering (6:21). The LXX, however, preserves the name of the Lord in this context, suggesting that God himself has acted wondrously [Septuagint]. Note this wordplay on the name of the angel: mapli' and peli'.

With the ascent of the Lord's messenger in the midst of the flames, both husband and wife realize for the first time the visitor's identity. Manoah, in true Israelite fashion, assumes that death is imminent (Gen. 32:30; Exod. 20:19; 33:20; Judg. 6:22-23; Isa. 6:5). Wisely, his wife recognizes that their deaths at this point in time would totally undercut all that has been promised. Given his ensuing silence, Manoah apparently agrees.

13:24-25 A Barren Woman Bears Samson

At some point following Samson's birth, *the Spirit of the Lord began to stir* (pa'am) him [Holy Spirit in the OT]. The verb pa'am literally involves "pushing" or "impelling" rather than merely "coming upon" or "empowering." By implication, the child who has had no say in his nazirite vows now perhaps offers resistance. Already, Samson's reluctance to take his role and vows seriously begins to surface; significant coaxing is required.

Samson's activities here and elsewhere center primarily in the vicinity of his hometown. *Zorah* was some fifteen miles west of Jerusalem, and *Eshtaol* about two miles northeast of Zorah [Maps, *pp. 240, 242].* Situated between the two was *Mahaneh-dan,* where Samson now finds himself. Since the name *Mahaneh-dan* can just as well be rendered *a camp (maḥaneh) of Dan,* the site may be a temporary settlement or encampment. Recalling the constant pressure placed upon the Danites by the Philistines, one can easily imagine such a dwelling. Another site referred to as *Mahaneh-dan* appears in 18:12, but the location there lies beyond the geographical limits of the present passage. Given the transitory nature of the Danites during these early years, this second site might itself be another temporary encampment. If so, the name lingers on well after the Danites have left the area (18:12-13).

THE TEXT IN BIBLICAL CONTEXT

Barrenness

Central to the story of Samson's birth is the barrenness of Manoah's wife. This is so, not primarily because of the pain and anguish associated in the ancient world with such a childless condition, but because of the recurring theological importance of barrenness in the Bible. Time after time, moments of grave difficulty serve as the context for wonderful conceptions. In this way, emphasis once again falls squarely upon God's role in the unfolding of salvation history:

Mother	Text	Associated Difficulties	Child
Sarai	Gen. 11:30; 18:1-15; 21:1-7	Promises to Abram in jeopardy	Isaac
Rebekah	Gen. 25:19-26	Descendant needed to preserve promises	Jacob & Esau
Rachel	Gen. 29:31; 30:1-24	Impending slavery in Egypt	Joseph
Manoah's wife	Judg. 13:1-25	Philistine oppression	Samson
Hannah	1 Sam. 1:1-28	Internal corruption and divine silence (cf. 1 Sam. 3:1)	Samuel
Elizabeth	Luke 1:5-25, 57–66	Preparation needed for the coming Messiah	John the Baptist

To these can also be added the climactic birth of Jesus himself. Although no passages associate barrenness with Mary, her pregnancy follows a divine pronouncement and is similarly attributed to God's intervention (Matt. 1:18-25; Luke 1:26-38; 2:1-7). Clearly, beginning with Abram's reception of the original promise and continuing to the coming of Jesus, the pages of Scripture reveal the Lord miraculously raising up human instruments through otherwise empty wombs.

THE TEXT IN THE LIFE OF THE CHURCH
Life from Barren Places

While the biblical record of so-called miraculous conceptions either ends or blurs with the birth of Christ, the truth of Scripture still rings with resounding clarity: God brings life from barren places. Pastors and other leaders, as important as they may be, come and go. Particular ministries and modes of outreach, though originally effective, eventually die. Sadly, countless individuals often make a mess of their lives.

From where, then, will help arise? From unseen corners. From dark closets. From virtually anywhere. A young seminary graduate, sent to "close" a dying congregation, surprisingly leads it back to health. An unknown visitor in a foreign country, looking for a place to stay, "stumbles" upon the local school for the blind. Remarkably, the school just happens to need a house mother for the older residents. An unexpected pat on the back and cup of coffee, given to a broken person, stimulate hope for the first time in recent memory. God, remember, brings water from rocks. God, as Manoah's wife reminds us, causes life to grow in otherwise barren places.

The Lord is the one who *works wonders* (13:19). Believers celebrate their awe through song, as in this piece from the Russian Orthodox liturgy: "Who is so great a God as our God? Thou art the God who doest wonders" (*Hymnal:* 62; cf. 149, "Great God of Wonders").

Samson Fancies a Philistine 14:1—15:20

Following the account of Samson's birth, the first of two symmetrical units now traces a series of events growing out of Samson's relationship with a Philistine woman from Timnah. In this unit, note the emphasis placed on the Spirit of the Lord coming upon Samson in power. All three references in the entire story to such an empowering appear in the present unit (14:6, 19; 15:14). In each case, the phrase constitutes an explanation of Samson's heroic feats of strength: the slaying of a lion, the slaughter of thirty Philistines, and the killing of a thousand Philistines [*Holy Spirit in the OT*].

Importantly, however, each incident of empowerment soon results in such tragic consequences as the breaking of vows and an unquenchable desire for revenge. What remains, then, is an uncomfortable and at times distressing mixture of divine enablement and human folly.

14:1-9 Samson Selects a Bride

Timnah was a town located six miles west of Zorah. Although Timnah fell within the Danites' original territorial allotment (Josh. 19:42), it clearly has since come under expanding Philistine control *[Map, p. 242]*. That Samson can travel there so freely, however, suggests what the overall narrative repeatedly implies elsewhere; relations between the Philistines and the Israelites are relatively cordial. A mixed marriage is not unthinkable. Although Samson himself makes the actual selection of a Philistine wife, depriving his parents of any role in the process, he leaves it to them to work out the details. Nowhere is there a request for counsel or instruction, let alone a concern for parental approval. Samson sees a Philistine woman, and he wants her as his wife.

Wedding plans go forward, in spite of legal and parental protests. Indeed, both the law as well as experience frown upon marrying foreigners (Exod. 34:15-16; Deut. 7:3; cf. Gen. 24:3-4; 26:34-35). Judges 3:5-6, in fact, implies that such intermarriages are a woeful deviation from accepted norms. Likewise, Manoah and his wife emphasize the gross incompatibility of Samson and this woman. After all, she is a *Philistine*, and he is not only an Israelite, but a nazirite at that. Among Israel's immediate neighbors, only the Philistines continually avoid circumcision (cf. Judg. 15:18; 1 Sam. 14:6; 17:26, 36; 31:4; 1 Chron. 10:4).

Nevertheless, Samson persists. Here, the NIV's "She's the right one for me" softens Samson's emotional state-of-mind, perhaps implying a genuine conviction about the woman's various merits. Instead, Samson desires her because "she is beautiful in my eyes." In this way, Samson's criterion closely approximates that of the Israelites in general in Judges 17–21. There, all the people "do what is right in their own eyes" (17:6; 21:25).

Samson thus shows rather blatant disregard for both the law as well as his parents. The writer, reflecting a time after Philistine domination came to an end, clarifies this potentially distasteful scene. The Lord, he suggests, stands behind these uncharacteristic activities, for *he was seeking a pretext to act against the Philistines* (14:4). Throughout the OT, God appears as the ruler of history, capable of working at any time and through any instrument. For the writer, hindsight indicates that that is just what the Lord was doing in this case.

Unlike Hosea, who was specifically instructed to marry a harlot (Hos. 1:2), Samson merely follows his natural instincts. Rather than disqualifying him from participating in the Lord's plans, however, Samson's roaming eyes provide an opportunity for divine intervention. As such, even these events must be read within the context of God's overall designs.

Manoah and his wife face their inability to discourage Samson from marrying the Philistine woman. They join their son in another trip to Timnah, to make the necessary wedding arrangements (14:5). Samson, the Spirit-empowered Danite, slaughters an attacking lion, but does *not tell his father or his mother what he had done* (14:6). Such concealment raises questions as to the whereabouts of the parents. Their unawareness of the event, in fact, has led various commentators to conclude that, in an earlier version of the story, they never made the journey. They hold that the references to the parents in 14:5-6 constitute a later attempt on the part of the writer either to merge two distinct accounts or to sustain the parents' presence following a family breakup over the Philistine woman (Gray: 328; Soggin: 239-240). More likely, all three individuals make the journey, but Samson alone turns into the vineyards (Boling: 230). Entering a vineyard, even though he may not consume anything from the vines, involves the type of "dabbling with fire" not uncommon to Samson.

Upon reaching his destination, Samson engages in what appears to be his first conversation with the desired Philistine woman (14:7). Previously, he has only "seen" her (14:1). Whether the conversation involves wedding arrangements goes unsaid, nor are the whereabouts of the parents disclosed. Importantly, however, neither the experiences along the way nor the present conversation does anything to change Samson's mind about the woman. She remains, as before, "beautiful in the eyes of Samson."

With this not-too-subtle reminder about Samson's determination, the narrative advances an indeterminate amount of time to yet another journey to Timnah (14:8). Samson leaves the main route to reexamine the lion's carcass, in which bees have constructed a honeycomb. Typically, bees avoid rotting bodies, preferring drier and more amicable conditions. In helping himself to the honey, in spite of the fact that it is encased within a dead body, Samson breaks one of the major stipulations of his nazirite vow. Not only does he refrain from disclosing his activities to his parents, he even goes so far as to share the unclean food with them (Lev. 11:24-25, 37-40). While casually disregarding his own responsibilities, Samson frivolously and secretly takes others along with him.

14:10-18 Samson Divulges His Riddle

For the fourth time in the span of these few verses, someone goes down (*yarad*) to either Timnah in general (14:1, 5) or the woman in particular (14:7, 10). Precisely what the father hopes to accomplish here remains unclear, particularly insofar as he has apparently made the necessary wedding arrangements earlier. Might he be making one final attempt to prevent what he painfully considers to be a terrible mistake? If so, he meets with no noticeable success.

The type of marriage envisioned here differs from the norm (cf. 15:1). In fact, it closely approximates the ṣadiqa relationship of Gideon with the concubine from Shechem, in which the woman remains in her father's house, and the man becomes a visiting husband (notes on 8:31). Given the formal arrangements and the attention to tradition, however, perhaps somewhat greater social status should be assigned to Samson's relationship. De Vaux suggests that, in contrast to Gideon's "liaison sanctioned by custom," Samson's union is "a true marriage but without permanent cohabitation" (29).

Samson throws a feast (mišteh) in the home of the bride, in accord with Philistine customs (14:10). In Israel, such a feast would be conducted in the house of the groom. Literally, a mišteh constitutes a "drinking session" or a "feast with a great deal of wine" (Gen. 19:3; 21:8; Esther 5:6; Dan. 1:5). The root of mišteh is šatah, meaning "to drink." Yet this is not the type of celebration for a nazirite to attend, let alone sponsor. In this joyful setting, then, the second of Samson's nazirite stipulations deliberately falls by the wayside (notes on 13:5).

At some point during the celebration, the locals provide Samson with *thirty companions*. Although such attendants normally came from the groom's own community, Samson apparently has arrived on the scene unaccompanied. These companions may simply constitute the type of friendly escort common in such ceremonies (cf. Matt. 9:15). Intriguingly, however, the LXX reads "when they [the local Philistines] feared him [Samson]" in place of "when the people saw him" (14:11); the roots yare' ("to fear") and ra'ah ("to see, appear") frequently have remarkably similar forms [Septuagint]. Clearly, in at least some circles, the companions are seen as a bodyguard, not "for" Samson, but "against" him! If the Philistines have no reason to fear Samson up to this point, they soon will have. Ironically, then, the bodyguard becomes a sort of self-fulfilling prophecy.

In the company of his new-found companions, Samson challenges them with a riddle (ḥidah). Riddles comprise a variety of forms, including probing questions (1 Kings 10:1; 2 Chron. 9:1) and perplexing problems (Ps. 49:4). What these forms all have in common, however, is the element of mystery or hiddenness. Hence, riddles become a type of entertainment or a test of insight. People renowned for their ability to decipher riddles are considered particularly wise (Prov. 1:6).

The stakes in Samson's riddle are exceptionally high. *Linen garments* are large sheets serving as either an outer covering during the day or a blanket at night. *Festal garments* refers to the best garments, worn only on special occasions. Generally speaking, a person has only one such set of the finest clothing. Samson's challenge, therefore, offers the opportunity for both significant profit as well as considerable loss. The companions, for example, can either double a portion of their holdings or lose the most valuable part of their wardrobe.

The stakes are even higher for Samson, however, who bears sole responsibility for either the gain or the loss of thirty garments. The riddle, therefore, goes well beyond the bounds of simple merriment. In spite of the risk, however, the companions accept the challenge, no doubt reasoning that their combined wits assure eventual success. *The seven days of the feast*, the traditional duration for such a celebration prior to the final consummation of the marriage, serve as the temporal parameters for them to discover a solution.

As to the riddle itself, it appears in the form of a couplet or bicolon. Following a precise rhythmic pattern, each line contains three beats:

> Out of the eater / came / something to eat.
> Out of the strong / came / something sweet.

As often with Hebrew poetry, however, the closing elements do not in actuality rhyme. The rhyme here results solely from translation.

The search for a solution is bound to fail, for the entire puzzle stems from a private encounter of which even the parents are unaware. In short, neither the companions nor anyone else can possibly discern the solution. The most obvious answer to the riddle, as Crenshaw points out, is "vomit":

> Thus the statement would refer to the aftermath of wedding festivities when even the valiant soldier, the eater and the strong, is unable to retain the unaccustomed delicacies, that is, something to eat and something sweet. (489)

The desired answer, however, remains elusive.

The companions, sensing the increasing risk of a financial setback, turn to Samson's wife *on the fourth day* (following the LXX; Hebrew incomprehensibly reads "seventh day"; cf. 14:17) and threaten to burn both her as well as her father's household unless she provides them with the answer (14:15). Even as Job's wife mysteriously remains and tests her beleaguered husband one final time, so too do the companions assume that the key to unlock Samson's mind lies in the hands of the woman (Job 2:9). She endures an apparent insult in which Samson reasons that not even his parents know the answer, so much less should his bride! Yet she gradually and methodically wears down her husband. Throughout her efforts, appeals are made to the love that Samson seemingly withholds. Delilah will later take a similar but subtly different approach (16:15). Finally, on the closing day of the celebration, he discloses the solution.

The thirty companions, now with an answer, themselves pose a riddle. Samson, realizing the source of their success, responds with yet another riddle, similarly expressed in two parallel lines of three beats each:

If you had not / plowed / with my heifer,
You would not / have found out / my riddle.

The term *heifer*, clearly a reference to his wife, can hardly be taken in any way other than a pejorative sense. Bitten by defeat and seemingly betrayed by his wife, Samson is reduced to name-calling. What begins as a day of great joy and anticipation ends, not with the consummation of the marriage, but with the assumption of a great debt.

14:19—15:6 Samson Loses His Wife

While reeling from the loss of his own wager, *the spirit of the Lord* once again comes upon Samson (14:19) *[Holy Spirit in the OT]*. Immediately, Samson makes the nearly twenty-five mile trip to Ashkelon, a major Philistine city located along the Mediterranean coast *[Map, p. 242]*. Presumably, he seeks to distance himself from the people of Timnah, hoping to gather the necessary garments without detection. Samson slaughters thirty anonymous and uninvolved Philistines and collects their gear. Details are of little consequence here: why are these unsuspecting Philistines wearing their best garments? Of more importance is the fact that Samson is now on the prowl, performing deeds against Israel's notorious enemy.

These deeds, of course, certainly take several days to complete. Nevertheless, Samson returns to Timnah at least as angry as when he left. Full of rage, he pays off his debt and stomps away from the scene, providing no further comment concerning either his destination or his intentions. By such action, Samson renounces all claims to his Philistine bride, who just a short time ago was "beautiful in the eyes of Samson" (14:7). As a result, this abandoned and embarrassed woman becomes the wife of Samson's best man (14:20; cf. John 3:29; van Selms: 65-75).

At the time of the wheat harvest, probably in late May, a more level-headed Samson returns to Timnah to see the woman he still believes to be his wife. He may be bringing the kid as a peace offering, to help heal the wounds of the past. Yet visiting husbands in marriages such as this typically bring gifts along, and a kid may be traditional (Gen. 38:17). Knowing full well that nothing can be done to undo his daughter's second marriage, the father offers Samson her younger sister instead (cf. Deut. 24:1-4). Whether this offer is extended out of fear or as a token of regret, Samson unexpectedly declines. Rarely does Samson act with such self-control! Rather than appeasing himself with another woman, he vows to vent his justifiable anger on the Philistines themselves.

The manner chosen by Samson to release his considerable frustration involves the use of foxes or, more likely, jackals; the Hebrew term šuʻal allows for either (15:4). Jackals, however, are considerably more plentiful in Palestine and, unlike solitary-minded foxes, live in packs. He ties a torch to each pair of tails, and sets the jackals/foxes loose in the fields. As a result, the uncut and the harvested grain (in shocks) is destroyed. The expanding fire scorches the vineyards and olive trees as well, curtailing the productivity of the trees for some time to come.

Samson's strategy is by no means unique. In the annual festival of Ceres in ancient Rome, for example, foxes with lighted torches were released and hunted. Behind this tradition stands an apparent rite intended to protect the fields from mildew prior to the harvest. Accordingly, the red foxes represented rust-fungus, and their capture symbolizes the removal of this significant agricultural threat. Insofar as this rite seemingly originated in or near Palestine and only later spread to Rome, some suggest that Samson's scheme reflects such a ceremonial practice. Samson, Martin writes, "lets loose the destructive rust-fungus which destroys the growing corn of the Philistines" (169) [Historicity and Truth].

More likely, however, Samson simply employs what might be called a guerrilla tactic (Gaster: 434-435). Essentially the same tactic appears elsewhere in ancient combat. In a battle against the Romans in 217 B.C., for example, the Carthaginian general Hannibal used cattle with burning torches attached to their horns (Livy: 22.16-17). In that case, as here, the strategy proved most effective. Such effectiveness, however, cannot conceal the fact that the episode has tragic consequences for Samson, his wife, and her father. Samson, who has legally lost his wife as a result of his earlier tantrum, now loses her to death through this latest outburst. Repeatedly, other people feel the burden of Samson's adventures.

15:7-20 Samson Gains His Revenge

The gaining of personal revenge clearly constitutes the sole motivating factor behind Samson's ongoing endeavors: "If this is the sort of thing you do, I swear I will be vindicated against you! But thereafter, I quit!" (15:7; Boling's translation: 234). Samson is running out of control, an addict hoping to quit after indulging one final time. For this escalating exchange of attack and counterattack, revenge and counterrevenge, then, no end lies anywhere in sight [*Violence and War in Judges*].

Samson now strikes the murderous Philistines *hip and thigh with great slaughter* (15:8). The precise meaning of the imagery here remains somewhat unclear, although the proverbial phrase "leg upon thigh" seemingly stems from a wrestling context. Samson, as it might be said today, "tied the Philistines in knots." Fearing yet another Philistine reprisal, he subsequently hides out in an otherwise unidentifiable cave somewhere in Judah. Centuries later, Rehoboam fortified a site known as *Etam*, but its location in the Bethlehem area lies well beyond the geographical setting envisioned here (2 Chron. 11:6).

The Philistine reprisal anticipated by Samson is not long in coming. Arriving in Judah, one thousand of them camp near the now unknown site of *Lehi* ("jawbone"; cf. 15:15). More important than Lehi's location, however, is its anticipatory connection with Samson's unusual weapon (15:15). The Philistines, who encamp at "Jawbone," will later die from a "jawbone." For now, all these forces gather in hopes of tracking down a single man! Even these are few, however, compared to the three thousand Judahites who subsequently approach Samson in his hiding place (15:11). Samson's reputation has increased in pace with his acts of violence.

At the center of these proceedings lie two dialogues, one going on between the Philistines and the men of Judah, and one between the men of Judah and Samson himself. The Judahites, first of all, inquire of the Philistines as to the reasons behind their latest military expedition. Undergirding both the question as well as the ensuing answer is the essential nature of the ongoing Philistine domination. Generally speaking, such domination, at least at this point in time, lacks the severe oppression so characteristic of many of the previous accounts. Instead, the affected Israelites converse with and in fact negotiate with the Philistines, much as Samson and his family did earlier with the people of Timnah. Oppression here is not so much violent and turbulent as it is subtle and even acceptable. From all indications, the Israelites have no essential arguments against being in this weakened state! Apparently, falling far short of the Lord's intentions causes no serious concern.

This attitude toward the Philistines is expressed in an even-more alarming way when the men of Judah confront Samson near his hide-out (15:11). Philistine domination, they suggest, is a genuine and tolerable part of life. As a result, Samson's confrontations are unhelpful and even totally unwanted. Rather than crying out for a deliverer, therefore, the Judahites hope to get rid of one! To do so, they first convince Samson into letting them tie him up. His lone request, that the men of Judah not kill him themselves, no doubt reflects his desire to avoid a physical engagement with fellow Israelites. Such an engagement would divert his energies away from the Philistines and cause considerable suffering for the Judahites. The *new ropes* employed in the process are considerably stronger than used ones. As a result, Samson's later escape appears even more miraculous.

As the men of Judah and their entwined prisoner return to Lehi, the Philistines rejoice in apparent victory. However, for the third time in this major unit *the spirit of the Lord rushed on him* (14:6, 19) *[Holy Spirit in the OT]*. In the ensuing celebration over the death of a host of Philistines, Samson once again displays his love for riddles and poetic expression (15:16). This brief poem includes a clear play on the words for *donkey* and *heap*, both of which translate the same Hebrew word (*ḥamor*):

> With the jawbone of a donkey (*ḥamor*),
> heaps (*ḥamor*) upon heaps (*ḥamor*)!
> With the jawbone of a donkey (*ḥamor*),
> I have slain a thousand men.

Lost during this personal celebration, however, is the fact that the weapon used to kill the Philistines has come from a "dead" donkey. The jawbone is *fresh* and therefore heavy and strong, clearly to Samson's advantage. Still, Samson again violates his nazirite vows, part of which is to avoid contact with corpses (notes on 13:5). In spite of his divine empowerment, then, Samson continues to operate by his own agenda.

With his personal conquest of the Philistines temporarily completed, Samson discards the deadly jawbone and renames the place where the encounter has occurred (15:17). The account, therefore, is at least in part what commentators typically refer to as an aetiology—a story intended to explain the origin of a name. In accord with recent events, *Ramath-Lehi* literally means "hill of the jaw-bone" *[Hero Stories; Historicity and Truth]*. As the curtain closes on this first major unit, Samson calls out to the Lord for the very first time (15:18); at no previous point has there been any dialogue between God and this deliverer, the last in Judges. What prompts Samson's call is hardly an event of national importance, such as pleas for communal deliverance seen earlier (3:9, 15; 4:3; 6:6; 10:10). Instead, his recent exploits have left Samson emotionally exhausted and exceptionally thirsty.

Somewhat reminiscent of the fleeing Elijah, who in most other ways differs from our present hero, Samson's condition leads to an anticipation of death (1 Kings 19:1-8). In contrast to Elijah's apparent depression, however, Samson's plea more closely resembles a dare: *Am I now to die of thirst?* (on the *uncircumcised*, see 14:3). Nevertheless, God unreservedly supplies the desired water, apparently through a small, rocky depression (*maktes̆*). Revitalized, Samson renames the site, even as he did at Ramath-Lehi (15:17). Later generations will therefore understand this otherwise curious name; *En Hakkore* literally means "The spring of the caller."

With the notification that *he judged Israel in the days of the Philistines twenty years*, we assume that the narrative has come to a close. In some earlier versions of the story, perhaps it did. Now, however, the journey just traveled is soon to be repeated (16:1-31) *[Preview]*. The present concluding statement, therefore, merely amounts to an intermission. Insofar as the Philistines oppressed the Israelites for forty years (13:1), the reference here to twenty years may underscore the incompleteness of Samson's deliverance.

THE TEXT IN BIBLICAL CONTEXT
Just One More Time!

With anger written all over his face, Samson shouts to the Philistines: "If this is the sort of thing you do, I swear I will be vindicated against you! But thereafter, I quit!" (Boling: 234). For Samson, each next expression of his vengeful anger will be the last. He is wrong. In fact, Samson later dies with thoughts of revenge still lingering on his mind (16:28).

The Bible elsewhere warns against this potentially fatal "one more time" mentality. Various narratives, for example, show that "one more time" typically becomes another "one more time." Indeed, the book of Judges itself repeatedly depicts the Israelites setting aside their evil ways, only to return to them shortly thereafter. Furthermore, selected passages specifically instruct groups and individuals to *stop* engaging in perpetual ungodly behaviors. "If you put your detestable idols out of my sight *and* no longer go astray," Jeremiah announces, "then the nations will be blessed by him, and in him they will glory" (4:1-2). Paul similarly exhorts his converts to "put to death" their former ways (Rom. 8:13; Col. 3:5). Finally, Jesus candidly instructs both the healed

invalid as well as the adulteress woman to "sin no more," not simply
to limit their deviant acts to one closing fling (John 5:14; 8:11).
According to Scripture, the "one more time" mentality is a paralyzing
illusion. In reality, there is no better time than now to stop vengeance
and sin.

Refreshment for the Weary

Without any hint of correction or reproof, the Lord gives Samson, his
burned-out instrument, the desired water. Refreshed and rejuvenated,
Samson is ready for his next assignment. God similarly supplied a
physically and emotionally exhausted Elijah with food and water. With
regained strength, the exhilarated prophet was off to the races!
Finally, the strong-willed Jonah experienced serious depression and
weariness, although for entirely different reasons (Jon. 4). Thoroughly
upset over the mass conversion of the Ninevites, Jonah withdrew to a
dusty and shadeless hill in hopes that God might destroy the city anyway. With remarkable patience, the Lord supplied Jonah with a
shade-giving vine as well as a series of thought-provoking questions.
Unlike the noted change in countenance associated with both Samson
and Elijah, however, the outcome of Jonah's ordeal remains for the
reader to decide.

Regardless of the outcome, each of these episodes demonstrates a
caring and compassionate God ministering to his exhausted and dis-
couraged servants. In apparent solitude following energy-draining
activities, moments of depression can become moments of refreshment. Jesus, who himself experienced quiet periods of divine nurturing, instructed his apostles to go away "by yourselves to a quiet place
and get some rest" (Mark 6:31). During such times, the God of
Scripture has more than enough food and drink to go around.

THE TEXT IN THE LIFE OF THE CHURCH

Dealing with Emotional Fallout

Weariness, discouragement, and even depression are familiar to all,
including the saintliest of saints. Both experience and research inform
us that discouragement and despair arise for a great variety of reasons. Such factors as improper diet, insufficient exercise, inadequate
rest and relaxation, excessive stress, unrealistic expectations, major
disappointments, and suppressed guilt—they all contribute to this type
of emotional imbalance. Likewise, depression often follows "high
points" or moments of notable accomplishments. Indeed, each of the
biblical examples cited above falls into this category: Samson's victo-

ry over the Philistines, Elijah's mastery over the prophets of Baal, and Jonah's crusade among the Ninevites. Unmistakably, some linkage exists between the enormous energy that goes into various tasks and the emotional fallout that ensues.

Given the pressures of life and the many demands of ministry, then, all need to learn to deal with the threat of emotional fallout in wholesome and constructive ways. As starters:

• *Know Yourself.* Gain a basic familiarity with yourself and how you respond to certain situations and circumstances. There is no substitute, according to Sarah Horsman, "for a basic awareness of our inner selves—knowing who we are and what makes us tick" (38).

• *Strengthen Problem Areas.* Pay closer attention to such things as diet, exercise, rest, and expectations. E. Stanley Jones, the great Methodist missionary to India, once suggested that the most spiritual thing a tired person can do is sleep.

• *Recognize the Occasion.* Read the warning signs before the moment takes control of you. On the basis of such signs and built-in indicators, make necessary adjustments, to circumvent avoidable pitfalls.

• *Let God Feed You.* Center every day around the living Christ, and eat freely from his table. As Thomas à Kempis so beautifully phrased it:

O my Lord Jesus! trusting in Thy great goodness and mercy, I come to Thee, as a sick man to him that shall heal him, and as he that is hungry and thirsty to the fountain of life, as one that is needy to the King of Heaven, as a servant to his lord, a creature to his Creator, and as a desolate person to his meek and blessed comforter. (Thomas: 4.2)

Samson Delights in Delilah 16:1-31

The second symmetrical unit (Preview) again follows with worsening consequences the pattern of events found in 14:1—15:20. The account grows primarily out of Samson's relationship with Delilah. As this particular unit unfolds, however, stress no longer falls on those special occasions of divine empowerment (cf. 14:6, 19; 15:14). Indeed, nowhere in 16:1-31 does the Spirit of the Lord come upon Samson. Instead, Samson's uncanny capabilities are specifically linked to his nazirite vows (notes on 13:5). Since as the primary event of this unit is the violation of his third and final vow, attention now centers, not on the divine origin of his strength, but on the seemingly naive manner in which Samson finally *loses* his strength.

16:1-3 Samson Sleeps with a Prostitute

Gaza was situated along the Mediterranean coast, some 35-40 miles south from both Timnah and Samson's hometown of Zorah *[Map, p. 242]*. The site may at one time have come under Israelite control (cf. 1:18); now it stands as the southernmost of the five major Philistine cities. Whatever the reasons for this latest expedition again, Samson soon strays from his course. Now, the altered destination is not a vineyard with either a roaring or a decaying lion, but the house of a *prostitute* (cf. 14:5, 8). Perhaps, after being bitten by his Timnite wife, Samson "has decided that the safest relationship with the lovely Philistine women is that of a man with a harlot" (Crenshaw: 497).

In spite of the considerable distance between Timnah and Gaza, however, Samson's reputation clearly has preceded him. Even the private conversation of the guards and their intentions are unmistakably clear: "At dawn we'll kill him" (15:2; see Bar-Efrat: 17-23). In the meantime, the Philistines wait throughout the night.

What transpires next has raised various questions among commentators. On the surface, Samson somehow discovers the plot, rises in the middle of the night, and passes undetected through the gate. The problem, of course, concerns his apparent ability to secretly circumvent the guards. To lessen the difficulty, some suggest reading "all day" in place of the first "all night" in 16:2. Accordingly, the Philistines guard the open gate throughout the day, but retire at night, assuming the gate sufficient to prevent any departure (Cundall: 174). Yet it must be recalled that the gate of an ancient Palestinian city only remotely resembles a contemporary door or entranceway. Rather than a relatively simple opening, the gate of a strongly defended Philistine city no doubt comprises a complex structure with a collection of rooms (Mazar: 317-319). As a result, the guards may well have withdrawn during the night to one of the gate's inner compartments. At such a moment, particularly with the gates closed, one might slip through the passageway unnoticed.

Not one to do anything casually or with moderation, however, Samson proceeds forcibly to disassemble the gate itself. Hoisting the doors and other pieces of the city gate upon his shoulders, Samson carries them away from the now-unprotected city. Precisely what such freight weighed is difficult to determine, nor is it clear where Samson finally deposited it. The town of *Hebron* lay some forty miles east of Gaza, forty miles uphill! Somewhere between Gaza and Hebron, then, stands the mountain in question. Samson's feat would normally be a job for several ordinary human beings. The point throughout the narrative is that, for the good or the bad, Samson is no ordinary human being. In departing from Gaza, he wishes to make a statement, which he does with characteristic flair *[Historicity and Truth]*.

16:4-17 Samson Divulges His Secret

In spite of the tragic ending to his marriage with the Timnite as well as the excitement surrounding his rendezvous with the prostitute, Samson soon establishes yet another relationship with a foreign woman (cf. 1 Kings 11:1-8). In this case, however, we are specifically informed that he *fell in love with . . . Delilah* (16:4). The Timnite has accused Samson of not loving her; his attraction to her is entirely physical (14:16). Similarly, the encounter with the Gazite prostitute constitutes nothing more than a sensual escape from reality, including the earlier breakup of his marriage and the uncanny events accompanying it. Samson's interest in Delilah, therefore, suggests a deepening level of attachment, at least on his part. If trouble surrounds his more-casual relationships, one can only imagine what lies in store for a person like Samson when the so-called blindness of love sets in.

Not much can be said about Delilah apart from what immediately surfaces in the present story, though she is the first of Samson's women to be given a name. Her home lies at some unspecified place in the *valley of Sorek*, the same valley that surrounds both Timnah and Zorah. The general setting of the story, therefore, remains essentially unchanged. Likewise, the meaning of the name *Delilah* is elusive, although plentiful etymologies and renderings have been suggested: "loose hair," "beloved," and "worshiper" (Soggin: 253). Even Delilah's ethnic background cannot be established with absolute certainty. She may, for example, have been either a Canaanite or a Hebrew with contacts to the Philistines. Yet the overall scope of the narrative and Samson's preference for Philistine women add up most acceptably to identify Delilah as a Philistine.

At some point after learning of this budding romance, the Philistines approach Delilah in hopes of cornering Samson. That they do so with great concern and seriousness is expressed in the fact that the rulers themselves establish the contacts on this occasion (16:5). By implication, the entire Philistine hierarchy is involved in this struggle with a single Danite. Furthermore, they specifically seek to discover *what makes his strength so great,* thus implying some apparent mystery surrounding Samson's incredible feats. The writer frequently attributes such feats to divine empowerment, but the pagan Philistines remain at a total loss. Apparently, Samson's own physique provides no solution; he must look far more "ordinary" than is typically assumed.

In negotiating with Delilah, each ruler promises to pay *eleven hundred pieces of silver* in exchange for the wanted information. Assuming that the rulers in question include the leaders of the five major Philistine cities, the total amount equals 5,500 shekels. To place this exorbitant sum in perspective, it need only be recalled that the gold rings confiscated by Gideon's men from the Midianites totaled 1,700 shekels (8:26; cf. Gen. 23:15; 2 Sam. 24:24; Jer. 32:9)! While various attempts have been made to lessen this seemingly exaggerated figure, the extent of the offer underscores the desperation of the rulers [Historicity and Truth]. The Philistines hope to rid themselves of Samson, once and for all.

Initially, Samson suggests that being tied with *seven fresh bowstrings* will render him defenseless (16:7). Such thongs are actually bowstrings constructed out of animal tendons, and their freshness assures that they are neither dry nor brittle (cf. 15:15). On the second occasion, Samson refers to *new ropes*, an approach which, although apparently unknown to both Delilah and the Philistine rulers, has failed in an earlier attempt to capture the Danite (16:11; cf. 15:13). Third, Samson draws frightfully close to the truth, claiming that by somehow weaving the braids of his hair on a loom, he can be incapacitated (16:13-14). In spite of her efforts, frustration, and increasing accusations, Delilah has yet to obtain the secret to Samson's strength (16:10, 13) [Hero Stories].

Finally, out of sheer desperation, Delilah calls into question the genuineness of Samson's professed love for her (16:15). If the attractive but unloved Timnite earlier felt abandoned, the adored Delilah presently feels betrayed (cf. 14:16). Insofar as Samson does in fact love Delilah, her reservations constitute a direct challenge to both his sincerity and truthfulness. Given Samson's dogged individualism as well as his affection for Philistine women, such a challenge cannot go unmet. As a result, he eventually wearies of Delilah's protracted prodding and reveals the secret of his strength (16:17; cf. 14:16). In this all-important battle of the wills, therefore, Delilah emerges as the victor.

Importantly, Samson prior to this point never alludes to his nazirite vows. In fact, he neither mentions them nor attempts in any serious way to abide by them. While casually disregarding the stipulations concerning the vine and corpses, however, Samson has yet to clip his flowing hair. On one level, long hair serves as a noticeable symbol, and cutting it would be easily detected by both his parents and friends. Similarly, letting his hair grow no doubt inconveniences Samson far less than abstaining from wine and carcass-encased honey. On another level, however, Samson apparently associates his incredible feats with his hair, betraying at least a crude and nonmoralistic conviction concerning the significance of his vows: *If my head were shaved, then my strength would leave me* (16:17). Therefore, by reluctantly disclosing his secret now, he not only prepares the way for the breaking of this third and final vow, but also for his own demise.

16:18-22 Samson Loses His Strength

The nature of Delilah's summons to the Philistine rulers suggests that the Philistines have grown weary of the game and therefore need convincing. When they finally do arrive, Samson, his hair cut, attempts to muster his formidable powers once again. In what must be a brief but terrifying moment, however, he soon realizes that things are not as they once were. Samson earlier experienced the invigorating presence of the descending Spirit (14:6, 19; 15:14); now he faces the horror of the Lord's withdrawal (16:20). With relative haste, he is captured, blinded (ironic, since his eyes had gotten him into so much trouble!), and taken to Gaza, the very scene of some of his earlier heroics (16:1-3).

Now, rather than using his strength to disassemble the city's gate in defiant triumph, Samson embarrassingly grinds grain with a prison millstone. Endlessly wandering around in circles, the strongman from Dan is but a shell of his former self. Only the writer's curious observation leads one to think that the story may not yet be over: *But the hair of his head began to grow again* (16:22). Apparently the Philistines have concluded that a single cutting is perpetually sufficient.

16:23-31 Samson Gains His Revenge

After the passing of an indeterminate period of time, the Philistine rulers coordinate a festival of sorts. That Samson's hair has at least partially grown back following his capture suggests that the occasion envisioned here is not primarily a victory celebration to commemorate his apparent demise (16:22). Generally, such a celebration would follow immediately after the event itself, thereby welcoming home the triumphant forces as well as humiliating the defeated foe. Instead, the taunting of Samson in this case constitutes only a part of a later and otherwise larger happening.

The god *Dagon* is seen here and elsewhere in the OT as the pre-eminent Philistine deity (1 Sam. 5:1-7; 1 Chron. 10:10; cf. 1 Macc. 10:83; 11:4). Dagon was actually venerated by Semites in northern Mesopotamia already in the late third millennium B.C. By the time of the Philistines' arrival on the Mediterranean coast in the twelfth century B.C., worship of Dagon had spread in varying degrees throughout the entire region. He appears, for example, in the archaeological record at such important cities as Ebla, Mari, and Ugarit, once as the father of the great storm-god, Baal. As part of his expanding influence, the Philistines themselves have elevated Dagon to a lofty position within their religious system. The name *Dagon*, at one time erroneously associated with the Hebrew *dag* ("fish"), more likely means "grain" (*dagan*). He was, therefore, an agricultural deity, the god of grain or vegetation *[Prohibition Against Images]*.

The recorded moments of the festival appear to be slightly out of order. For one thing, a prison is hardly the place for a sizeable crowd to view a notorious personality. Furthermore, the sportive taunt-song would be far more stirring following Samson's arrival. Most likely, therefore, the events in 16:24 actually follow those in verse 25. Accordingly, as the people grow increasingly exuberant (and intoxicated!), they summon Samson from the prison (v. 25). As he arrives and subsequently performs, the many spectators join in a resounding chorus of rhyming lines (cf. 14:14), in which they celebrate the dreaded Danite's downfall (16:24). In the midst of such merrymaking, no one except Samson even considers a possible change in fortunes.

Samson eventually stations himself next to the primary support columns. Clearly, Samson possesses at least a basic understanding of Philistine architectural designs. Though no Philistine temples have been uncovered at Gaza, one has been excavated at Tell Qasile (Mazar: 319-323). There, the eleventh century B.C. cultic center includes a ceiling supported by two cedarwood pillars. The structure, however, could scarcely accommodate the number of people mentioned here, nor is it clear how those on the roof can see the activities taking place at the base of the columns below. In short, the scene of Samson's final and fatal feat remains problematic.

Positioned between the supporting pillars, Samson uncharacteristically calls upon the Lord (16:28; cf. 15:18). On the surface, such a gesture suggests a deepening understanding of the true source of his strength. The motivation, however, is sinister, frighteningly similar to the Samson of old. Samson seeks divine intervention, not because the Philistines pose a monumental threat to the people of Israel, but to gain revenge *for my two eyes* (16:28). Even as Samson earlier has sought to balance the scales for the death of his Timnite wife, now he thinks solely of his own mistreatment. In spite of his own deficiencies, however, his prayer receives a favorable response: Samson experiences divine empowerment one final time. As a result, Samson accomplishes more in dying than in living (16:30; cf. 14:19; 15:8, 15) *[Hero Stories]*.

The entire narrative of Samson's activities comes to a close with an announcement of his burial and a restatement of his period of service (cf. 15:20). Samson's grave is situated *between Zorah and Eshtaol*, the general location for many of the previous events and the same area where the Spirit of the Lord initially stirred him (13:25). While the writer refrains from commenting on the thoughts and feelings of Samson's kinsmen who retrieve his body, one can imagine a certain ambivalence. Like the tribes of Israel, Samson experienced an unusually promising beginning (1:1-21; 13:1-25). Yet, as Israel continues to unravel in the presence of pagan deities, so too does Samson squander his potential in the face of self-serving attractions. For both Israel and Samson, then, the outcome is disturbingly similar. The few vanquished foes pale in comparison to the imagined possibilities, possibilities ravaged by ever-increasing faithlessness.

THE TEXT IN BIBLICAL CONTEXT
Self-Control

The Samson of these chapters is a person running out of control. In particular, Samson has a thirst for women, especially foreign women: a Philistine from Timnah, a prostitute from Gaza, and Delilah from Sorek. Samson is hardly alone in lacking self-control. Other biblical personalities are in his company.

Text	Character	Situation
Gen. 34:1-4	Shechem	Takes and rapes Dinah, the daughter of Jacob
Gen. 38:2-3, 15-18	Judah	Has sexual relations with both a Canaanite woman and his disguised daughter-in-law
1 Sam. 2:22	Eli's sons	Sleep with the women who served at the entrance to the Tent of Meeting
2 Sam. 11:1-5	David	Commits adultery with Bathsheba
2 Sam. 13:1-22	Amnon	Rapes his sister Tamar
Mark 6:17-18	Herod	Marries his brother's wife
1 Cor. 5:1-5	Unnamed man	Has sexual relations with his father's wife
Eph. 4:17-19	Gentiles	Engage in impurities of every kind

To these can be added such passages as John 4:17-18 and 8:1-11, where the presence of promiscuous women demands the existence of equally promiscuous men!

In contrast to all of the above, Joseph stands out as a resounding example of unwavering self-control. Even when confronted with repeated advances from Potiphar's apparently beautiful wife, Joseph refuses to compromise either his own godly standards or his earthly master's trust. His refusal costs him his prestigious and influential position (Gen. 39:7-20). Joseph, therefore, embodies the type of self-control celebrated in Scripture, fleeing from sexual immorality in precisely the way that Paul later suggests (1 Cor. 6:18; cf. Gal. 5:23; 1 Thess. 5:6-8; 2 Tim. 3:3; Titus 1:8; 1 Pet. 1:13; 4:7). Samson's lack of self-control, however, leaves him "like a city whose walls are broken down" (Prov. 25:28).

Misused Abilities

Much like Samson, unfulfilled potential and self-centered desires characterize other significant figures in Scripture. King Saul, though anointed and divinely empowered, sinks to the suicidal depths of human despair (1 Sam. 9-31). Solomon, overflowing with wisdom, wealth, and piety, exchanges it all for personal gain (1 Kings 3:1—11:43). Gehazi, apprentice to Elisha himself, dies a leprous individualist (2 Kings 5:20-27). Judas Iscariot, one of the twelve disciples of Jesus, forfeits his position and eventually his life in an unforgettable act of betrayal (Matt. 26:14-16; 27:3-5).

Yet as pitiable as each of these examples is, none quite captures the moving sense of unmet expectations that emerge from Isaiah's "Song of the Vineyard" (5:1-2):

> My loved one had a vineyard
> on a fertile hillside.
> He dug it up and cleared it of stones
> and planted it with the choicest vines.
> He built a watchtower in it
> and cut out a winepress as well.
> Then he looked for a crop of good grapes,
> but it yielded only bad fruit.

Finally, with tearful despair, God's prophetic mouthpiece turns to his fellow Judahites and concludes (Isa. 5:3-4):

> Now you dwellers in Jerusalem and men of Judah,
> judge between me and my vineyard.
> What more could have been done for my vineyard
> than I have done for it?
> When I looked for good grapes,
> why did it yield only bad?

Painfully, Isaiah's community as a whole embodies so much of what appears in Samson centuries before: squandered potential, wasted opportunities, and self-serving ambitions. With God, we are left in silence to imagine what might have been.

THE TEXT IN THE LIFE OF THE CHURCH
Misdirected Ambitions

"Ignorance is bliss," people sometimes say. Not for Samson, about whom Judges makes one of the saddest statements in all of Scripture: *But he did not know that the Lord had left him* (16:20). Inevitably, his reckless behavior and blatant disregard for his God-given vows were his undoing (on vows, see TBC after 12:7).

This disfigured deliverer stands as a powerful and unforgettable symbol for all of God's people. With Samson, one has a permanent reminder of what *could become* of even the most important and gifted. In Samson, one may see a talented orator who speaks everywhere but in church, a musician who plays only in nightclubs, a thinker who thinks only of and for himself. In Samson, one may see a servant of God sell out to temporal pleasures and passionate fancies. In Samson, one may see a multitude of expectations give way to a lingering and nagging "if only." In Samson, we see ourselves apart from a continuing commitment *to* and reliance upon the living Lord.

Nevertheless, this forceful symbol is just a reminder of what *could be*, not of what *must be*. Indeed, by reflecting on Samson, the community of faith at all times can more effectively resist the enticements of the world. Samson demonstrates how foolish and deadly is the uncontrolled quest for earthly pleasure. Surely, life must be more than this! In his essay entitled *The Weight of Glory*, C. S. Lewis, addresses this issue:

> We are all half-hearted creatures, fooling around with drink and sex and ambition when infinite joy is offered us, like an ignorant child who wants to go on making mud pies in a slum because he cannot imagine what is meant by the offer of a holiday at sea. We are far too easily pleased. (2)

God has far better things in mind for his people than "mud pies." In the words of the Westminster Confession, the Lord wants nothing less for men and women than for them to "enjoy him forever."

Perverted Sexuality

In the words of a certain Christian leader who, like Samson, found himself running uncontrollably to satisfy the cravings of his flesh:

> I've experienced enough of the unquenchable nature of sex to frighten me for good. Lust does not satisfy; it stirs up. I no longer wonder how deviants can get into child molesting, masochism, and other abnormalities. Although such acts are incomprehensible to me, I remember well that where I ended up was also incomprehensible to me when I started. (Anonymous: 1982:34)

Yet as striking as this individual's comments might appear, both experience and research confirm that struggles with pornography, lust, and infidelity are prevalent, not only in society as a whole, but within the Christian community as well.

Two surveys underscore the severity of the problem. According to a 1988 poll conducted by Christianity Today, Inc., 23 percent of the pastors surveyed had done something sexually inappropriate with someone other than their spouse since entering local church ministry. Twelve percent admitted having extramarital intercourse. In that same poll, 45 percent of the surveyed Christian laity acknowledged having engaged in sexually inappropriate activities outside of marriage, and 23 percent said they had had extramarital intercourse (Muck: 12).

In another study recently conducted by the University of Chicago, only 50.5 percent of conservative Protestants, 30.9 percent of mainline Protestants, and 22.2 percent of Catholics affirmed that "religious belief always guides their sexual behavior and that premarital, extramarital, and homosexual sex is wrong" (Moeller: 31). From all indications, something has gone tragically wrong with the human appetite for sex.

In response to this problem, the Christian community must increasingly be characterized by two fundamental convictions. First, we must reaffirm a biblical view that both celebrates and restricts human sexuality. "Sex," as Philip Yancey describes it, "is not an end in itself but, rather, a gift from God. Like all gifts, it must be stewarded to God's rules, not ours" (80). Second, we must cultivate a culture of forgiveness in which the struggling members among us can leave their closets and experience genuine hope and transformation.

Part 3

Final Outcome: The Depravity of Israel

Judges 17:1—21:25

OVERVIEW

In the same way that the book of Judges begins with two parallel introductions, the writer now ends his work with two parallel conclusions. Furthermore, each of these conclusions complements the respective introductions by dealing with the same general motifs, the conquest and covenant. However, the situations depicted here indicate that a lengthy and morally downward journey has indeed taken place. Whereas the introductions seek to explain the reasons for Israel's decline, the conclusions reveal the climactic and chaotic results (Stone: 471-477).

First, 17:1—18:31 portrays the furnishing of an idolatrous family shrine as well as the northerly migration of the Danites. The migration might appear to be a successful political and military endeavor. In reality, it is nothing of the kind. The writer carefully insinuates that the Danites' "achievements" are directly the opposite of what is desirable. Briefly stated, the Danites invert the conquest.

Following this, 19:1—21:25 focuses on the abuse of an unnamed concubine and the ensuing disorder permeating all aspects of Israelite society. This second episode demonstrates that nothing in Israel's moral fiber remains untouched by the escalating corruption. The community has consistently and comprehensively desecrated the covenant.

While each of these two conclusions comprises a distinct unit, various elements suggest that they have been intentionally joined together here. Both, for example, appear within the same thematic time period in which *there was no king in Israel,* and *all the people did what was right in their own eyes.* Likewise, both refer to Bethlehem, the hill country of Ephraim, and significant Levites.

Finally, from a structural perspective, one can again recognize the same type of symmetry between them that appeared earlier in the introductions. In this case, both conclusions begin with a localized and seemingly secondary story. Yet in each instance this story gives way to and directly influences an event of far greater magnitude. Through this process, each portrays the contagious and ever-worsening nature of Israel's condition.

OUTLINE

Micah's Family Shrine,
17:1-13

↓

The Danites' Tribal Sanctuary,
18:1-31

A Concubine's Abuse,
19:1-28

↓

The Benjaminites' Annihilation,
19:29—21:25

Judges 17:1—18:31

The Danites' Alternate Conquest

PREVIEW

Relocation, even on a large scale, is nothing new. Here an entire Israelite tribe searches for and finds a homeland. One must not prematurely conclude, however, that greater living space means the move is ultimately beneficial. The following narrative focusing on the northerly migration of the Danites consists of three distinct episodes. These episodes are clearly separated from each other by the recurring statement *In those days Israel had no king* (17:6; 18:1).

In the opening scene an idolatrous family shrine is established in the hills of Ephraim; the closing scene portrays the subsequent construction of a tribal sanctuary further north, at the city of Dan (17:1-5; 18:1-31). These two scenes, which may at first glance appear unrelated, are carefully connected in the second episode with the introduction of a wandering Levite who successively serves at each of these religious centers (17:7-13). Through this linkage, the writer subtly seeks to demonstrate that the northern sanctuary at Dan unmistakably rests upon an idolatrous and degenerate foundation.

OUTLINE

Micah Erects a Family Shrine, 17:1-13
    17:1-6   Micah Fashions His Idols
    17:7-13   Micah Hires a Levite Priest

The Danites Secure a Homeland, 18:1-31

18:1-7   The Danites Spy Out Laish
18:8-13   The Danites Mobilize for Action
18:14-21   The Danites Confiscate Micah's Idols and Priest
18:22-26   The Danites Rebuke a Beleaguered Micah
18:27-31   The Danites Capture Laish

EXPLANATORY NOTES

Micah Erects a Family Shrine 17:1-13

17:1-6 Micah Fashions His Idols

The geographical setting envisioned here is exceptionally vague. While the descriptive phrase *hill country of Ephraim* places the story in the mountainous region north of Judah, no precise location is provided. On the basis of later events, however, Micah's home apparently stands in proximity to the major route connecting the northern and southern regions of the country (cf. 18:2).

As for Micah himself, the writer leaves unsaid everything unrelated to the immediate happenings. The name *itself* actually appears here in longer and shorter forms, *Micahyehu* (17:1, 4) and *Micah* (elsewhere), analogous to such name-pairs as "David/Dave" and "Debra/Deb." Since the name literally means "Who is like Yahweh?" Micah seemingly represents a faithful and devout segment within the society. The actual picture presented here, however, is unbecoming (Amit, 1990).

Micah, according to the story line, previously stole a sizeable sum of money from his own mother. The text fails to specify the intended unit of weight (literally, "eleven hundred of silver"); it is likely the shekel (cf. 8:26). If so, the amount of silver snatched by Micah equals that promised to Delilah by each of the Philistine leaders (16:5). Upon realizing that her money is missing, the mother pronounces a curse in Micah's hearing. Some commentators suggest that this implies a hidden suspicion of her son's guilt. More likely, the curse is pronounced publicly so as to increase its potential effectiveness. In the ancient Near East, as in various contemporary societies, curses carry significant influence. In response to an alterable crime, therefore, a curse and its accompanying threats may well encourage the guilty party to confess and make restitution.

As a modern case in point, the Kikuyu of central Kenya at times announce a cursing ceremony in advance so as to let the offender know of the impending consequences. Such a ceremony constitutes not simply a possible punishment for the crime, but also adds an incentive to surrender.

In this case, the curse proves highly effective; Micah confesses his guilt. Immediately, the mother, no doubt bewildered, pronounces a blessing over her son (17:2). While such an act may reflect a typical parental instinct all-too-quickly to forget the offense, the mother's motivation no doubt involves an attempt to protect her son from misfortune. The antidote for such a curse, after all, is the pronouncement of a blessing by the same person who has offered the original spell.

The predominantly negative picture presented here, however, does not end with the resolution of Micah's thievery. First, the mother announces her intention to dedicate all of the recovered funds to the Lord. While such a vow may appear commendable, it is actually swarming with difficulties (see TBC after 12:7). Included within the vow, first of all, is a provision for her son to maintain control of the goods. Regardless of the mother's pledge, therefore, none of the property in question will ultimately leave the family!

Second, this act of dedication involves the construction of *an idol of cast metal* (17:3-4). The Hebrew phrase (as in KJV and RSV: *a graven image and a molten image*) is an example of hendiadys, where *and* connects two words referring to the same thing. The second noun explains the first. Thus, what is envisioned here is likely not a pair of figures but a single image. Both the singular pronoun *it* in 17:4 and the references to a single image elsewhere in the narrative (18:20, 30-31) support such a view. The figure is perhaps carved from wood and subsequently covered with metal. In any case, all such images are explicitly prohibited in the law and therefore unacceptable in Israelite worship (cf. Exod. 20:4, 23; Deut. 4:16) *[Prohibition Against Images]*.

Finally, the actual outlay of silver used in the construction of the idol significantly totals only two hundred shekels (17:4). The full dedicated sum amounts to eleven hundred shekels. Is the remainder reserved for the maintenance of the shrine, as Martin tentatively proposes, or is it instead withheld for personal benefit (185)? Silence on this matter at least raises further doubts about the sincerity behind the dedication. Property consecrated to God must not be diverted to any other purpose (cf. Acts 5:1-11).

Following the questionable fulfillment of the mother's thorny vow, the increasingly negative picture now reaches completion in 17:5. Micah, seemingly unsatisfied with the newly fashioned image, makes *an ephod* (see notes on 8:27) *and teraphim*. Teraphim appear elsewhere in the OT, typically as household deities of varying sizes (Gen. 31:19, 34-35; 1 Sam. 19:13; 2 Kings 23:24). In this case, both the *ephod* as well as the *teraphim* perhaps serve divinatory functions, used inappropriately by Micah to seek supernatural messages (cf. Deut. 18:10-12; Isa. 44:25; 47:12-15; Acts 13:6-11; 19:13-20; Rev. 22:15). If not, they at least add to his list of forbidden images *[Prohibition Against Images]*.

With his entire collection of religious objects now intact, Micah finally positions them within his personal shrine. Micah, in other words, owns and operates his own sanctuary, a sanctuary that perhaps attracts a following from among the neighbors (18:22). Importantly, however, such a sanctuary has no clear claim to legitimacy. Nothing, for example, associates it in any way with genuine Israelite worship and tradition (Exod. 20:24).

Furthermore, Micah appoints one of his own sons to serve as a priest over these venerated objects. More literally, he "filled the hand of" his son, a technical expression for ordination, rooted in the actual filling of the priest's hands with portions of a sacrifice (Exod. 28:41; 29:9; Lev. 8:33; 16:32; 1 Kings 13:33; cf. Exod. 29:24). Such family priests were not unknown in ancient Israel, but the Levites more and more have replaced them (Num. 3; cf. 2 Sam. 8:18). Although Micah later secures the services of a Levite when the opportunity presents itself, he apparently makes no serious attempt to do so initially. From all indications, then, Micah's shrine is an idolatrous center, a convenient alternative to those of a more legitimate nature (18:31).

Throughout, the writer has studiously refrained from excessive condemnation. He has simply recounted the story, assuming no doubt that Micah's evil practices are self-evident. From a later vantage point, he attributes such confusion in these earlier periods to the lack of a king (17:6). In the absence of monarchical restraints, *all the people did what was right in their own eyes*. With such a conclusion, the writer condemns the behaviors described.

17:7-13 Micah Hires a Levite Priest

All the while that Micah was erecting his family's shrine, a certain Levite was apparently experiencing difficult times further south in Judah. Likewise, the description of this Levite, whose name appears as Jonathan far later in the story, presents the modern reader with a certain difficulty. According to the text, he was both a Levite as well as a member of the *clan of Judah* (17:7). Since he could hardly have been born into two distinct tribes, various commentators conclude that the term *Levite* here constitutes an occupational category or class of people rather than a tribal designation (Boling: 257; Soggin: 270). In this view, the man was a Judahite who also happened to serve vocationally as a Levite.

To further complicate the problem, however, the later genealogical information concerning Jonathan suggests that he was a direct descendant of Moses (18:30). Moses, of course, was from the tribe of Levi, specifically through the line of Kohath (1 Chron. 23:12-15). Therefore, while acknowledging a certain ambiguity in the language of 17:7, it seems appropriate here to retain a more traditional understanding of Jonathan's status. Jonathan was from the tribe of Levi, but he resided within the territory of Judah.

Admittedly, however, this straightforward understanding fails to do justice to the writer's subtle description of Jonathan (17:7-8). To fully appreciate this particular Levite, one must first consider various references to the so-called Levitical cities. Of the several cities awarded to the Levites instead of a single territorial allotment, nine were situated within the borders of Judah and Simeon (Num. 35:1-5; Josh. 21:9-16; 1 Chron. 6:54-81). These southern cities are all associated with those Kohathites who were direct descendants of Aaron. The remaining Kohathites, including the descendants of Moses, received cities further west and north in the regions of Dan, Ephraim, and Manasseh [Map, p. 240].

Accordingly, Jonathan has no business living in Judah. He is a sojourner (ger) in the land, residing far away from the cities traditionally assigned to him. This helps explain why he eventually decides to leave Judah in search of a more stable position. As a drifter of sorts, his economic situation must be somewhat precarious.

After leaving his predicament in Judah, Jonathan travels north, perhaps with the intention of returning to his homeland. While en route, he stumbles upon Micah, who extends a most respectful offer of employment to the youthful Levite: *Be to me a father and a priest* (17:10; cf. Gen. 45:8; 2 Kings 2:12; 6:21; 13:14). Since Micah has recently ordained his own son for the same position, the offer comes as a surprise (17:5). This sudden willingness to disregard the previous appointment, however, simply underscores the preference given to Levites in such situations. Anyway, no serious conflict between the two appointees appears likely. One may expect, given the idolatrous nature of Micah's sanctuary, that the Levite will surely decline the offer.

Nevertheless, the Levite turns out to be as opportunistic as Micah himself. In Micah's case, the presence of a Levite over his sanctuary is a sure guarantee that even greater blessings lie ahead (17:13). Jonathan, the Levite, will provide the legitimacy that the shrine has previously lacked, and the popularity of the place will no doubt increase accordingly. If nothing else, God can hardly withhold his favor from the employer of a genuine Levite.

In the Levite's case, even the unorthodox character of the position does not lessen the security of the offer. For someone who has recently left a life of uncertainty, a dependable salary plus room and board offers a welcome change. As a result, this section of the narrative concludes with what would have been unthinkable earlier: a Levite overseeing an idolatrous shrine, and a proprietor expecting God's blessings because of it.

THE TEXT IN BIBLICAL CONTEXT

Idolatry

Micah, with his assortment of images, does not stand alone among the biblical characters. Following the exodus from Egypt, a sizeable number of Israelites joined their collective energies and resources in constructing the infamous golden calf (Exod. 32). Later, Jeroboam I furnished the major shrines at Dan and Bethel with similar figures (1 Kings 12:28-30). Yet neither of these noteworthy examples matches the singular audacity of Manasseh, who goes so far as to place a homemade idol within the Jerusalem temple itself (2 Kings 21:7; 2 Chron. 33:7)! Clearly, Israel and idols are not strangers.

The presence of these and other idols, however, runs directly against the pervasive teaching of the OT. In this regard, two specific and fundamentally different commandments appear within Israel's legal traditions. First, the people of Israel are to construct no such images themselves (Exod. 20:4; Lev. 26:1; Deut. 4:16, 25; 5:8; 27:15). Second, they are to destroy any already-existing idols if and when they find them (Deut. 7:5, 25; 12:3). These commandments find nothing but reinforcement from the psalmist and the prophets, who denounce idolatry with great force and regularity (Pss. 78:58; 97:7; Isa. 42:17; 44:9-17; Jer. 10:14; Mic. 1:7; 5:13; Nah. 1:14; Hab. 2:18). Idols, whether constructed (as in Micah's case) or preserved (as with the Danites in Judg. 18), always represent a deviation from the norm *[Prohibition Against Images]*.

False Security in Religious Rites

When given the choice, Micah quickly installs a Levite over his shrine. This, he imagines, guarantees the Lord's blessing. Comparable sentiments find expression elsewhere in various forms. The Israelites, for example, call for the ark following their initial defeat at the hands of the Philistines. In their mistaken view, the mere presence of the ark will prevent another defeat in the second phase of the battle (1 Sam.

4:3). Likewise, the community at large eventually comes to consider Jerusalem itself as totally impregnable simply because it is the so-called city of the Lord (Jer. 7:4; Lam. 4:12). Finally, equally presumptuous thoughts become affixed to the outward exercising of such practices as fasting and the offering of sacrifices (Isa. 58; Hos. 6:6; Amos 5:21-24; Mic. 3:11; 6:7).

In these and other cases, the people of Israel simply equate God's blessing and acceptance with either the possession of religious property or the performance of religious rituals. Somewhere along the way, they apparently have forgotten what the prophets continually emphasize: God delights, not so much in religiosity, but in those who act justly, love mercy, and walk humbly before him (Mic. 6:8).

In the NT, Jesus similarly rejects the notion that external behaviors or characteristics alone in some way earn God's favor. Whether it be praying, fasting, Sabbath observance, or social action—the condition of the human heart takes on paramount importance (Matt. 5–7; 12:1-8; Mark 7:1-23). The same holds true for Paul, who elevates internal circumcision over the simple circumcision of the body (Rom. 3; Gal. 5:6). If anyone can place confidence in external criteria, Paul argues that he can (Phil. 3:1-11). Such things, however, are relatively worthless in and of themselves. Of greater importance is this: "Love the Lord your God with all your heart, and with all your soul, and with all your mind, [and] your neighbor as yourself" (Deut. 6:5; Lev. 19:18; Matt. 22:37-39).

THE TEXT IN THE LIFE OF THE CHURCH

On Misreading God

Both the veneration of idols and the equation of divine favor with external religious practice have this in common: God is reduced to a controllable and totally predictable deity. In the case of idols, God takes on whatever form we humans desire. We do the shaping and the fashioning. We determine the expectations and demands. We regulate the sphere of influence. We handle God, move God, spend God, control God, and play God. As a result, the God we worship is in reality nothing more than what Martin Luther labels an idol concocted for ourselves (1960:273; cf. Ps. 115:4).

When people associate divine favor simply with religious possessions and behaviors, they put God into the role of a convenient and manageable checklist. From the beginning of time, people have sought after gods who are consistent and predictable, gods with unambiguous likes and dislikes. In this way, everyone knows precisely what to do and when to do it. We may assume that God automatically delights in regular church attendance, hour-long prayers, and the sharing of financial resources, for example. Then we confidently go ahead and do them, fully anticipating his blessings in return. What results, all too often, is a contract or bargain. Such a contract is then typically applied in one of two distinct but equally destructive ways:

• *Evaluative Tool.* With the terms of the agreement neatly defined, we need only review the list each day to determine our spiritual standing. Spirituality, in other words, is simplistically and naively equated with performance. Lost somewhere in all of this is the intimacy that God so much wants to share with his people.

• *Insurance Policy.* By keeping the terms of the contract, failures in more important areas go unnoticed or unattended.

By simply observing various religious externals, one subtly concludes that God has little interest in whatever else one does. In Isaac Bashevis Singer's novel *The Slave*, a former Jewish captive named Jacob struggles with this issue. He comments on the behavior of a townsman named Gershon:

> Men like Gershon cheated, but they ate matzoth prepared according to the strictest requirements. They slandered their fellow men, but demanded meat doubly kosher. They envied, fought, hated their fellow Jews, yet still put on a second pair of phylacteries. (202)

Elsewhere, after much reflection and experience, Jacob profoundly recognizes the folly of such a theological position:

> Despite the thirty-odd years he had lived in the world, Jacob was continually astonished at how many Jews obeyed only one half of the Torah. The very same people, who strictly observed the minor rituals and customs which were not even rooted in the Talmud, broke without thinking twice the most sacred laws, even the Ten Commandments. They wanted to be kind to God and not to man; but what did God need of man and his favors? What does a father want from his children but that they should not do injustice to each other? Jacob, leaning over the well, sighed. This was the cry of the prophets. Perhaps it was the reason the Messiah did not come. (180-181)

As former British archbishop William Temple once said, "It is a mistake to assume that God is interested only, or even chiefly, in religion." Similarly, God's favor cannot be bought with a list of "religious" behaviors.

What makes all of this so tricky, finally, is that the God of Scripture is by no means utterly confusing and chaotic. He does have certain likes and dislikes, and he does at times act in predictable ways. Furthermore, God does invite our creative input and participation, and he unashamedly encourages us to use such earthy images as a shepherd or king when we reflect upon him. Yet God also refuses rigid categorization, and he likewise vetoes all attempts to reduce his marvelous gospel to a mere set of even the best behaviors. In spite of his act of self-revelation, God maintains an unmistakable sense of freedom, wonder, and mystery. Among other surprises, he prefers living in malleable and stretchable human hearts rather than living in simplistic and restrictive theological boxes.

EXPLANATORY NOTES

The Danites Secure a Homeland 18:1-31

With Micah's shrine firmly in place, the narrative now shifts to the Danites' northerly migration and their eventual conquest of Laish. On this subject, the writer frequently mentions various similarities between these occurrences and the earlier Israelite conquest of Canaan. In fact, Abraham Malamat points out ten specific points of correspondence between the two events: in both, the people acquire a priesthood, send out spies, and build sanctuaries (1970:2-16). From all indications, the writer of Judges did indeed pattern his portrayal of the present story according to the Israelite conquest.

Nevertheless, this portrayal is not set forth to applaud the Danites' achievements. On the contrary, the points of correspondence merely serve to highlight grave differences between the two events. Webb's analysis (185-186) includes these differences:

Israel	Dan
Advancing	Retreating
Claiming an inheritance	Seeking a more attainable alternative
Operating during Yahweh's involvement in the conquest	Operating following Yahweh's withdrawal, 2:20-21
Encounters great, fortified cities	Seeks isolated, defenseless opponent
Joshua and Caleb demonstrate faithful confidence	Spies' report reflects easy prey

The actions and achievements of the Danites, in other words, constitute the direct antithesis of the Israelites' march to the Promised Land.

Precisely when the events recorded here take place remains difficult to say. The Samson stories seem to reflect a setting following this Danite migration; only an impotent and sluggish remnant of the tribe lingers behind. If so, then the Danites settle in the north somewhat earlier in the period than the positioning of the present episode at first suggests. In truth, we simply do not know for sure. If, however, these events did occur earlier, then theology again supersedes chronology as the ordering device [Historicity and Truth].

18:1-7 The Danites Spy Out Laish

Reference has already been made to the inability of the Danites to subjugate the territory allotted to them (1:34-35). According to Joshua 19:40-46, the Danites originally received the area situated just west of Benjamin [Map, p. 240]. Due to extreme pressure from both the Amorites (1:34) and the Philistines (Judg. 13–16), however, they never secured their position there [Sea Peoples]. Now, finding themselves in an ever-narrowing corner, the Danites ultimately acknowledge defeat and seek refuge elsewhere.

In a manner reminiscent of previous conquest narratives, the account begins with the Danites sending selected representatives to spy out the land (18:2; cf. Num. 13–14; Josh. 2). The reference to Zorah and Eshtaol indicates a localized context similar to that of Samson's adventures (13:2, 25). This area apparently constitutes the primary portion of the original territory which actually has come into Danite hands.

Soon after beginning their northerly journey, the spies arrive at Micah's house, much in the same way that Jonathan did earlier (17:8). Just how they recognized the voice of the young Levite, however, goes unmentioned. It's doubtful, of course, that they knew Jonathan personally, nor did they simply overhear him performing a familiar priestly ritual. If they had, their later question concerning Jonathan's activities in the area would be unnecessary. Instead, the young Levite likely spoke a distinctive but unspecified dialect, one he has learned during his stay in Judah. Such a dialect, after all, may well be familiar to the Danites, who originally shared a common border with the Judahites.

The spies ask the Levite for a word from God concerning their expedition (18:5). Once again, the precise method of receiving such a message goes unstated (cf. 1:1). Jonathan has a variety of means at his disposable, including the ephod (17:5; cf. notes on 8:27). Given the idolatrous nature of Micah's shrine, however, one wonders about the origin of the favorable response. Such apparent trivialities are obviously of no concern to the Danite explorers, who surely welcome the message and continue on their journey.

The city of Laish (18:7), referred to in Joshua 19:47 as Leshem, was situated some twenty-five miles north of the Sea of Galilee. Mentioned in various ancient texts, including the Egyptian Execration

Texts (ca. 1850-1825 B.C.) as well as those from Mari (ca. 1825-1765 B.C.), Laish was already a significant city early in the second millennium B.C. *[Ancient Near Eastern Texts].* Furthermore, archaeological evidence reveals a sizeable and prosperous community there during the period of the Judges (Biran, 1980:172-173).

Beyond such background information, however, the writer himself provides at least two significant characteristics of Laish. First, the people of Laish live *after the manner of the Sidonians,* an apparent reference to a peaceful way of life that emphasizes commerce over combat. Sidon was a Phoenician settlement on the Mediterranean coast known primarily for trade and commerce rather than war. Second, Laish is relatively isolated, both geographically and politically. Not only is the city far removed from the more westerly Sidonians, but it also has no treaty with the Aramaeans to the north and east (reading *'aram* from the versions at the end of 18:7, in place of *'adam,* "men"). The people of Laish, in other words, have no allies who can readily offer assistance if the need arises. Both of these crucial factors will contribute to the city's destruction at the hands of the approaching Danites.

18:8-13 *The Danites Mobilize for Action*

Given both the positive word from the young Levite as well as the apparent susceptibility of Laish, the Danite spies return home with considerable confidence. This, of course, differs greatly from the pessimism that so pervaded the Israelite explorers returning to Kadesh (Num. 13:26-29). In the context of such unbridled optimism, the spies give an impassioned plea to their fellow Danites, encouraging them to move without delay. Insofar as the Danites have known nothing but contention and defeat in the south, such encouragement is surely welcomed.

Upon receiving the report from the spies, *six hundred men,* prepared for battle and accompanied by their families, immediately leave Zorah and Eshtaol (18:11; cf. 18:21). If this occurrence precedes the events associated with Samson, then it is apparent that at least a few Danites choose to remain behind. In any case, the total number of participants seems to constitute a sizeable portion of what remains of the tribe after several years of conflict (cf. 18:19, *a tribe*).

Kiriath Jearim, remembered in history primarily as the place where the ark of the Lord was positioned following its return by the Philistines (1 Sam. 7:2), lay some seven miles northwest of Jerusalem. The Danites, therefore, set up camp about nine miles from their original point of departure *[Map, p. 242].* This camp, memorialized in the name *Mahaneh-dan,* "a camp of Dan," should not be confused with a similarly named site in 13:25. Rather, the descriptive label likely refers to multiple temporary encampments rather than to any single, permanent settlement.

18:14-21 The Danites Confiscate Micah's Idols and Priest

Upon arriving at Micah's house, the former spies bring to everyone's attention the well-stocked sanctuary that they had stumbled upon during their previous visit (see notes on 17:3-6). Micah and the Levite apparently live in separate quarters, although they are near each other. No doubt due to the Levite's earlier word of encouragement as well as the positive outcome of their original scouting expedition, the spies now seek renewed contact with the displaced priest. As events soon indicate, however, they have more grandiose and sinister things in mind this time around.

With the rest of the company standing by the gate to the complex, the former spies swiftly empty Micah's sanctuary of all its venerated contents. The list of objects appears four times in this section and thus vividly rekindles notions of how severe Micah's idolatrous behavior is (18:14, 17, 18, 20). In a sense, the sanctuary is "overflowing" with images. Yet, while Micah ignores Israelite legal traditions in fashioning such images, the Danites similarly abandon the law by not destroying them (Deut. 7:5, 25; 12:3).

During the proceedings, the Levite himself stands by, seeking to ascertain the motives behind such thievery (18:18). Any attempt on his part to abort the robbery, however, quickly fades when the Danites invite him to join their party. By accepting their offer, an offer that sounds strangely similar to the one made earlier by Micah in 17:10 (*be to me a father and a priest*), the wandering Levite chooses to wander once more. In the face of a clear professional promotion, opportunism displaces prior commitments.

The ordering of the Danite procession betrays an anticipation of some type of reprisal (18:21). By positioning both the members of their families as well as their possessions *in front of them,* the armed men stand ready to defend against an attack from the rear. In their minds, this entire episode is far from over.

18:22-26 The Danites Rebuke a Beleaguered Micah

Traveling without any cumbersome paraphernalia, Micah's recruits soon approach the much-slower Danites. In spite of their opening question, the Danites obviously know why Micah is chasing them (18:23). Micah's impassioned plea, however, has no apparent effect.

Rather than returning all or even a portion of the sacred images, the now-angry Danites threaten their pursuer (18:25). The phrase *hot-tempered men*, literally, "bitter of soul," elsewhere denotes a wild bear robbed of her cubs (2 Sam. 17:8). Recognizing both the numerical advantage and the ruthless determination of his adversaries, Micah abandons hope and returns home. Ironically, the tables have completely turned. Micah, himself a former thief, is now left to endure the painful and lingering consequences of thievery (cf. 17:1-2).

18:27-31 The Danites Capture Laish

With Micah's handmade images—the writer again emphasizes that the sacred objects are actually human creations—as well as the vagabond Levite firmly in their custody, the Danites finally reach their desired destination (18:31). Encountering little or no resistance, they destroy a people quiet and unsuspecting (18:27) *[Maps, pp. 240, 242]*. The Danites brutally attack an exemplary and nonthreatening group of people, a people who stand essentially defenseless *[Violence and War in Judges]*. Archaeologists have noted some evidence pointing to an interruption of cultures at Laish during the Late Bronze period (Biran, 1987:105-106) *[Archaeological Periods]*. Such evidence possibly reflects the arrival of the Danites to the area.

Little is known concerning *Beth-rehob*, and its precise location remains uncertain (18:28). The site might well be equated with the Rehob mentioned in Numbers 13:21, the northernmost place visited by the Israelite spies. Furthermore, the fact that it was under Aramaean control during David's reign raises the possibility that it was also an Aramaean city during the time of the Danite migration (2 Sam. 10:6). If so, then the proposed lack of a treaty between Laish and the Aramaeans takes on even-greater significance (cf. 18:7). Perhaps assistance was within the reach of Laish after all, assistance that never materialized due to this political vacuum.

After conquering Laish, the Danites not only rebuild and inhabit the city, but rename it after their own tribal forefather (18:29; cf. Gen. 30:1-6). Within the city, they establish a sanctuary of sorts and furnish it with at least Micah's handmade image. For whatever reason, neither the ephod nor the teraphim are mentioned. To oversee the operation of the new sanctuary, the Danites make good on their former promise and install the young Levite as priest.

Here for the first time, the narrative refers to this priest by name: *Jonathan son of Gershom, son of Moses* (18:30). Apparently, however, the horror of associating this wandering Levite with the great lawgiver himself was too much for the early scribes to ignore. As a result, they inserted a raised *n* in the name, thereby altering *msh* ("Moses") to *mnsh* ("Manasseh"). As the *Talmud* explains it:

> Was he the *son of Manasseh?* Surely he was the son of Moses, for it is written, *the sons of Moses: Gershom, and Eliezer*; but [you must say that] because he acted [wickedly] as Manasseh, the Scriptural text ascribed his descent to Manasseh. (Simon and Slotki: Baba Bathra 109b).

In the view of the scribes, in other words, Jonathan follows two lines of descent. While he is a literal descendant of Moses, he is a moral descendant of the despicable king Manasseh (2 Kings 21:1-9).

Finally, the story comes to a close by connecting the events here with two outside reference points in Israel's history. In the first, the writer suggests that Jonathan and his sons continue their priestly activities *until the land went into captivity* (18:30). By implication, the idolatrous priesthood in Dan apparently maintained some level of operation and influence until either 734 or 722 B.C. On the first of these dates, a large percentage of the Northern Kingdom of Israel's population was deported by the Assyrians (2 Kings 15:29). On the second, the nation itself succumbed (2 Kings 17:3-6).

In addition to associating the longevity of the priesthood to the captivity of the land, the writer informs us that Micah's idol remains in use *as long as the house of God was at Shiloh* (18:31). Shiloh, located some ten miles north of Bethel, served as both the religious and administrative center for the Israelite tribes during the settlement period (Josh. 18:1; 19:51; 21:2; 22:12) *[Map, p. 242]*. It was there, in fact, that the ark of the covenant was initially housed (1 Sam. 4:3). Shiloh's significance during this early period finds corroboration in the ever-developing archaeological landscape. Among other things, recent excavations indicate considerable religious structures there from at least the beginning of the eleventh century B.C. (Finkelstein: 170). Precisely when "the house of God" ceased functioning at Shiloh, however, is difficult to know.

Within the biblical text itself, no account describes the actual destruction of Shiloh. The prophet Jeremiah refers to the ruined sanctuary there, but he provides no clear indication as to the date of its devastation (Jer. 7:12-15; 26:6). Therefore, we simply know that at least the sanctuary lay in ruins by the late seventh century B.C. According to the archaeological record, Shiloh itself continued to be occupied in one form or another throughout the Iron Age and into the time of the exile *[Archaeological Periods]*. There is evidence of a destruction, however, dating back to the middle of the eleventh century B.C., the same general period in which the ark was confiscated by the Philistines (1 Sam. 4; Finkelstein: 173-174). Perhaps the devastation of the sanctuary described by Jeremiah occurred in connection with these events.

At least, Shiloh forever lost much of its importance following both the removal of the ark of the covenant as well as this apparent attack on the site itself. It may well be to this momentous decline, then, that the writer of Judges refers. If instead he has in mind some later happening, then that happening cannot yet be specified.

In spite of the apparent uncertainty in establishing such particulars, the intent of these concluding verses seems clear enough. First, the effects of the Danite shrine are long-lasting, continuing well beyond the time of its inception. Such a long-lasting influence reinforces the notion that the Danite sanctuary was to some degree continuous with the major northern shrine established later by Jeroboam I (1 Kings 12:29). That shrine repeatedly receives similarly negative evaluations in the biblical text (e.g., 1 Kings 12:30; 16:26; 2 Kings 10:29).

Second, the need for the Danite shrine is undermined insofar as a legitimate religious center exists at Shiloh during the same period. Regardless of the precise time when Shiloh's importance ceased, the fact that an authentic sanctuary exists there *when* the Danites construct their own underscores the extent of their wrongdoing. Therefore, what begins as an idolatrous but relatively localized family shrine culminates in an equally idolatrous tribal sanctuary of fargreater influence.

THE TEXT IN BIBLICAL CONTEXT

Opportunism

The wandering Levite from Bethlehem never passes up an opportunity to improve his immediate situation. Though initially displaced in Judah, his professional savvy leads him through a sequence of promotions that ultimately ends with him serving as priest for the entire tribe of Dan. In terms of influence and financial security, at least, the Levite's opportunism pays off. Much the same can be said for Abner, who years later seizes the chance to secure a firm position within David's administration (2 Sam. 3:12).

Opportunism, however, did not pay off for either the unnamed Amalekite or Simon the Sorcerer. For the Amalekite, his opportunistic attempt to claim credit for Saul's death results in his own execution rather than the anticipated favor of David (2 Sam. 1:1-16; cf. 1 Sam. 31:1-6). As for Simon, he fares somewhat better, escaping with nothing more than a severe tongue-lashing (Acts 8:9-25). Opportunism, therefore, brings mixed results.

Of more importance than potential effectiveness, however, are the conditions under which opportunism is exercised. Scripture encourages the development of God-given gifts and abilities; it never celebrates advancement through illegitimate and self-serving means. Models more worthy of emulation than the Levite appear in both David and Jesus. When given the opportunity to murder Saul and thereby accelerate his own rise to power, David flatly refuses to harm "the Lord's anointed" (1 Sam. 24).

Similarly, Jesus rejects the devil's invitation to bypass the cross, even though he longed for a less-painful alternative (Matt. 4:8-10; 26:39). In each instance, integrity and faithfulness take precedence over advancement. Biblically speaking, if an opportunity is clean, pure, and God-given, then seize it. Otherwise, "Better a poor man whose walk is blameless than a rich man whose ways are perverse" (Prov. 28:6).

Sin's Snowballing Effect

A process that begins with Micah's manufacturing of a household idol eventually culminates with the construction of an illegitimate tribal sanctuary. An originally localized and private wrongdoing gives way to corruption of far-greater magnitude. Once introduced, evil has an uncanny tendency to reproduce itself in ever-expanding ways.

There is much biblical evidence for evil's reproductive capacity. The relevant passages indicate both qualitative and quantitative aspects of evil's contagious nature. With respect to quality, people who engage in sinful behavior tend to perform increasingly wicked deeds. Cain's jealous anger, for example, rapidly leads to the ruthless murder of Abel (Gen. 4:1-8). David, after committing adultery with Bathsheba, has little trouble eliminating her husband, Uriah (2 Sam. 11). Judas' act of betrayal leads eventually to his suicide (Matt. 26:14-16; 27:1-5). Even Peter, in disavowing his relationship with the Lord Jesus, compounds his first denial with an oath and then a series of curses (Matt. 26:69-75)!

In terms of quantity, the sins of an individual or minority often result in ongoing and deepening consequences for the community at large. Already in the opening chapters of Genesis, evil widens its sphere of influence. What begins with a single act of rebellion, ends with an international quest for self-glorification (Gen. 3:6; 11:1-9). Likewise, what begins in Eden soon reaches to the farthest corners of the earth. This motif repeats itself later with noteworthy regularity. As cases in point, Gideon's construction of an ephod swiftly infects the bulk of his supporters (Judg. 8:27). Jeroboam's wicked practices serve to suffocate spiritually the Northern Kingdom of Israel throughout its history (e.g., 1 Kings 12:30; 15:26, 34; 16:26). Finally, Manasseh's inestimable wickedness tarnishes Judah beyond repair (2 Kings 21:1-18; 23:26-27).

In reflecting on a similar situation developing in Corinth, Paul forcefully asks the church there if they do not know that "a little yeast works through the whole batch of dough" (1 Cor. 5:6, NIV)? Unchecked evil rarely remains stagnant. The first offense typically gives way to greater and more-disastrous encroachments, reproducing like a nasty computer virus.

THE TEXT IN THE LIFE OF THE CHURCH

Curtailing Corruption

Big sins typically grow out of little ones. In King David's case, what began with a second glance at a bathing woman eventually resulted in adultery and murder (2 Sam. 11). As Menno Simons describes the sequence, "As soon as [David] gave in, . . . he, without hesitation, went from one deadly sin and wickedness to another" (982). To similar and equally sorrowful examples of escalating corruption in today's world, the gospel provides at least three invigorating responses:

• *Avoid beginning the cycle.* Those uninvolved in such an escalating process must carefully refrain from instigating one.

• *Break the cycle.* Those already caught in evil's net must prayerfully set their sights on breaking the cycle and, with the help of other believers, moving on to holier ground.

• *Assist those in the cycle.* Both local congregations and the wider church must supplement their view of ethics with a profound understanding of God's grace. Christians need to engage in what Walter Brueggemann refers to as "prophetic energizing" (62-79). They must, in other words, provide oppressed and imprisoned people with visions of what could be.

Exposing Corruption

Memorials commemorating the Holocaust, including one recently constructed in Washington, D.C., can be found in various cities throughout the world. A similar exhibit recalling the near extermination of the Armenians is situated in the old city of Jerusalem. To these could be added countless other examples. Each of these memorials serves the same essential purposes: (1) to recall times when those in power dealt treacherously with commoners, and (2) to plead with subsequent generations not to repeat such atrocities again. Each memorial, in other words, exposes past corruption in the hope of establishing a more benevolent society for future generations.

So it is with many biblical texts, including Judges 17–18. In recounting such sordid stories from the past as the Danite conquest of the *quiet and unsuspecting* citizens of Laish (18:7), the writer calls into question all subsequent attempts to advance one's own purposes through the confiscation of another's property and possessions. At the same time, he summons the people of God to serve similarly as watchpersons who, by critically evaluating events of the past and retelling even the painful stories, warn against encroaching ungodliness in their own time.

Similarly, the church must use history to protect the future. Believers can do this through recounting such events as these: how the Crusaders recaptured the Holy Land for the cause of Christ (Bainton: 112-113); how the Spanish dislodged native cultures in Latin America in the name of their religion (Bonino: 57); how Europeans obtained land in North America from Native Americans or the Inuit; how Israelis seized more Palestinian territory to fulfill "prophecy"; how the Americans impoverished Iraq to secure oil; and how "ethnic cleansing" has devastated peoples in many places and times, including the present.

Judges 19:1—21:25

The Death of Morality

PREVIEW

The book of Judges closes with bizarre scenes of individual and corporate violence. Violence fits hand-in-glove with the apostasy and degradation of religious practices witnessed in chapters 17 and 18. Now, within the span of these final few chapters (19–21), the reader encounters a perversion of hospitality, sexual immorality, murder, mass abduction, and the near annihilation of an entire tribe. Apparently, no sphere of life stands unaffected by this corruptive torrent. As a result, the entire covenant lies in shambles.

This final narrative consists of three primary episodes. The first focuses on a localized event involving the brutal rape and killing of an unnamed concubine (Judg. 19). The event sets the stage for the coming civil war in much the same way that Micah's deeds are preparatory to the founding of the Danite sanctuary (Judg. 17–18). In the second episode, the drama expands as the combined forces of Israel repay evil with even greater evil (Judg. 20). As a result, the tribe of Benjamin finds itself on the verge of extinction. Finally, episode three concludes the narrative by recounting how this threat of extinction is averted (Judg. 21).

Throughout the entire sequence, the solution to one problem merely creates yet another crisis. Accordingly, the narrative ends precisely where it begins: *In those days there was no king in Israel* (19:1; 21:25).

OUTLINE

A Concubine Loses Her Life, 19:1-28
    19:1-10   A Levite Regains His Concubine

192

19:11-15   Gibeah Denies Hospitality
19:16-21   An Elderly Sojourner Extends Hospitality
19:22-28   Men of Gibeah Abuse the Concubine

Israel Debates a Grievous Crime, 19:29—20:11
19:29-30   A Levite Broadcasts the Deed
20:1-7   The Israelites Assemble at Mizpah
20:8-11   The Israelites Plan Their Response

Israel Repays the Wayward Benjaminites, 20:12-48
20:12-17   The Israelites Confront the Benjaminites
20:18-28   The Benjaminites Defeat the Israelites
20:29-48   The Israelites Ambush the Benjaminites

Israel Preserves the Shattered Benjaminites, 21:1-24
21:1-4   The Israelites Mourn the Loss of the Benjaminites
21:5-14   The Benjaminites Receive Wives from Jabesh-gilead
21:15-24   The Benjaminites Seize Wives at Shiloh

Restatement of a Discouraging Appraisal, 21:25

EXPLANATORY NOTES

A Concubine Loses Her Life 19:1-28

The beginning episode, characterized by the dastardly treatment of the concubine, gains momentum through contrasting images of ancient Eastern hospitality (Matthews, 1992). In other words, the writer accentuates the concubine's ill fortune by placing it within the overall context of extended hospitality (at Bethlehem), unexpected hospitality (at Jebus), and expected but denied hospitality (at Gibeah). Clearly, far more is expected of Gibeah than what actually transpires. Therefore, the evil treatment of the concubine, though worse than anything else that has happened *since the day that the Israelites came up from the land of Egypt* (19:30), is itself a painful symptom of a more pervasive condition.

19:1-10 A Levite Regains His Concubine

The opening clause, *In those days, when there was no king in Israel,* serves both to introduce the following narrative as well as to connect it with what has gone before. The impact, however, is not so much chronological as impressionistic. By implication, although the events of chapters 19–21 may not have taken place after those of chapters 17–18, they do fit within the same general period of confusion and lawlessness.

As in the earlier story of Micah and the Danites, the present account refers to both Bethlehem and Ephraim and similarly includes the activities of a certain Levite (17:1, 7-9). Here, however, the Levite resides in *the hill country of Ephraim* (literally, "a remote section of the hills of Ephraim") and only temporarily descends into Bethlehem *[Map, p. 240]*. Accordingly, he does not appear as another wandering priest seeking more suitable accommodations. Rather, he is probably older and at least somewhat more established. In addition, no obvious importance is attached to his tribal affiliation.

As to the former Levite, his priestly identity further aggravates the situation: even Israel's "religious leaders" are corrupt (cf. Jer. 8:10-12; Mic. 3:11). In the present instance, however, no such insinuations immediately stand out. At most, the label heightens the drama by emphasizing the social distance between an "honored" Levite and the surrounding characters, particularly the concubine (Trible: 66).

The action of the account begins with an apparent rift between the Levite and his *concubine*. A concubine constitutes a legitimate though secondary marital partner (cf. 8:31). Unlike Gideon's concubine, however, who continued to reside elsewhere with her parents, the concubine in this case has left her home in Bethlehem and settled with the Levite. At some point in time, problems have erupted.

According to the Hebrew text and the NIV, the concubine instigates the difficulties by being *unfaithful* to him (19:2). Such unfaithfulness, however, seems somewhat incompatible with both the Levite's cordial quest for reconciliation (he went *to speak tenderly to her*) as well as the warm reception provided by her father. If unfaithfulness is the issue, then great embarrassment awaits the father, and death awaits the daughter (Lev. 20:10; Deut. 22:13-21). The Septuagint preserves another reason for the rift, supporting the NRSV's reading that the woman in fact *became angry with* the Levite *[Septuagint]*. In other words, an unspecified family squabble occurred, perhaps over abuse or mistreatment (cf. 19:25, 28). Insofar as Israelite law made no provision for a woman to divorce her husband, the concubine flees home.

After a time lapse of four months, the Levite arrives in Bethlehem in hope of regaining the runaway woman. What follows is a believable but perhaps comical—at least for those alien to the Near East—depiction of genuine hospitality. The father alone, as head of the household, can offer hospitality, which he does with great exuberance. Such apparent excitement, however, may partially mask a fear of returning a bride price if the marriage relationship ultimately dissolves (Matthews, 1992:7). In any case, the Levite remains a guest in his father-in-law's house for an initial period of three days (19:4). When his attempts to return home at that point meet with pressing pleas to remain, this initial period soon lengthens into five days! Finally, late on the fifth day, the Levite abandons conversation and, accompanied by his concubine and his servant, begins the journey home.

Nothing whatsoever is said about the woman's interests in all of this, nor do we encounter the Levite actually speaking *tenderly to her* (19:3), as he has clearly intended. Instead, the entire exchange involves only the Levite and his father-in-law. As Boling bluntly reminds us, "It was a man's world" (274; cf. Judg. 5).

The anxious travelers leave Bethlehem late in the afternoon. Even under the best of circumstances, insufficient daylight remains for the entire trip home. A decision will need to be made on where to spend the night. As events soon show, that decision, ironically brought about by the father-in-law's coaxing and the Levite's willingness to risk late-day travel, will change the entire course of events.

19:11-15 Gibeah Denies Hospitality

Some five miles into their northerly journey, the Levite and his companions approach the city of *Jebus* (19:11). Given the parenthetical comment in verse 10, *Jebus* is apparently the original name for Jerusalem prior to the Israelite conquest of the city under David (2 Sam. 5:6-16). In truth, however, the name *Jerusalem* already appears in both the Egyptian Execration Texts as well as the Amarna Letters, hundreds of years before the time of David *[Ancient Near Eastern Texts]*. The name *Jebus* never appears outside the Bible. In all likelihood, then, the city of Jerusalem never officially bore this alternate name. Rather, the name *Jebus* either serves as a secondary label describing the Jebusite population in pre-Davidic Jerusalem, or else it belongs to a site just north of Jerusalem, perhaps even the city's northern suburb (Miller: 115-127). In either case, Jebus is clearly a community of foreigners during the period of the judges.

Regardless of the ethnic makeup of the city, the servant quickly suggests that the group spend the night in Jebus (19:11). The Levite, by immediately dismissing such a suggestion, makes the fateful decision. In his mind, the Israelite towns of *Gibeah* and *Ramah* constitute more appropriate and no doubt more hopeful alternatives. Gibeah, probably contemporary Tell el Ful, was located some fives miles north of Jerusalem. Remembered primarily as the hometown of Saul and the center of activities during his reign (1 Sam. 10:26), the city belonged to the tribe of Benjamin. Ramah, also in Benjaminite territory, was situated about two miles north of Gibeah *[Map, p. 242]*. The remaining distance to these cities, despite the continually descending sun, is not sufficient reason for the Levite to risk the potentially unfriendly surroundings of Jebus. In his view, safe and secure quarters lay relatively close ahead.

By the time the group reaches Gibeah, the slightly more distant Ramah no longer remains an option; city gates close at sunset, and darkness is imminent. The Levite and his companions hope for a gracious host in Gibeah (19:15). Ancient cities typically had narrow streets; limited space prevented the construction of anything remotely resembling a modern town square. Instead, the interior section of the gate itself generally served as the congregating point; it is likely here that the weary but expectant travelers wait. Surprisingly, their waiting goes unnoticed—a remarkable and unanticipated violation of hospitality customs (19:15).

19:16-21 An Elderly Sojourner Extends Hospitality

The kindly old man who welcomes them is merely a sojourner (*ger*) in the area rather than a citizen; this forcefully underscores the social ineptitude of the Benjaminites themselves, who fail to offer hospitality. As a sojourner, the Ephraimite likely has no legal right to offer such accommodations (Van Nieuwenhuijze: 287). In the dialogue, the Levite alludes to an intended but previously unmentioned trip *to the house of the Lord* (Heb.: *bet yhwh;* 19:18, NIV). Though an eventual stopover at an unspecified sanctuary is possible, the phrase likely constitutes a simple misreading of the text at some point during transmission. Since the LXX reads *to my house,* the original form in Hebrew was likely *beti,* "my house" (as in NRSV) *[Septuagint].* However, a later scribe mistook *beti* as an abbreviation of *bet yhwh,* "house of the Lord," thereby exchanging the forms (Moore: 415-416). If so, then the Levite simply and understandably refers to his journey home (cf. 19:29).

The Levite's insinuation that he and his companions need nothing more than a roof over their heads may constitute a social insult, as Matthews suggests; yet its purpose in the present narrative remains clear enough (19:19; Matthews, 1992:8). The writer heaps further ridicule upon the uncaring people of Gibeah. The citizens of Gibeah could offer accommodation to the visitors without cost. What the citizens fail to do, the old man does: he opens his house, cares for the animals, extends the appropriate social graces, and promises to *care for all your wants* (19:20-21).

19:22-28 Men of Gibeah Abuse the Concubine

In a scene strikingly similar to that of Lot and his heavenly guests (Gen. 19), local *hoodlums* charge the door of the house (19:22). While the precise etymology of *beliya'al* ("hoodlums") remains uncertain, the sense is clear enough. These are *perverse* individuals who pay no regard to either the law or acceptable norms of human conduct (cf. 1 Sam. 2:12; 10:27). The term Belial later became a popular name for Satan in the writings from Qumran and elsewhere, appearing also in the NT (2 Cor. 6:15) *[Ancient Near Eastern Texts]*. The unwelcome intruders at the sojourner's house, it can be said, are "sons of the devil."

The hoodlums of Gibeah demand, *Bring out the man who came into your house, so that we may have intercourse* (*yada'*) *with him* (19:22). In spite of its various and well-documented nuances, here there can be no doubt about the meaning of the verb *yada'* (generally "to know"). "To know" may mean to acquire information. However, it also means to have close familiarity with and so, idiomatically, to have sexual relations with someone. The hoodlums have no friendly intent. They make no attempt, first of all, to meet the travelers during the initial waiting period by the city gate. Furthermore, they willingly receive an alternative victim with a lengthy sequence of sexual activities (19:25). The hoodlums' advance, therefore, is unquestionably sexual in nature (cf. Gen. 4:1; 19:5; 1 Kings 1:4).

The Ephraimite protests on the grounds of social decency. The Levite, after all, is a guest in the house and a visitor to the city. For the entire city to deny him hospitality is appalling enough. To add to that by committing a sexual atrocity is for the old man unthinkable. Remarkably, however, he unhesitatingly offers both the concubine as well as his *virgin* daughter as alternatives (19:24)! The concubine, of course, is not his to give, and the daughter constitutes his own flesh and blood (Lasine: 39; Trible: 74). Once again, an Israelite father endangers his virgin daughter in a moment of desperate thoughtlessness (cf. 11:29-40).

In spite of such impassioned pleading, the hoodlums reject the old man's proposal. Before they can act further, however, the Levite himself forcibly delivers his concubine to the waiting mob. Clearly, the concubine finds no support from the man who only days earlier journeyed to Bethlehem *to speak tenderly to her* (19:3). Somewhere, lost in the shuffle, stands the virgin daughter. What is for the concubine a night of horror becomes for the Ephraimite's daughter a night of reprieve.

Gibeah's hoodlums disregard their former intentions concerning the Levite and ruthlessly abuse the concubine throughout the night.

Eventually she stumbles back to the house where she has been forsaken just a few hours before. Bargained away by the old man, abandoned by her husband, and exploited by the hoodlums—she has lost everything. All that remains is the inevitable discovery of her return and the accompanying hope for assistance.

Such hope, however, is unfulfilled. Everything suggests that the Levite fully intends to return home without her (19:27)! Stumbling upon the woman in the morning, the Levite, without any hint of compassion or concern, instructs, *Get up; . . . we are going* (19:28). When no response is forthcoming, the Levite loads her like baggage on one of his donkeys and begins the trip home. Is the woman dead? Is she comatose? Is she asleep? Although the LXX officially announces that the woman is dead, the Hebrew text is more ambivalent, leaving the concubine's immediate fate up to the reader's imagination (Polzin: 200-201) *[Septuagint]*.

THE TEXT IN BIBLICAL CONTEXT

Domestic Violence

At times, people unknowingly assume that biblical characters always lived exemplary lives. The shocking scene in Judges 19 quickly dispels any such assumptions. Not only do characters in the Bible sometimes fail to live godly lives, but they occasionally save their worst behavior for members of their own families. Examples of what might generally be called domestic violence or abuse appear already in Genesis, when Cain slays his brother Abel (4:1-16), Sarah and Abraham abandon Hagar and Ishmael (21:8-14), Jacob torments his other sons by showing favoritism to Joseph (37:1-4), and these same sons in turn sell Joseph to a group of caravaneers heading toward Egypt (37:25-36).

To these can be added several other instances from elsewhere in the Bible, including Amnon raping his half-sister Tamar (2 Sam. 13:1-22), David neglecting his son Absalom (2 Sam. 14:28), and various religious leaders failing to care for aging parents (Mark 7:9-13).

In the biblical world, family life is often as turbulent as life in society at large. Yet the Bible seeks to speak a fresh and countercultural word. Children are a gift from God (Ps. 127:3; Prov. 17:6), a wife is cause for celebration (Gen. 2:23; Prov. 31:10; Mal. 2:15), and elderly parents are worthy of honor (Prov. 20:20). Instructions are repeatedly provided to encourage healthy and harmonious relationships within family contexts (Deut. 21:15-17; Prov. 23:22; Eph. 5:21—6:4; Col. 3:18-21; 1 Pet. 3:7). Caring for one's family is so highly regarded in Scripture that a failure to do so constitutes nothing less than a denial of the Christian faith (1 Tim 5:8).

THE TEXT IN THE LIFE OF THE CHURCH
Abusing Our Own

"Among other mammals," writes Andrew Vachss, a lawyer specializing in child abuse cases,

> non-protective parents are considered defective by other pack members, . . . and so they are expelled. Likewise, predators within a species will not be tolerated. They are banished, avoided, or killed. These are not moral judgments; they are biologically driven and, among all species but our own, compelling. (5)

The fundamental problem of the human species, Vachss adds, is that "we are not protecting and preserving our own" (4).

While Vachss focuses on child abuse issues in particular, the problem of domestic violence encompasses victims of various ages and situations. Such abuse, according to R. M. Hanson, refers to "the perversion/misuse of the privilege of caring for another person, e.g., a child, elderly relative, or spouse" (136). Further, abusive behaviors need not be physical in nature. Categories of abuse include but are not necessarily limited to sexual, emotional, physical neglect, and nonaccidental injury. People can do considerable harm to family members in a great variety of ways.

To face the problem of domestic violence head-on, Christians need to keep several things in mind:

• Incidences of domestic violence are plentiful and increasing. While precise statistics are difficult to determine, over 200,000 cases of child abuse alone are reported in the United States each year. Others estimate that as many as 1 out of 10 people in America suffer from domestic abuse of one type or another (Hanson: 136). To make matters worse, accounts from other countries indicate that the problem spreads well beyond national borders (Poling). One can only wonder how many of the victims sit in the pews of local churches on any given Sunday. The church simply cannot ignore the issue anymore. We must make pastoral efforts to reach out to the wounded victims.

• Christians must stop using selected biblical texts to condone or even encourage various forms of domestic abuse. As Riffat Hasson points out, "Religion has been used very widely historically . . . as a legitimization for the abuse that women suffer" (Religious News Service: 123). When interpreting and applying passages dealing with submission, for example, great care must be taken not to open the door to destructive behaviors. People's welfare and very lives are at stake.

• In our efforts to minister to the victims of abuse, we must not casually forget the culprits who stand behind the crimes. Vachss is surely justified in criticizing society's current tendency to worry about the rights of the predators more so than the prey (4). Yet the church simply cannot ignore the abusers, many of whom were themselves victims of similar abuse earlier in life. As Joyce Hollyday so thoughtfully writes,

> I fear rape, and humiliation, and the physical power of men who batter and bruise—and sometimes kill. I don't know any woman who hasn't at some point in her life had to face the truth of her vulnerability. But I also consider it a great privilege to be allowed into the thoughts and feelings of the men in that room. Somehow, it seems to me, we are all—women and men—entangled in this brokenness together. And we need to find our way out together. (29)

Hospitality

While traveling through Jordan a few years ago, I was offered a ride by a Palestinian truck driver. After gladly accepting, Nyfe (the driver) and I stumbled through a conversation severely limited by a language barrier. That barrier, however, did not prevent him from extending to me the greatest demonstration of hospitality I have ever experienced. What began with a simple ride ended up including an impromptu dinner with his extended family, a night's lodging, breakfast, and a valuable farewell gift! In much of the Middle East, hospitality is not a secondary and often-neglected social grace, but a way of life.

How different this is from life as many Westerners know it. Given busy schedules, rampant individualism, and the apparent lack of safety in many of our neighborhoods, hospitality has often become a forgotten art. At best, hospitality is relegated to occasional visits from those who are already family and friends. What we can learn from many Middle Easterners is what the Bible has been teaching all along: hospitality involves extending life to those who are otherwise unknown to us (Janzen: 43). Hospitality, according to Joan Chittister,

> is the act of giving what you have to everyone in sight. It is not a series of grand gestures at controlled times. It is not a finishing-school activity. It is an act of the recklessly generous heart. (132)

EXPLANATORY NOTES

Israel Debates a Grievous Crime 19:29—20:11

With the previous hideous scene in mind, the writer now turns his attention to the crucial intertribal conflict between Benjamin and the remaining Israelites. One assumes that Gibeah's gross mistreatment of the Levite's party in general and the concubine in particular give rise to the ensuing and extensive military adventures. A parallel to these events is found in chapters 17–18, where Micah's personal activities similarly give rise to the Danite sanctuary.

The civil war may date earlier than is implied. The stationing of the ark of the covenant at Bethel, for example, apparently alludes to a time before its arrival at Shiloh (20:26-28; cf. 18:31). Likewise, Phinehas, still alive and serving as the priest at Bethel (20:28), has played a key role already during the wilderness wanderings and conquest (Num. 25; 31:6; Josh. 22:10-34).

Finally, the tribe of Benjamin, though typically small, is relatively strong and well-established as the period of the Judges actually comes to a close. Indeed, the Benjaminite Saul becomes Israel's first king, and his hometown serves as the center of operations (1 Sam. 9:1-2, 21; 10:20-21; 2 Sam. 21:14). If the central events here do occur early in the period, then the writer has once again positioned materials on the basis of theology rather than chronology. More important than the precise sequence of events is the unmistakable qualitative decline that so characterizes the times.

19:29-30 A Levite Broadcasts the Deed

Upon arriving home, the Levite secures a butcher knife and methodically and ritualistically dismembers the concubine. Then, in a manner similar to Saul's method of notifying the Israelites concerning the troubles of Jabesh-gilead, all of the twelve resulting pieces are sent via messengers throughout the land (1 Sam. 11:7). Each of the twelve tribes, including Benjamin, receives one section of the mutilated body.

According to the Hebrew text, the messengers who deliver the bizarre packages remain speechless; only the astonished recipients speak (19:30, NRSV footnote). The LXX, however, suggests that the Levite has instructed each messenger to challenge the Israelites: *Thus shall you say to all the Israelites, "Has such a thing ever happened since the day that the Israelites came up from the land of Egypt until this day? Consider it, take counsel, and speak out"* (NRSV) *[Septuagint].* Only then do the horrified onlookers make a response.

20:1-7 The Israelites Assemble at Mizpah

The collective gathering of Israel *before the Lord at Mizpah* is an example of the intertribal alliance operative prior to the monarchy. The phrase *Dan to Beersheba* constitutes a later standardized expression based upon the limits of Israel's territorial holdings during David's time and beyond (2 Sam. 17:11; 24:2; 1 Kings 4:25) *[Map, p. 242].*

The editorial remark, therefore, updates the geographical setting for subsequent generations.

The name *Mizpah* ("watchtower") actually refers to no less than five distinct places in Palestine, but the context here points to the Mizpah of Benjamin. Two contemporary sites frequently associated with this place are Nebi Samwil, some five miles north of Jerusalem, and Tell en-Nasbeh, three miles further north of there. Of the two, the current archaeological record speaks more supportively of Tell en-Nasbeh.

In this setting, Mizpah functions simply as the place of assembly. Bethel, as the following verses indicate, serves as the sanctuary where oracles are sought.

At this gathering, *four hundred thousand* armed soldiers are present, a number that exceeds imaginable limits (20:2). Some suggest understanding the term *'elep* ("thousand") as a military unit, thus meaning "four hundred contingents" (Boling: 280). For that matter, the function of such large figures throughout the OT remains frustratingly evasive. At least, the writer seeks to emphasize the overwhelming response given to the summons. Of equal importance to the large number of participants, however, is the noteworthy absence of the Benjaminites. Assuming that they too have received a portion of the woman's dismembered body, their absence constitutes a refusal to participate in the tribal confederation's proceedings. Later events will point to the same conclusion (20:13).

In summarizing his experiences, the Levite adds or reshapes two bits of information. First, he suggests that the hoodlums of Gibeah actually have sought to take his own life (20:5). This may be a purely interpretive conclusion, for the culprits never said any such thing. In fact, the death of the concubine herself appears at most as a later consequence of their sexual activities rather than an intended outcome.

Second, the Levite now verifies that the woman was dead when he found her outside of the house that morning. Since there is no one to refute his testimony, both the Israelite leaders as well as later readers have no choice but to accept what the Hebrew text earlier refused to mention (cf. 19:28).

20:8-11 The Israelites Plan Their Response

In an emotionally charged atmosphere, the Israelites unanimously direct their attention against Gibeah (20:9). Until the problem finds resolution, no one will return to either his tent (*'ohel*) or house (*bayit*), an inclusive pair of parallel terms depicting Israel's nomadic past and sedentary present. No attempt is made to ascertain the Lord's direction; no oracle is sought until the decision to fight has already been established (20:18). From all indications, the tribal assembly has itself assumed the responsibility of declaring war.

The leaders cast lots to determine the marching orders. Since 10 percent of the fighting forces are delegated the responsibility of overseeing the distribution of rations, a quick victory is not anticipated. The Israelites will march against Gibeah—the Hebrew text of 20:10 reads *Geba* (cf. 20:33), which actually lies nearly three miles further northeast—and repay its citizens for the *disgrace* (*nebalah*). The term *nebalah* typically designates a blatant and disgusting disregard of God's will or law, at times specifying sexual offenses (Gen. 34:7; Deut. 22:21; 2 Sam. 13:12). As subsequent events make plain, at least in the minds of the combined Israelite forces, such a hideous crime merits the severest of punishments, even if the unified Israelites have the statement of only one man (cf. Deut. 17:6).

THE TEXT IN BIBLICAL CONTEXT
Ratings on Wrongs

Denied hospitality. Emotional and sexual abuse. Murder. Mutilated remains. The shock of this entire scandal at Gibeah did not pass quickly, becoming instead an ugly benchmark in Israel's history (Hos. 9:9; 10:9).

In paying particular attention to the way biblical characters and writers react to grotesque evil, one notes a sense of amazement from beginning to end. The writer of Kings, for example, measures the degree of evil: Jeroboam establishes a religious system of his choosing (1 Kings 12:25-33), Omri "sinned more than all those before him" (1 Kings 16:25), and Manasseh "has done more evil than the Amorites who preceded him" (2 Kings 21:11; cf. 2 Chron. 33:9).

In the prophetic literature, the same note of disbelief rings again and again. Isaiah considers Israel's level of understanding to be less than that of an ox or donkey (1:3). Jeremiah cannot locate even one just person in all of Jerusalem (5:1). Malachi, groping for suitable metaphors, suggests that Judah treats God in a manner that would be totally unacceptable to either a father, master, or governor (1:6-8). Finally, in sheer exasperation, Jeremiah concludes, "Most devious is the heart; it is perverse—who can fathom it?" (17:9, Jewish Publication Society).

This sense of amazement continues on the pages of the NT. Jesus categorizes the vast assortment of wicked deeds performed by human beings (Matt. 15:19). So too with Paul, who prefaces a lengthy list of his own with the sweeping statement that the godless "were filled with every kind of wickedness" (Rom. 1:29). Worse yet, such evil infiltrates the community of faith itself. Just as the Israelites reacted in horror to something that took place within their own tribal alliance, now Paul exclaims to the people in Corinth: "It is actually reported that there is sexual immorality among you, and of a kind that is not found even among pagans" (1 Cor. 5:1). Evil retains its shocking ugliness. Indeed, the array of ghastly feats achievable by human beings appears to know no limits. Clearly, nothing short of God's grace can put an end to such unthinkable confusion (Rom. 3:21-26; 5:12-21).

THE TEXT IN THE LIFE OF THE CHURCH
Sensitivity and Balance

With constant reports in Western news media of corruption in government, poverty, and an assortment of other ills worldwide, Christians must avoid two extreme responses. Some people "get used to it." What would previously have caused great concern now appears ordinary and even tolerable. Others may wring their hands in fear and despair, forgetting the power of God to redeem even the worst of situations. Somewhere between these two extremes lies a more balanced and biblical perspective.

In reflecting upon their own experiences in various places around the world, Henri Nouwen, Donald McNeill, and Douglas Morrison arrive at just such a perspective. "Exposure to human misery on a mass scale," they write,

> can lead not only to psychic numbness but also to hostility. This might seem strange, but when we look more closely at the human response to disturbing information, we realize that confrontation with human pain often creates anger instead of care, irritation instead of sympathy, and even fury instead of compassion. . . . In the most horrendous way, this was the case in the Nazi, Vietnamese, and Chilean concentration camps, where torture and cruelty seemed easier the worse the prisoners looked. (54)

The question then is, how can we who follow Christ see the agony and evil in the world and yet be moved to sympathy as he was when confronted by a crowd of hungry people (Matt. 14:14)? To this, Nouwen, McNeill, and Morrison respond,

> As long as we depend on our own limited resources, the world will frighten us, and we will try to avoid the painful spots. But once we have become the participants in God's compassion, we can enter deeply into the most-hidden corners of the world and perform the same works Christ did; indeed, we may perform even greater works (John 14:12)! (57)

EXPLANATORY NOTES

Israel Repays the Wayward Benjaminites 20:12-48

In spite of apparent unity and optimism, the Israelites actually suffer two setbacks before finally emerging victorious in the conflict. Importantly, each of these two defeats follows specific instructions from the Lord to proceed with the battle. Through the entire ordeal, therefore, God actually punishes both the Benjaminites and the remaining tribes for their increasingly unfaithful behavior (Webb: 194). What at first appears to be a triumph for Israel's combined forces, is in reality a cauldron for mutual suffering and correction.

20:12-17 The Israelites Confront the Benjaminites

Prior to the military campaign, the Israelites rightfully encourage the people of Benjamin to surrender the guilty individuals. No investigative inquiry of any kind is initiated. Both the verdict and sentence have already been determined, again on the basis of a single testimony (cf. Deut. 17:6).

The Benjaminites express a solidarity of their own, perhaps to demonstrate an indifference to the crime and identify themselves with the men of Gibeah. More likely, the Benjaminites simply accuse the Israelites of turning an otherwise interfamily dispute into an intertribal one by circumventing lower judicial channels, including the exercising of vengeance by a close relative (McKenzie: 166). Either way, the Benjaminites refuse to surrender the culprits and instead prepare themselves for war.

In contrast to the combined forces of the opposing tribes, the Benjaminites muster some *twenty-six thousand armed men*, itself a large number (20:15). Beyond these general troops, they also mobilize a special contingent of *seven hundred picked men*. Each of these men has been particularly trained both to fight with his left hand as well as to handle a sling with consummate skill (notes on 3:15). Such training, coupled with the Benjaminites' familiarity with the surrounding landscape, would serve them well in most confrontations. Nevertheless, the Benjamite troops appear negligible in comparison to the more numerous opposition (20:17).

20:18-28 The Benjaminites Defeat the Israelites

With the battle lines drawn, the Israelites for the first time seek an oracle from God at *Bethel* (20:18). The name Bethel (*bet 'el*) literally means "house of God." There is some debate as to whether the city of Bethel or an unnamed sanctuary is actually referred to here. Boling, for example, suggests that the Israelites seek this first oracle at the lesser-known "house of God" at Mizpah (285). Typically, however, references to sanctuaries include *'elohim,* the longer term for God, rather than the shorter form *'el.* Furthermore, as Boling himself acknowledges, both the allusion to the ark of the covenant as well as the road information clearly indicate that the city of Bethel itself appears later in the story (20:26-27, 31). It seems best, therefore, to read "Bethel" throughout. Mizpah, once again, constitutes the gathering place for the tribal assembly (20:1). Bethel serves as the sanctuary where oracles are obtained (20:18, 26-28).

The Israelites specifically ask, *Which of us shall go up first to battle against the Benjaminites?* Frighteningly, this is the same question that the community asked at the outset of the book, though under entirely different circumstances (1:1). Rather than embarking on an offensive campaign against the Canaanites, the Israelites now turn to destroy themselves! The Lord's answer is identical to the earlier one: *Judah shall go up first* (1:2; 20:18). Is Israel on the verge of starting over again? Here, however, there is no promise of success.

The Benjaminites abruptly rout the Israelites, leaving them broken and theologically confused. Virtually all commentators agree that, for some reason, verses 22 and 23 have been inverted. By adjusting the order, the story flows far smoother. Following their initial defeat, the deflated Israelites seek yet another message from the Lord (20:23). On this occasion, they do not ask who should go first, but "Shall we go?" Clearly, doubts as to their original strategy have begun to set in. In response to the inquiry, God once again instructs them to confront the Benjaminites. Only after receiving this apparent word of confirmation—we still find no promise of success—do they return to the battle line *where they had formed it on the first day* (20:22).

As before, the Benjaminites inflict severe casualties upon Israel in the second attack. Mournfully, the Israelites return to Bethel, for both *the ark of the covenant of God* and *Phinehas son of Eleazar* are currently stationed (20:27-28). Mentioned nowhere else in the book of Judges, the ark was a portable chest containing at least the tablets of the law (Deut. 10:2, 5; cf. Heb. 9:4). Importantly, it serves as a tangible expression or symbol of God's presence. The Israelites occasionally attributed magical qualities to it (e.g., 1 Sam. 4:3). Following a time of some movement, including the situation depicted here at Bethel, the ark came to rest more permanently in Shiloh and still later in Jerusalem (1 Sam. 4:3; 2 Sam. 6:12-19). Phinehas has served a significant and acclaimed role during both the wilderness wandering as well as the conquest (notes on 19:29—20:11). Together, the ark and

Phinehas underscore the influence and importance of Bethel in the story.

While at Bethel, the increasingly desperate Israelites weep, fast, and engage in sacrificial rites. *Burnt offerings*, the most common variety, either serve as a means of securing atonement or accompany petitions (Lev. 1). *Sacrifices of well-being*, frequently referred to as "peace offerings," involve either the giving of thanks or the general desire for harmonious relations (Lev. 7:11-18). With two military defeats and God's disfavor, the presentation of both types seemingly reflects the Israelites' desire for forgiveness as well as acceptance. Such offerings also set the stage for the third and final inquiry concerning a potential attack against the Benjaminites.

The recurring inquiries directed to the Lord, as legitimate as they may at first appear, cannot conceal the true horror of the situation. The actual wording of Israel's successive petitions betrays the underlying pain. Whereas the opening appeal simply refers to *the Benjaminites*, the final two add the qualifier *our kinsfolk* (20:18, 23, 28). Now, rather than offensively attacking their external opponents, as in Judges 1:1, the Israelites point their weapons at each other. This is, therefore, a resounding illustration of internal conflict and self-extermination.

20:29-48 The Israelites Ambush the Benjaminites

In the narrative describing the third conflict, two largely parallel accounts appear. In 20:29-36a, the writer presents a general overview, concluding with a tally of the casualties. Then he provides a second depiction in which greater attention is given to both the ambush as well as the Benjaminites' eventual retreat (20:36b-48).

Precisely where the Israelite ambush lies in waiting remains unclear. The Hebrew of 20:33 actually reads "Geba," a city some three miles to the northeast, rather than "Gibeah" (cf. notes on 20:10). If the reading "Geba" stands, then the ambush is situated somewhere just to the northeast of Gibeah. On the other hand, if the text is emended to read "Gibeah" (so NIV), an alteration that finds some support in the LXX and other manuscripts, then the ambush lies just to the west of Gibeah *[Septuagint]*.

What follows is an encounter in which the Israelites achieve a total victory. Since the writer is more interested in impressions and impact than in a full description of battle detail, he makes no attempt to smooth off the number of casualties and survivors. According to the initial statement, 25,100 Benjaminites die in the fighting (20:35). In the second account, a total of 25,000 perish (20:46). Eighteen thousand of these die during the initial confrontation. The remaining 7,000 are cut down during an easterly chase scene that concludes near the unidentifiable site of *Gidom* (20:44-46). There are *six hundred* survivors, but in neither reckoning do they remain from the original 26,000 (20:15). What is clear, however, is that the overwhelming majority of Benjaminites lose their lives *[Historicity and Truth]*.

With the battle clearly over, a small and exhausted remnant of Benjaminites escape their attackers and take refuge at *the rock of Rimmon* (20:47); its exact location remains uncertain. A modern town preserving the name Rammun is located approximately four miles east of Bethel. This fact, coupled with references to the desert in the narrative, points to a general area northeast of Gibeah (20:45, 47). There they remain, no doubt sheltered in caves like thousands of others throughout the centuries, for a period of *four months.* Although the length of their sojourn is perhaps of no particular significance, it is an interesting parallel to the runaway concubine remaining in Bethlehem for four months before the Levite seeks her return (19:2-3). Four months after this intertribal catastrophe, the Israelites will similarly approach the remnant of Benjaminites (21:13).

Meanwhile, however, the combined Israelite forces make no apparent attempt to chase down the few surviving soldiers. Instead, they turn their attention to the surrounding Benjaminite towns, populated at this point by older men, women, and children. These towns, after all, supplied the troops who have since been killed in the fighting. By slaughtering every living thing and subsequently burning the cities (20:48), the Israelites seemingly place the entire tribe of Benjamin under what is typically referred to as "the ban."

The ban, *ḥerem,* was part of Israel's understanding of holy war: various enemies had to be "devoted to the Lord for destruction" (as in Josh. 6:17). This act of destruction helped to keep Israel from later contact and contamination. Normally, such drastic measures were either taken against Israel's external opponents or reserved for internal cases involving pervasive idolatry (notes on 1:17; 21:11; cf. Deut. 2:34; 3:6; 13:12-18; Josh. 6–7) *[Violence and War in Judges].*

In the present instance, however, the procedure stems from Gibeah's abuse of the concubine. Is this a case of grossly inflated retaliation? Do the Israelites actually implement this form of punishment in compliance with a divine oracle? The deep regret, change of policy, and preventive measures that soon follow suggest otherwise. Israel will actually attempt to undo or at least minimize the lingering effects of the deed.

THE TEXT IN BIBLICAL CONTEXT
God as Commander-in-Chief

The Israelites' formal inquiry of the Lord about military strategies (20:18, 23, 28) reflects what Boling refers to as a "commander-in-chief" view of God (54; cf. 1:1). God, who many times in the Bible is called the "Lord of hosts (armies)," leads the way (e.g., 2 Sam. 5:10; Ps. 24:10; Isa. 47:4; Jer. 2:19; Amos 5:14; Hag. 1:5). Precisely the same view frequently appears in the later strategizing of Israel's leaders, although with varying degrees of sincerity. David, for example, inquires of the Lord with respect to both his impending kingship as well as a potential attack against the Philistines (2 Sam. 2:1; 5:19). So too do Ahab, Jehoshaphat, and Zedekiah, all of whom seek counsel in the face of military confrontations (1 Kings 22:8; 2 Kings 3:11; 2 Chron. 18:7; Jer. 21:2; 37:7).

Finally, both Josiah and the elders of Israel solicit divine messages, not due to the threat of immediate invasion, but because of serious religious corruption infesting their constituencies (2 Kings 22:13, 18; 2 Chron. 34:21, 26; Ezek. 20:1, 3). In each of these instances, the heavenly commander provides some response, although not necessarily what the inquirer hopes to hear. Not so with Saul, whose sole and overdue attempt to inquire of the Lord ends in divine silence (1 Sam. 28:6; cf. 1 Chron. 10:14). As a result, this otherwise self-serving and increasingly desperate king inquires of a witch instead (1 Sam. 28:7)!

In-House Fighting

Conflict among the people of Israel neither begins nor ends in Judges 20. Rarely, however, does it reach greater proportions. The dissension poisoning Jacob and Esau is followed by the massive demonstration at the foot of Sinai (Gen. 27:41-45; Exod. 32). Shortly thereafter, significant contention arises during the wilderness wandering over the question of leadership (Num. 12:1-16; 16). Similar difficulties surround the inception of kingship. The eventual transmission of kingly rule routinely results in severe competition, repeated assassinations, and extensive popular unrest (1 Sam. 8; 1 Kings 2:13-46; 15:27; 16:10, 15-19). In fact, the entire nation splits in two when such communal unrest defies a congenial resolution (1 Kings 12).

Finally, subsequent events reveal increasing class distinctions, preferential treatment in the courts, and constant disputes between political and religious officials (1 Kings 16:13-14; 2 Chron. 18:11-27; Isa. 10:1-4; 31:1-9; Jer. 26:7-9; 28; 38:1-13; Amos 2:6-8; 7:10-17).

From beginning to end, the OT depicts recurring scenes of these and
other squabbles that permeate the people of Israel.

Sadly, the community of faith in the NT continues at times this
unenviable manner of internal operation. Indeed, Jesus himself senses
the weight of such conflict and specifically prays for the unity of those
who follow him (John 17:20-21). Nevertheless, the disciples argue
over their status in the kingdom of God (Matt. 18:1; 20:20-28; Mark
9:33-37; Luke 9:46). The believers in Corinth compete over varying
religious leaders (1 Cor. 1:10-17). The church at large apparently
alienates the poor in favor of the rich (James 2:1-13). Although unity
and love remain the distinguishing characteristics of the followers of
Jesus, dissension and conflict frequently linger (1 John 4:7-12).

THE TEXT IN THE LIFE OF THE CHURCH

Denominational Divisions

"Better a dry crust with peace and quiet," declares an ancient sage,
"than a house full of feasting, with strife" (Prov. 17:1). Jesus chal-
lenged his disciples to live and work together harmoniously. Love, he
declared, is the fundamental indication that individuals are really his
followers (John 13:35). Such love has not always typified the life and
work of the church over the centuries.

To understand the point, one need only recall the breaks between
the Eastern and Western churches as well at the subsequent rift separating the Catholic and Protestant traditions in the West. Segments
within the church at large have forcibly repressed alternative voices.
The persecution of such groups as the early Anabaptists at the hands
of other Christians, for example, eerily resembles the near destruction
of the Benjaminites by the remaining tribes. Even now, the resulting
wounds and scars of multiple conflicts continue in the form of innu-
merable disjointed and disfigured traditions that rarely have dealings
with each other. Even when intergroup interaction occurs, derogato-
ry tones can be expected.

To illustrate the painful irony of such disunity, Tom Skinner
employs Paul's vocabulary about the "armor of God" (Eph. 6:10-20).
This armor, as Skinner points out, is intended to assist the church in
carrying out the redemptive and at times endangering work of Christ
in the world. All too often, however, otherwise inactive Christians turn
and use the various weapons against each other. Protestants repeatedly stab all Catholics. Dispensationalists draw blood from
Charismatics. Methodists refuse to eat at the same table with
Episcopalians. Fundamentalists and Liberals simply disown each
other. And on and on. While such caricaturing may at first glance be

amusing, the painful truth is that God's kingdom bears the dirty stain. After all, a house divided eventually falls (Matt. 12:25; Mark 3:24; Luke 11:17).

The cry of Menno Simons, a sixteenth-century reformer, lingers to this day:

> The anguish of my soul is at times so great, greater than I can write. May the mighty God strengthen me. And this because I see that the house of the Lord has to endure so many offenses, not only from without, but, alas! also from within. (996)

EXPLANATORY NOTES

Israel Preserves the Shattered Benjaminites 21:1-24

With the Benjaminites on the verge of extinction, the remaining Israelites face the overwhelming prospect of losing an entire tribe from their number (21:1-4). To avert such a tragedy, two distinct and seemingly parallel measures are taken to provide the surviving Benjaminite soldiers with wives. The first of these involves the annihilation of yet another group of Israelites, sparing only the virgins (21:5-14). The second entails the kidnapping of dancing girls during an annual festival (21:15-24).

21:1-4 The Israelites Mourn the Loss of the Benjaminites

The preceding extermination of the Benjaminites, with only the six hundred soldiers hiding in the desert remaining (20:47), constitutes the virtual loss of a related tribe. This already-serious situation is all the more serious in the light of an otherwise unknown *oath* taken previously at *Mizpah* (notes on 20:1). According to that oath, none of the other Israelites will be permitted to allow their daughters to marry a Benjaminites (21:1). Inevitably, the six hundred remaining soldiers would therefore die out.

To appreciate more fully the severity of such a situation, one need only remember that an entire social safeguard existed in ancient Israel to prevent a single family from dying out! According to the levirate law, if a man died childless, his brother was required to marry the widow and produce an heir for him (Deut. 25:5-10). Otherwise, the deceased man's name would be forever forgotten, and him with it. How much worse, then, is the prospect of watching an entire tribe disappear.

It is precisely this prospect that sends the weeping Israelites back to *Bethel*. Once there, they again present *burnt offerings and sacrifices of well-being* (21:4; notes on 20:26). Why they need to build another altar, however, remains unclear. It may have some specific

association with the coming events, or perhaps it actually stands at
Mizpah rather than Bethel (Burney: 488; Cundall: 208). In any case,
no response from God is forthcoming. From all indications, the
Israelites are left to handle this situation on their own.

21:5-14 The Benjaminites Receive Wives from Jabesh-gilead

To secure wives for the remaining Benjaminites, the Israelites first
check the attendance records from their original assembly at Mizpah
(21:5, 8; cf. 20:1). Apparently, the participants at that gathering have
taken a second oath that similarly comes to bear on the present
predicament. In addition to withholding their own women from the
Benjaminites, the Israelites have agreed that the severity of Gibeah's
crime has made participation in the tribal assembly mandatory. As a
result, the entire community has sworn that any group failing to
attend will *be put to death* (21:5). In spite of the enormous ongoing
complications created by such decisions, both the absolute importance
of the spoken word as well as the solemnity of a vow prevent either
oath from now being rescinded (TBC after 12:7, on vows).

Through some unspecified means, the Israelites recount the participants and eventually determine that the people of *Jabesh-gilead*
boycotted the assembly (21:9). As the qualifier "Gilead" indicates,
Jabesh was situated somewhere east of the Jordan River. Scholars
have suggested various sites in northern Gilead, where the Wadi el-
Yabis clearly preserves the name; yet the precise location of the town
remains uncertain.

After determining Jabesh-gilead's absence, the Israelites send a
contingent of *twelve thousand soldiers* for what must have been a
distance of nearly forty-five miles, to carry out the oath (21:10).
Nowhere are these men told to seek reasons for the Jabeshites' failure to come. Likely the assembly simply assumes that earlier marital
connections between Gilead and Benjamin are to blame (cf. 1 Chron.
7:12, 15). Rather, the contingent is instructed to utterly destroy (ḥrm)
every living thing, sparing only the young virgins [*Violence and War
in Judges*]. The young virgins are protected solely for utilitarian reasons; they will marry the Benjaminites. For the second time in this
sequence of events, then, the Israelite community places other
Israelites under the ban, *ḥerem* (notes on 1:17; 20:48).

With their mission completed, the soldiers escort *the four hundred young virgins* back to *Shiloh* (21:12). Precisely why the assembly has restationed at Shiloh, however, is unmentioned. Context suggests, once again, that Shiloh is not yet the central sanctuary it will
later become. In fact, precise directions are required to explain its geo-

graphical position (21:19)! Perhaps its more northerly location simply makes easier the return of both the soldiers as well as the Benjaminite survivors. After all, Shiloh, identified with modern Khirbet Seilun, lay nearly ten miles northeast of Bethel, in the general direction of Jabesh-gilead [Map, p. 242]. For whatever reason, the tribal assembly waits there and receives the returning party.

With the young women of Jabesh-gilead now in their custody, the Israelites finally summon the beleaguered Benjaminites (21:13; cf. 20:47). With the summons comes an offer to normalize relations and establish *peace* (*šalom*). Word of the virgins from Jabesh-gilead no doubt adds credibility to the offer, so the escapees abandon their hideout.

The intermarrying between the two tribes at least partially explains later events. The Benjaminite Saul, for example, protects the people of Jabesh-gilead in the face of Ammonite aggression (1 Sam. 11). Similarly, the citizens of Jabesh-gilead remove the bodies of Saul and his sons from their humiliating perches in Beth Shan (1 Sam. 31:11-13). Sadly, however, any celebration associated with the present events soon fades in the light of grim reality: *but they [virgins] did not suffice for them* (21:14). As the following story makes clear, the Israelite assembly will soon rectify that.

21:15-24 The Benjaminites Seize Wives at Shiloh

With two hundred Benjaminites still in need of wives, the assembly is forced to consider other options. Since the people of Jabesh-gilead were apparently alone in boycotting the original gathering, intertribal massacres no longer remain an alternative. Instead, the Israelites must find an entirely different approach. Quickly, just such an approach presents itself.

In this latest solution to the Benjaminite problem, attention turns to an unnamed and obscure *yearly festival of the Lord . . . at Shiloh* (21:19). The writer consistently implies that the ceremony involves Israelites who worship the Lord and who can likewise be held accountable for the infamous oath at Mizpah (21:1, 18, 22). If the Shilohites are in fact Israelites, however, then why are they unaware of the ongoing proceedings? Did they not have representation at the intertribal assembly? Or if the people of Shiloh constitute a Canaanite settlement not yet under Israelite control, then how can they be held accountable for honoring the oath (21:18, 22)? Worse yet, if they are Canaanites, then why are they considered desirable for marriage? Such questions find no immediate answers in the narrative itself (Gray: 363; Soggin: 304-305).

Of more significance, given the writer's purposes, is the fundamental unfamiliarity implied in the precise description of the location
of both the festival and Shiloh (notes on 21:12). On one level, such
an unfamiliarity stems from the fact that Shiloh has not yet gained the
importance associated with it later (1 Sam. 1–4). On another level,
however, the need for explanations and directions insinuates that the
people of Israel during the time of these events pay far too little attention to things of religious importance, including Shiloh and the festivals (Boling: 293). Such matters remain largely unknown.

Enough is known, however, for the Israelite strategists to design a
devilish plan that at least calls to mind the fate of the Levite's concubine. According to the plan, particular attention focuses on a period
during the festival when the local girls join in the celebratory dancing
(21:21). Before this event, the two hundred unmarried Benjaminites
are to find suitable hiding places in the surrounding vineyards. When
the girls of Shiloh appear, each waiting Benjaminite can suddenly
seize the woman of his choice.

Finally, the Israelite leaders themselves promise to handle the
expected backlash from the men of Shiloh (21:22). In so doing, they
will appeal to both mercy as well as innocence. With respect to mercy,
the failure of these remaining Benjaminites to receive wives during the
earlier assault on Jabesh-gilead ought to encourage a gracious
response now. Concerning innocence, the fact that the Shilohites
have not actually given their young women to the Benjaminites means
that they themselves have never violated the first oath (21:1). Clearly,
the plan covers all the details, even the anticipated responses.

Without any noticeable hesitation or reluctance, the Benjaminites
go and methodically carry out the plan (21:23). Whether or not the
men of Shiloh ever respond in the envisioned manner, however, goes
unmentioned. Indeed, nothing suggests any resistance or hindrance
whatsoever. Instead, the Benjaminites seize their wives, return home,
and rebuild their cities. With countless people stampeded in the
process, the pressing problem concerning the potential extermination of the tribe of Benjamin finds resolution. As a result, the
Israelites themselves can finally disassemble, head home, and perhaps rest easier.

Restatement of a Discouraging Appraisal 21:25

In spite of the multitude of sins extending from the community, the
writer contents himself with a final restatement of his all-embracing
conclusion: *In those days there was no king in Israel; all the people
did what was right in their own eyes*. From his later vantage point,

possibly four hundred years after these events, the period of the Judges ends in nothing short of chaos [Formation of the Book]. No discernible standards exist. Even the apparently effective operations of the intertribal assembly merely mask the godless choices and strategies employed. In short, the covenant community embraces a non-covenantal way of life.

By concluding in this way, however, the writer does more than simply depict the past. Actually, the statement itself anticipates a brighter future. Such chaos, after all, will eventually give way to the type of stability and order that must have characterized the writer's own time. Therefore, one can almost sense him taking a deep breath, consoling himself with the realization that *those days* are thankfully part of the past.

THE TEXT IN BIBLICAL CONTEXT
The Danger of Human Solutions

When confronted by the apparent silence and withdrawal of God, a silence that continues into Samuel's day, the Israelites devise their own schemes and construct their own solutions (cf. 1 Sam. 3:1). In doing so, they annihilate the people of Jabesh-gilead and kidnap the women of Shiloh. Often, human beings throw fuel on the fire when they take matters into their own hands.

Grasping for a quick fix, especially in the face of a silent God, has been a temptation to which many have succumbed. Abraham fathers a child by Hagar, his concubine, rather than waiting for God's provisions (Gen. 16). When faced with Moses' lengthy absence as well as an apparent desire for a tangible expression of God's presence, the Israelites collect their valuables and erect a golden calf (Exod. 32). If only they had waited just a short while longer! Moses soon returns, and the tabernacle serves as God's answer to their longings for a sign of his presence.

In a much later episode, Judas, sensing God's inactivity in the face of Roman oppression and desiring that Jesus forcefully change all of that, collects the chief priests' valuables and in essence helps them erect a cross for Jesus (Matt. 26:14-16; Mark 14:10-11; Luke 22:4-6). In his haste and misconceptions, little does Judas realize that God actually has things well in hand. Clearly, making sound decisions and prayerfully exercising one's renewed mind constitute biblical virtues (Prov. 2:1-11; 3:5-6, 21-26; 11:12; 14:8; 16:9; Matt. 7:24-27; Rom. 12:1-2; 1 Peter 1:13). Self-reliance and self-directed action, however, are entirely different matters.

The Influence of Leadership

In assessing Israel's pitiful condition at the close of the period, the writer repeatedly points out that these are kingless days. By implication, the Israelites' woes are at least partly due to a leadership vacuum. God is always the supreme Ruler of his people, but he makes allowances for humanity's need for earthly leaders. Whether priests, prophets, judges, kings, or apostles, the Scriptures regularly depict leaders as vital gifts to the community of faith. In their absence, chaos has a greater opportunity to reign.

Clearly, leaders can be a great boon. Godly leaders, for example, have the capacity to move their people to new and glorious heights. Moses oversees the transformation of Israel from a group of motley slaves into a covenant community primed for entrance into the Promised Land. Josiah thwarts the onslaught of religious corruption and institutes a far-reaching reform movement (2 Kings 23). Ezra and Nehemiah supervise the return of the exiles and the rebuilding of both Jerusalem's walls as well as the people's religious identity (Ezra 7:1-10; Neh. 2:1-18; 6:15). Paul carries out a comprehensive missionary movement and trains needed church leaders throughout the known world. So often in the testimony of biblical writers, significant accomplishments and advances go hand-in-hand with godly leadership.

Nevertheless, the reverse is also true; leaders can be a source of great trouble. Solomon, though renowned for the grandeur of his accomplishments, unfairly taxes his people and even conscripts laborers from among his fellow Israelites; he is a bad example for the people by marrying many foreign women and worshiping their gods (1 Kings 4:7-28; 5:13; 11:1-13). Jeroboam II and his associates live in luxury while a fair number of their subjects wallow in poverty (Amos 3:15; 5:11-12). Jeroboam I and Manasseh lead their respective constituencies into virtually unredeemable spiritual morasses (1 Kings 12:30; 2 Kings 21:1-9; 23:26). Similarly, the influence of various religious leaders brings confusion and misdirection for a host of individuals during the days of Jesus and beyond (Matt. 7:15, 29; Acts 7:51-53; Gal. 1:7). In these and other instances, the people would almost surely have fared far better had the leader in question never gained authority.

In short, earthly leaders have the capacity to influence their people in both positive and negative ways. The mere presence of authorities, therefore, is no guarantee that good days lie ahead.

THE TEXT IN THE LIFE OF THE CHURCH
God at the Center

In *Things Fall Apart*, Nigerian novelist Chinua Achebe describes the moving and indeed heartbreaking undoing of a powerful tribesman named Okonkwo. With the coming of white people to the area, one unfortunate occurrence after another takes place, leaving this once-proud leader humiliated and defeated. Out of sheer desperation, Okonkwo takes his own life rather than risk prolonged imprisonment. In reflecting on Okonkwo's personal collapse in the midst of a seriously threatened tribal society, Achebe concludes that "when the center cannot hold, things fall apart."

According to the divine plan, the Lord alone stands at the center of his people's identity and mission. He creates, sustains, guides, and empowers, and he alone is worthy of honor and glory. Leaders, as important and influential as they might be, serve only as instruments in God's hands. Tragically, the people of ancient Israel during the period of the judges increasingly abandon their "center," choosing instead to follow their own instincts and desires. When the center fails to hold, things simply fall apart. In the resulting turmoil, neither judges nor kings, as later experience will verify, can provide the ultimate solution. Indeed, no humanly contrived schemes can possibly correct the problem. Nothing less than a genuine return to God will do.

Neither time nor modern advances have in any way altered the basic biblical notion that God reserves the center position for himself alone. Although he graciously and willingly invites human beings to assume roles within his kingdom, he simply will not share his rightful position as "Lord" with anyone or anything else. If, like Israel during the period of the judges, the church abandons its fundamental identity and refocuses on competing deities and personages, then trouble inevitably follows. For the church of today, both Israel's experience as well as Achebe's pronouncement serve as prophetic warnings: When "the center cannot hold, things fall apart."

The Crisis of Leadership

Now as always, the community of faith depends in part upon the instruction and direction provided by its various leaders. Likewise, the godly character and spiritual commitment of such leaders remains absolutely essential. People, after all, are no less easily influenced than in the past. Too often in recent years, notable church workers have legitimately been called into question and found morally and spiritually wanting. In her book entitled *Talking About God Is Dangerous*, for example, Russian dissident Tatiana Goricheva writes,

> Since I've been living in the West, it has become clear to me that the crisis of faith here for the most part rests on the fact that there are no true clergy, or almost none; there are no true pastors who can really heal and give good advice and say "Yes" or "No" with authority. (28)

Menno Simons said much the same thing nearly five centuries earlier, but with even greater anguish:

> The heathen have entered the sanctuary and have spoiled the temple of the Lord. Our princes are rending lions; our fathers betray us; our pastors deceive us; our shepherds are wolves; our watchmen are thieves and murderers of our souls. We find nothing but thistles and thorns. (316-317)

As with ancient Israel, the church needs more than people filling influential positions. The church needs godly men and women who possess both the faith and courage to lead in a genuine way, faithful to the Lord.

Outline of Judges

PART 1. PRINCIPAL CAUSE:
THE DISOBEDIENCE OF ISRAEL   **1:1—3:6**
The Conquest Abandoned:
A "Political" Introduction   **1:1—2:5**
Joshua's Death   1:1a
Judah's Accomplishments   1:1b-21
  Simeon Assists Judah   1:1b-3
  Judah Captures Adoni-Bezek   1:4-7
  Judah Conquers Jerusalem   1:8
  Judah Overtakes Many Foes   1:9-18
  Judah and Benjamin Suffer Setbacks   1:19-21
The Northern Tribes' Failures   1:22-36
  Joseph Overtakes Bethel   1:22-26
  The Remaining Tribes Experience Defeat   1:27-36
  The Messenger's Rebuke   2:1-5
The Covenant Forsaken:
A "Theological" Introduction   **2:6—3:6**
A Generation's Faithfulness   2:6-9
A New Generation's Unfaithfulness   2:10-19
The Lord's Indictment   2:20—3:6

PART 2. WORSENING EFFECT:
THE DETERIORATION OF ISRAEL   **3:7—16:31**
The Pattern Established: Othniel   **3:7-11**
The Pattern Affirmed: Ehud and Deborah   **3:12—5:31**
A Positive Portrait: Ehud's Escapades   3:12-31

Crisis Introduced   3:12-15a
Ehud Pays Eglon   3:15b-19
Ehud Slays Eglon   3:20-25
Ehud Leads Israel   3:26-30
Shamgar Handles the Philistines   3:31
A Positive Portrait: Deborah's Adventures   4:1—5:31
  Deborah in Story   4:1-24
    Crisis Introduced   4:1-3
    Deborah Prophecies to Barak   4:4-11
    Barak Pursues Sisera   4:12-16
    Jael Pegs Sisera   4:17-24
  Deborah in Song   5:1-31
    Song Introduced   5:1
    Israel Praises the Lord 5:2-3
    Israel Recalls the Lord's Arrival   5:4-5
    The Canaanites Oppress Israel   5:6-12
    Various Tribes Arise from Israel   5:13-18
    The Lord Fights for Israel   5:19-23
    Jael Strikes Sisera   5:24-27
    A Worried Mother Awaits Sisera   5:28-30
    Israel Prays to the Lord 5:31
The Pattern Threatened:
Gideon and Abimelech   **6:1—10:5**
An Ambiguous Portrait (Scene 1): Gideon's Quests 6:1—8:32
  Crisis and Criticism   6:1-10
    Crisis Introduced   6:1-6
    A Prophet Rebukes Israel 6:7-10
  Gideon Prepared for Leadership   6:11-40
    The Lord Calls Gideon   6:11-24
    Gideon Demolishes Baal's Altar   6:25-32
    Gideon Summons the Israelites   6:33-35
    Gideon Tests the Lord   6:36-40
  Gideon Triumphant in Combat   7:1—8:3
    The Lord Reduces Gideon's Troops   7:1-8a
    The Lord Encourages Gideon   7:8b-15
    Israel Conquers the Midianites   7:16-25
    Gideon Consoles the Ephraimites   8:1-3
  Gideon Revengeful in Victory   8:4-21
    Succoth and Peniel Rebuff Gideon   8:4-9
    Gideon Pursues Zebah and Zalmunna   8:10-12
    Gideon Repays Succoth and Peniel   8:13-17
    Gideon Slays Zebah and Zalmunna   8:18-21

Gideon Corruptive in the Spotlight 8:22-32
    Gideon Constructs an Ephod 8:22-27
    Gideon Fathers Abimelech 8:28-32
An Ambiguous Portrait (Scene 2):
    Abimelech's Atrocities 8:33—10:5
Crisis Introduced 8:33-35
Abimelech Becomes King 9:1-6
Jotham Shouts a Fable 9:7-21
Shechem Betrays Abimelech 9:22-33
Abimelech Destroys Shechem 9:34-49
A Woman Stones Abimelech 9:50-57
Tola and Jair Lead Israel 10:1-5
The Pattern Ignored: Jephthah and Samson 10:6—16:31
A Negative Portrait: Jephthah's Undertakings 10:6—12:7
Israel Bargains with God 10:6-16
    Crisis Introduced 10:6-10
    The Lord Rebukes Israel 10:11-16
Jephthah Bargains with Israel 10:17—11:11
    Israel Seeks a Leader 10:17-18
    Jephthah Recruited as Leader 11:1-11
Jephthah Bargains with Ammon 11:12-28
Jephthah Bargains with God 11:29-40
    Jephthah Makes a Vow 11:29-31
    Jephthah Subdues the Ammonites 11:32-33
    Jephthah Fulfills His Vow 11:34-40
Jephthah Bargains No More:
    Ephraim Destroyed 12:1-7
Negative Portraits:
    Ibzan's, Elon's, and Abdon's Operations 12:8-15
Ibzan Leads Israel 12:8-10
Elon Leads Israel 12:11-12
Abdon Leads Israel 12:13-15
A Negative Portrait: Samson's Stunts 13:1—16:31
Samson Predicted and Produced 13:1-25
    Crisis Introduced 13:1
    A Messenger Announces Samson's Birth 13:2-5
    The Messenger Pays a Second Visit 13:6-14
    Manoah Offers a Sacrifice 13:15-23
    A Barren Woman Bears Samson 13:24-25
Samson Fancies a Philistine 14:1—15:20
    Samson Selects a Bride 14:1-9
    Samson Divulges His Riddle 14:10-18

Samson Loses His Wife   14:19—15:6
Samson Gains His Revenge   15:7-20
Samson Delights in Delilah   16:1-31
   Samson Sleeps with a Prostitute   16:1-3
   Samson Divulges His Secret   16:4-17
   Samson Loses His Strength   16:18-22
   Samson Gains His Revenge   16:23-31

PART 3. FINAL OUTCOME:
THE DEPRAVITY Of ISRAEL   **17:1—21:25**
The Danites' Alternate Conquest   **17:1—18:31**
Micah Erects a Family Shrine   17:1-13
   Micah Fashions His Idols   17:1-6
   Micah Hires a Levite Priest   17:7-13
The Danites Secure a Homeland   18:1-31
   The Danites Spy Out Laish   18:1-7
   The Danites Mobilize for Action   18:8-13
   The Danites Confiscate Micah's Idols
     and Priest   18:14-21
   The Danites Rebuke a Beleaguered Micah   18:22-26
   The Danites Capture Laish   18:27-31
The Death of Morality   **19:1—21:25**
A Concubine Loses Her Life   19:1-28
   A Levite Regains His Concubine   19:1-10
   Gibeah Denies Hospitality   19:11-15
   An Elderly Sojourner Extends Hospitality 19:16-21
   Men of Gibeah Abuse the Concubine   19:22-28
Israel Debates a Grievous Crime   19:29—20:11
   A Levite Broadcasts the Deed   19:29-30
   The Israelites Assemble at Mizpah   20:1-7
   The Israelites Plan Their Response   20:8-11
Israel Repays the Wayward Benjaminites   20:12-48
   The Israelites Confront the Benjaminites 20:12-17
   The Benjaminites Defeat the Israelites   20:18-28
   The Israelites Ambush the Benjaminites   20:29-48
Israel Preserves the Shattered Benjaminites   21:1-24
   The Israelites Mourn the Loss of the
     Benjaminites   21:1-4
   The Benjaminites Receive Wives from
     Jabesh-gilead   21:5-14
   The Benjaminites Seize Wives at Shiloh   21:15-24
Restatement of a Discouraging Appraisal   21:25

Essays

ANCIENT NEAR EASTERN TEXTS   Until the last century, the Bible was essentially the only written document dealing with the world of the OT. What was known about ancient Israel and the surrounding nations, therefore, depended almost entirely upon what the biblical writers recorded. At the same time, what they only briefly mentioned or else omitted altogether remained beyond contemporary understanding.

During the last hundred years or so, however, both planned archaeological excavations as well as accidental discoveries have uncovered various additional texts from the ancient Near East. From time to time, such texts mention and perhaps evaluate actual events previously known from the OT. More frequently, they enhance our general understanding of the ancient world by depicting with greater interest and detail the affairs and beliefs of Israel's neighbors. As a result of these discoveries, far more is known today about the world of the Bible than ever before.

Among the more important texts relating to the OT in general and the book of Judges in particular are the following:

Amarna Letters. Tell el-Amarna is the modern name for what remains of the ancient city of Akhetaten. Located in middle Egypt and built during the fourteenth century B.C., Akhetaten served briefly as the capital of Egypt during the reign of Pharaoh Akhenaton. Discovered there in 1887 were various literary texts and a collection of some 350 letters. Written primarily in cuneiform Akkadian, the vast majority of these letters were sent to the Egyptian rulers from kings ruling over city-states in Syria and Palestine. Such valuable correspondence depicts the political situation in the region during the fourteenth century. Among other things, the correspondence clearly reveals Egypt's declining influence there and the subsequent rise in local unrest.

Execration Texts. Execration, a practice widely followed throughout much of ancient Egypt's history, involved the cursing of various individuals and their homelands. Typically, the names of such people were written on ceramic vessels that would be smashed during the pronouncement of the curse. The remains of many of these vessels, now known as Execration Texts, have since come to light. Of them, certain texts from the nineteenth and eighteenth centuries B.C. list various places in Palestine, including Jerusalem. While the full social and political implications of these lists remain somewhat unclear, they at least help to verify the early existence of certain cities in the region.

Moabite Stone. Discovered in 1868 in the city of Dhiban, Jordan, this basalt stone contains an inscription of Mesha, the king of Moab during the ninth century B.C. With linguistic similarities to biblical Hebrew, the inscription has proved useful in understanding the language of the OT. Furthermore, it shows that the Moabites were speaking about their god Chemosh while using categories common among the Israelites; this evidence has helped place the OT more firmly within its cultural and religious context. Chemosh, for example, grows angry with his people, permits oppression, and secures military victories.

Ugaritic Texts. Ugarit, known today as Ras-Shamra, was a major city along the Syrian coast of the Mediterranean Sea until its destruction ca. 1200 B.C. Accidentally discovered in 1928 by a local farmer, the site subsequently underwent several seasons of archaeological excavations. The most significant artifacts unearthed there were cuneiform texts written in Akkadian as well as a previously unknown language. This language, now referred to simply as "Ugaritic," proved to be an alphabetic script with many similarities to biblical Hebrew. Such similarities have greatly assisted scholars in understanding various Hebrew terms and expressions that had remained problematic. In addition, the texts from Ugarit shed light upon the history and beliefs of the local inhabitants. Included among these are depictions of such deities as El, Baal, Asherah, and Anat—deities mentioned in the OT but left largely unexplained.

ARCHAEOLOGICAL PERIODS The history of Palestine is typically divided into several archaeological periods. The earliest of these periods derive their names primarily from materials used in manufacturing tools and weapons. Following the Iron Age, however, names are based upon significant events. The list below includes only the general periods up to and including the Persian Period, each of which can be further subdivided (Mazar: 30). Furthermore, since precise transition points rarely exist, most of the dates are approximate.

Neolithic Period/New Stone Age (8500-4300 B.C.). Such developments as the domestication of animals, production of grain, and manufacturing of pottery enable Palestine's nomads to settle down. As a result, organized and more permanent villages increasingly replace temporary encampments.

Chalcolithic Period/Copper-Stone Age (4300-3300 B.C.). The discovery and trade of copper reduces isolation between the villages and stimulates greater interaction and connectedness.

Early Bronze Age (3300-2200 B.C.). Fortified cities appear in the plains, Jordan Valley, and the Negev during this period of notable urbanization. Likewise, international trade routes passing through Palestine bring to the area both Egyptian as well as Mesopotamian influences. Among the most important developments in these places is the ever-expanding role of writing, resulting in a variety of legal and religious texts [Ancient Near Eastern Texts, above].

Middle Bronze Age (2200-1550 B.C.). Various groups of Semites arrive in Palestine, likely including Abraham and his followers. After moving about in the region's mountainous areas, some of them continue on to Egypt to find needed food. In Palestine itself, small city-states dot the landscape. In contrast to both Egypt and Mesopotamia, no larger organizational structure appears in Palestine.

Late Bronze Age (1550-1200 B.C.). The entire region of Palestine, including its fortified city-states, lies under Egyptian domination. That domination increasingly wanes as the period progresses. During this time, descendants of Abraham leave Egypt with Moses in the Exodus, and they begin to settle in Palestine.

Iron Age (1200-586 B.C.). The Israelites establish their position in Palestine, but pressure from the Philistines and the Canaanites initially forces them to remain in the hill country. Following the period of the Judges, Israel's loose tribal system gives way to a centralized monarchy. The remainder of the Iron Age witnesses a significant variation in developments: a notable consolidation of power under David, a split in the kingdom following Solomon, times of religious unfaithfulness and reawakening, the prophetic movement, and the eventual destruction of first Israel (722/1) and then Judah (587/6). Many of these events take place against the background of a power struggle between Egypt and the Assyrians or Babylonians of Mesopotamia.

Persian Period (586-332 B.C.). Following the destruction of Jerusalem and the exile of Judah's inhabitants, Palestine falls under the control of the Babylonians. Within a short time, however, the Persians conquer Babylon and allow the Jews to return home. Throughout the period, the region constitutes a small section of the sprawling Persian Empire.

ASHERAH In the Ugaritic texts, this Canaanite goddess appears as the wife of the chief god, El, and the mother of other gods, including Baal [Ancient Near Eastern Texts, above; Baal, below]. Her depiction in the OT, however, is somewhat different. Rather than Baal's mother, she stands by his side in much the same way that the goddess Ashtoreth does elsewhere [Ashtoreth, below]. Asherah thus serves as one of Baal's consorts (Judg. 3:7; 1 Kings 18:19; 2 Kings 23:4). In addition to naming this Canaanite goddess, the term Asherah appears elsewhere in the OT with reference to unspecified wooden poles that symbolize her (Judg. 6:25, 28, 30; 1 Kings 15:13; 2 Kings 21:7). These poles function as cult-objects used in worship. Because of their idolatrous character, the presence of such poles similarly symbolizes Israel's increasing unfaithfulness to the Lord. As a result, destroying the cult-objects became a sign of fidelity to God himself (Judg. 6:25-27; 2 Kings 23:6).

ASHTORETH Ashtoreth is the OT name for the Canaanite goddess known outside the Bible as Astarte or Ishtar. Many scholars think the unexpected o-e vowel pattern in the present form "Ashtoreth" reflects a deliberate alteration of an original a vowel ("Ashtart"). According to this position, the vowels o-e derive from the Hebrew term boseth, "shame." If so, then early Hebrew scribes apparently broadcast their utter disdain for Astarte by mockingly changing her name (Day: 492)!

Appearing in many texts throughout the ancient world, Ashtoreth shows up most frequently in the OT alongside Baal himself (Judg. 2:13; 10:6; 1 Sam. 7:4; 12:10) [Baal, below]. She was, in other words, another one of his consorts. When written in the plural form, Ashtaroth (1 Sam. 7:3, NRSV: Astartes), the term does not imply multiple goddesses. Instead, it likely alludes to and lumps together the various local expressions of Ashtoreth-worship.

BAAL In Hebrew and related languages, the term *baal* (*ba'al*) means "husband," "lord," or "owner." Frequently, however, *baal* appears as a proper noun and is actually the name of a Canaanite deity. While the OT refers to the god Baal on several occasions, and repeatedly in the book of Judges, it never clearly explains who he was or what he did. Apparently, the original readers, all too familiar with Baal, needed no such information! Happily, the texts from Ugarit have filled in many of the gaps *[Ancient Near Eastern Texts, above]*.

According to these texts, Baal was the second-highest ranking deity in the Canaanite pantheon, beneath only El himself. Baal was a storm-god, and his followers described him as "the Rider on the Clouds," who was assisted by the "clouds, wind, bolts, and rains." Baal, in other words, was a fertility god who controlled the weather. Given such status, it becomes far clearer why the Israelites continually yielded to the temptation of worshiping him. By the time of Elijah, Baal worship had even temporarily become the dominant religion in the Northern Kingdom of Israel (Hos. 2:1-8).

Living in a land void of major rivers, the Israelites depended entirely upon the rain for their sustenance. In times of drought, times when the Lord seemed quiet and distant, Baal was thought to be the right god to know. Rather than merely falling down at the feet of carved figures, then, the worship of Baal often constituted a quest for economic security and survival during times of difficulty.

Ultimately, this apparent usefulness of serving Baal led to his increasing popularity and the development of various local forms of Baal worship. The OT mentions such forms as Baal-Berith (Judg. 9:4), Baal of Peor (Num. 25:3), and Baal-Zebub (2 Kings 1:2-3). When the biblical writers at times use the plural noun "the Baals," therefore, they do not refer to multiple gods bearing the same name. Rather, they blend together the various local forms of worshiping one god, Baal.

BREAKDOWN OF THE JUDGES CYCLE According to the summary presented in Judges 2:6—3:6, six specific stages or recurring events constitute what is often referred to as the "Judges Cycle":
1. The Israelites do evil in the eyes of the Lord.
2. The Lord brings upon the people a foreign oppressor.
3. The Israelites cry to the Lord for assistance.
4. The Lord raises up a judge or deliver to rescue the people.
5. The judge leads Israel to freedom.
6. The land has rest.

Once summarized, this cycle then serves as the building material for the various accounts recorded in 3:7—16:31.

Judge	Evil	Oppressor	Cry	Deliverer	Freedom	Rest
Othniel	3:7	3:8	3:9	3:9	3:9-10	3:11
Ehud	3:12	3:14	3:15	3:15	3:29-30	3:30
Deborah	4:1	4:2	4:3	4:6-8, but hesitation	4:23-24	5:31
Gideon	6:1	6:1ff., and very severe	6:6	6:12, but call is long & delayed	8:28	8:28
Jephthah	10:6, and total	10:7	10:10, but God is weary	11:6, but called by the people	11:33	NO

Judge	Evil	Oppressor	Cry	Deliverer	Freedom	Rest
Samson	13:1	13:1	NO, and no help wanted (15:11)	13:5, but will only begin the work	NO	NO

The Judges Cycle, however, does more than hold the individual narratives together. The writer uses the cycle as a primary means of demonstrating Israel's ever-worsening decline during the period. This he does by either delaying various stages or omitting them all together. In other words, the literary consistency and flow of the cycle decreases along with Israel (see chart on previous page). Clearly, while the entire system functions smoothly, swiftly, and effectively under Othniel, gradual erosion leaves the cycle in shambles by the time of Samson.

CANAANITES   In spite of some ambiguity, the term *Canaanite* typically refers to a somewhat diverse collection of people residing in Palestine. Such diversity resulted from both the constant flow of varying groups through the region and the jagged terrain that prevented unification. During the Late Bronze Age (1550-1200 B.C.), the Canaanites established a city-state type of organizational system in which smaller towns encircled larger and more important cities [*Archaeological Periods, above*]. Each of these city-states was self-governed, resulting in a collection of independent political units. In such a context, no overarching or comprehensive governmental structure existed. Only the external authority imposed by the Egyptians superseded such local home rule. By the onset of the Iron Age, however, that external authority had evaporated.

Generally speaking, the Canaanites occupied the fertile valleys and coastal areas of Palestine. They thus controlled the most fertile portions of Palestinian real estate. Along with this control and their agricultural way of life came the worship of the fertility god Baal and his cohorts [*Asherah, above; Ashtoreth, above; Baal, above*]. Such worship naturally involved a formal system of practices and rituals that embodied their beliefs. The Canaanites, therefore, constituted an established physical and religious presence in Palestine, both before and during the period of the Judges.

CHRONOLOGY   Determining the chronology in the book of Judges necessarily begins with the task of establishing parameters for the time period the book depicts. The period of the judges falls between the conquest of Canaan and the rise of the monarchy under Saul. Of these two events, a date of ca. 1020 B.C. for Saul's coronation seems clear enough. The conquest of the land, however, presents a far greater problem. Situating the conquest chronologically depends upon the date of Israel's exodus from Egypt, and such a date continues to arouse some discussion. While the intricacies of this discussion can hardly be examined here, mention will be made of the major alternatives.

Generally speaking, two distinct and conflicting views emerge concerning the date of the Exodus. The first of these, the so-called "early date," begins with a literal reading of 1 Kings 6:1:

In the four hundred eightieth year after the Israelites came out of the land of Egypt, in the fourth year of Solomon's reign . . ., he began to build the house of the Lord.

Since the fourth year of Solomon's reign was ca. 966 B.C., the Exodus apparently occurred in about 1446 B.C. Additional biblical support for this date is drawn from Jephthah's statement in Judges 11:26. If Israel had in fact been in the land for three hundred years prior to Jephthah's activities, then such an early date is required.

In contrast to this view, the dominant position among scholars today places the Exodus some two hundred years later (ca. 1250 B.C.). According to the proponents of this "late date," archaeological and textual evidence outside of the Bible situate the exodus from Egypt sometime during the reign of Pharaoh Ramses II in the thirteenth century B.C. Such biblical passages as 1 Kings 6:1 and Judges 11:26, then, are seen as schematic figures of some sort. The number 480, for example, might well be the product of the popular numbers twelve and forty. Likewise, the number 300 represents a stylized attempt to summarize all the preceding figures mentioned in the book of Judges.

In the face of such drastically different positions, at least two key points must be kept in mind. First, while a more literal reading of the biblical text perhaps implies a relatively lengthy period of time between the exodus and the monarchy, the OT is not unanimous in pinpointing a date. Indeed, by simply totaling other biblical numbers, one arrives at a period of between 550 and 600 years rather than 480!

Second, the overall archaeological picture concerning the matter is both complicated and at times frustratingly imprecise. As a result, proponents of both views have little trouble "digging up" support for their positions. Suffice it to say that, given the present state of understanding, the weight of the evidence still favors placing the exodus in the middle of the thirteenth century B.C (ca. 1250 B.C.; cf. Kitchen). Accordingly, after allowing for the wilderness wanderings as well as the conquest under Joshua, the period of the judges began ca. 1200 B.C.

Having concluded that the book of Judges deals with the Israelites' fortunes and misfortunes during the twelfth and eleventh centuries B.C. (ca. 1200-1020 B.C.), yet another problem immediately arises. By simply adding the various figures that the writer assigns to the respective periods of oppression as well as to the individual judges, one arrives at a total of 410 years:

Oppressors		*Judges*	
Cushan-rishathaim	8 years (3:8)	Othniel	40 years (3:11)
Moab	18 years (3:14)	Ehud	80 years (3:30)
Philistines	? years (3:31)	Shamgar	? years (3:31)
Jabin	20 years (4:3)	Deborah	40 years (5:31)
Midian	7 years (6:1)	Gideon	40 years (8:28)
		Abimelech	3 years (9:22)
		Tola	23 years (10:2)
		Jair	22 years (10:3)
Ammon	18 years (10:8)	Jephthah	6 years (12:7)
		Ibzan	7 years (12:9)
		Elon	10 years (12:11)
		Abdon	8 years (12:14)
Philistines	40 years (13:1)	Samson	20 years (15:20; 16:31)

Obviously, 410 years is a far cry from the suggested 180 for the entire period! Nor will it do simply to revert to the early date for the exodus to minimize this apparent discrepancy. To do that, one would first need to add to the 410 years at least 40 years for the wilderness wanderings and the conquest, 40 years for Eli's ministry (1 Sam. 4:18), an unknown number of years for Saul's reign (1 Sam. 13:1 is problematic), and a final 40 years for David's kingship (2 Sam. 5:4). This, once again, totals over 550 years, not the 480 years recorded in 1 Kings 6:1.

At least two significant observations shed light on this final difficulty. First, it is immediately apparent that several of the figures recorded in Judges are multiples of the number twenty. Indeed, these numbers equal a full 280 of the 410 total years. While the precise function of such round figures in the OT awaits further clarification, it seems clear enough that they serve some purpose other than precise record-keeping. Second, selected individual episodes within the main body of the book no doubt occurred simultaneously or overlapped *[Localized Accounts, below]*. As a result, the figure 410 represents the *combined* number of years, not the number of *consecutive* years.

ENVELOPE STRUCTURE (INCLUSIO) Referred to also by the term *inclusio*, envelope structure is a literary technique popular among the ancient Hebrew writers. According to this type of arrangement, significant terms or phrases appearing at the beginning of a section or even an entire composition are later repeated at the close. As a result, the intervening materials are framed or bracketed, forming a comprehensive whole.

Envelope structure shows up with considerable frequency in both narrative and poetic sections of the Bible. References to David, Joab, and the Israelite attack against Rabbah, for example, enclose the story of David and Bathsheba and set it apart from the surrounding materials (2 Sam. 11:1; 12:26-31). Likewise, virtually the entire book of Ecclesiastes is enveloped by the recurring expression "'Meaningless! Meaningless!' says the Teacher. 'Everything is meaningless!'" (1:2; 12:8). Finally, Psalm 8 provides a clear poetic illustration of the technique, beginning and ending with the proclamation "O Lord, our Lord, how majestic is your name in all the earth!" In each case, this pattern assists the reader in recognizing the limits of the enclosed literary unit. In identifying these limits, one can better evaluate and appreciate the overall design and meaning of the composition instead of simply focusing upon isolated verses.

With respect to the book of Judges, envelope structure appears with some frequency. Geographical references to Ophrah (6:11; 8:27) and Zorah and Eshtaol (13:25; 16:31), for example, tie together the Gideon and Samson narratives, respectively. Similarly, the phrase *In those days there was no king in Israel* (19:1 and 21:25) marks both the beginning and the end of the crisis with Gibeah. Finally, the entire book of Judges is itself enveloped by scenes in which the Israelites seek marching orders from the Lord (1:1-2; 20:18).

FORMATION OF THE BOOK According to Jewish tradition, the book of Judges was written by none other than Samuel himself. Today, however, virtually no one embraces this position. Likely such a connection reflects the well-known rabbinic tendency to attach sacred writings to important prophetic figures more than it does any serious conclusion concerning the book's actual origins. Judges remains an anonymous work.

In spite of such anonymity, however, various elements within the book help us better understand how Judges probably came to be. These elements fall naturally into the following categories:

Specific Indications of Time. The book contains a number of both early and late elements. The continuing dominance of the Jebusites at Jerusalem (1:21) and the Canaanites at Gezer (1:29), for example, point to a time period no later than the eleventh and tenth centuries B.C. Additional early elements include the ongoing status of Sidon as the leading Phoenician city (3:3) as well as the linguistic antiquity of the Song of Deborah (Judg. 5).

With respect to later elements, various editorial comments clearly suggest that certain events had already transpired by the time the book reached its final form. Included here are both the destruction of Shiloh (18:31) and the inception of kingship (17:6; 18:1; 19:1; 21:25). One additional item in this context is the reference to the land's captivity (18:30), likely meaning the destruction of the Northern Kingdom of Israel at the hands of the Assyrians in 721 B.C. If so, then the book of Judges could not have reached completion before that time.

By connecting these final two occurrences, the inception of kingship and the destruction of the Northern Kingdom of Israel, an interesting possibility arises. The writer's comments concerning kingship reveal a positive view of the monarchy—a king could have prevented the rampant and deadly individualism so typical at the end of the judges' period. The writer, in other words, apparently lived during the reign of a *good king*. Following the fall of Israel, only two of Judah's kings fit that category: Hezekiah (ca. 716-687 B.C.) and Josiah (ca. 640-609 B.C.). As such, a good deal of work may have gone into the book of Judges during one of their reigns.

The Nature of the Materials. The various hero stories that comprise the body of the book reflect many of the characteristics common to heroic literature [Hero Stories, below]. Since such literature was well-known throughout the Mediterranean World up until ca. 1000 B.C., the stories themselves no doubt originated at roughly the same time as the events they describe.

Beyond these stories, however, selected introductory and reflective comments clearly show that the earlier tales have since been placed in a later and more comprehensive framework. Not only does each individual story receive its own preliminary comments, but the entire collection of stories is now sandwiched between introductory and concluding sections. In other words, while the various stories themselves originated during or near the actual time of the judges, the book contains additional materials that did not.

On the basis of these observations, at least a general process of formation can be suggested:

1. Various independent and localized hero stories were told and retold during roughly the same time period as the events themselves (ca. 1200-1020 B.C.) [Hero Stories, below; Localized Accounts, below].

2. At some point thereafter, probably in the tenth and ninth centuries B.C., these individual stories were preserved in written form.

3. Eventually, some of these stories were gathered into a collection, what now comprises at least a major part of the present book's central section.

4. Finally, various introductory and concluding sections were added to the collection, and the stories themselves were placed within an interpretive framework. This work took place sometime after the fall of Israel in 721 B.C., probably during the reforming reign of King Josiah, toward the end of the seventh century.

At the close of this process, the book of Judges no doubt appeared much as it does today. Rather than a free-standing volume, however, it took its place within what most scholars call the "Deuteronomistic History," a multivolume work including the books of Joshua, Judges, 1–2 Samuel, and 1–2 Kings. Such an overarching history, revised once again in the sixth century B.C. to include the destruction of Jerusalem and the exile, sought to explain the ups and downs of Israel's journey in the light of Deuteronomy's teaching ("Approaching Judges," p. 15).

HERO STORIES   As to their literary form, the many stories appearing in Judges 3:7—16:31 have received various descriptive titles. R. Boling, for example, labels such accounts "historical romances" (31), while N. Gottwald brands them "sagas" (237). Others simply refer to them as either "deliverer" or "savior stories." Regardless of the precise terminology, however, the narratives dealing with the individual judges do bear some resemblance to the so-called heroic literature present elsewhere throughout the Mediterranean World between ca. 1500 and 1000 B.C. Therefore, although the ancient Israelites never developed heroic tales to the same extent or with the same fervor often found among their neighbors, these accounts might best be described as "hero stories" [Violence and Warfare in Judges, below].

Generally speaking, heroic literature unambiguously focuses significant attention on the individual hero. The hero, as C. Armerding expresses it,

> is the man of action *par excellence*. He is the aristocratic leader of a band of faceless nobodies. He is proud, powerful, crafty, and unforgiving. But he is also loving, chivalrous, and deeply emotional. His country and even his tribe remain in the background. He is the story. He and his character provide the content for literature. (25)

More fully, heroic literature typically displays many of the following:

Detailed Reporting. Whereas Hebrew narrative normally avoids excessive details, hero stories delight in graphic depictions. In the tale of Ehud, for example, the Moabite king Eglon's extreme obesity serves to surround the deadly dagger with layer upon layer of fat (3:22). Indeed, the vividness of the description virtually enables the reader to "touch" Eglon's rotund physique.

The Hero's Physical Characteristics. As cases in point, Ehud is a left-handed fighter (3:15), Gideon a "mighty warrior" (6:12), and Samson a human dynamo (Judg.14–16).

The Hero's Craftiness. Ehud, for example, devises a devilish scheme in which he totally outsmarts his Moabite counterpart (3:15-23). Likewise, Gideon leads his miniscule army to victory with only trumpets, torches, and empty jars (7:16-21). Samson befuddles his listeners with tantalizing riddles (14:1, 18; 15:16).

The Hero's Shortcomings. Barak, for instance, foolishly hesitates in the face of a prophetic commission (4:8). In addition, Jephthah bargains away his only child (11:30-39). Samson repeatedly forfeits everything at the sight of beautiful women (14:2; 16:1, 4-21).

The Hero's Love for Revenge. The timid Gideon of chapter 6 and the faithful Gideon of chapter 7 remarkably become the bloodthirsty Gideon of chapter 8. Similarly, one of the dominant driving forces behind Samson is his unquenchable desire for revenge (15:7).

The Hero's Remarkable Accomplishments. Samson's slaughtering of one thousand Philistines with the jawbone of a donkey is but the most conspicuous example of several hard-to-imagine achievements gained by Israel's various heroes (15:15-16).

The many stories preserved in the book of Judges, therefore, exhibit various heroic characteristics common to the literature of the day. The biblical storytellers and writers made use of familiar and captivating devices to communicate significant ideas and truth statements about themselves and God. In so doing, they both wonderfully entertain as well as insightfully instruct.

HISTORICITY AND TRUTH Since the Enlightenment of the eighteenth century, questions about the historical nature of the Bible have been asked with increasing frequency. Some interrogators have concluded that the Bible in general and the OT in particular include little of what we today call "history." Others argue that virtually every detail in the Bible is historically reliable and accurate. Still others, including Alan Cooper, suggest that it simply does not matter either way; the meaning and truth of the Bible do not depend on its historical accuracy (65-66).

In addressing this complex issue, several key points must be kept in mind:

The Bible's Claims to Historicity. Even the casual reader will quickly observe that the Bible presents its message couched in an overarching historical framework. The Bible does not consist simply of isolated ideas and religious principles; instead, it is a drama that unfolds along a broad, chronological time line. Included along this time line are many events, including key ones such as Israel's exodus from Egypt and Jesus' death and resurrection, that the biblical writers repeatedly present as actual historical occurrences. Minimally, then, the Bible claims to present a broad historical overview rooted in a series of crucial events (Long: 93).

Literary Forms. In addition to materials of a more historical nature, the Bible contains such other literary forms as parables, fables, and hymns (Dongell: 93-113). At times, these various forms are clearly set apart and introduced, as when Jesus employed parables in his teaching. On other occasions, however, the writer may simply include varying literary forms and devices in the larger account without specifically informing the reader. What results is a general historical framework that is supplemented or enriched with a wide range of other materials. The biblical writers thus do more than preserve archival records. They vividly present their message through multiple forms.

The Meaning of Truth. People in the West tend to define *truth* as that which is historically verifiable. A true story, for example, tells of events that have actually happened. For other people in the world, including many from the Middle East, *truth* has an additional meaning. For them, something is true if it reliably depicts human experience, if it presents a picture in which people can honestly see themselves and the world around them. John Bunyan's *Pilgrim's Progress*, for instance, is a true story, not because it actually happened, but because it faithfully portrays the struggles of following Christ.

When some readers come to the Bible, they come with only the first meaning of *truth* in mind. The Bible is true only if all of its contents can be historically verified. Yet this is too limiting a view, and it fails to do justice to the Bible itself. God can and does speak through channels other than historical documents, and truth by its very nature is too wonderful and complex to be reduced to a single form (Vanhoozer: 85). Therefore, while affirming the essential historicity of the Bible, readers must learn to recognize and appreciate the various techniques and materials that the biblical writers employ.

HOLY SPIRIT IN THE OT Unlike the NT writers, the Hebrews rarely link the terms *holy* and *spirit*. In fact, the expression "Holy Spirit" appears only three times in all of the OT (Ps. 51:11; Isa. 63:10-11). Far more frequently, the OT makes use of "the Spirit of God" or similar expressions. In such cases, no clear distinction yet appears between the various persons of the Godhead. Instead, these expressions are alternative ways of referring to God.

Generally speaking, the Spirit of God appears in the OT in three distinct contexts. First, the Spirit of God actively participates in both the creation and the preservation of the world (Gen. 1:2; Job 26:13, KJV and Heb.; Ps. 33:6; 104:30). In this way, the Spirit powerfully brings order and life out of chaos.

Second, the Spirit of God frequently serves to energize and inspire Israel's leaders (e.g., Exod. 31:3; Num. 11:25-29). The Former Prophets typically envision the Spirit in this way—coming upon and empowering selected individuals assigned to perform specific tasks (Judg. 6:34; 11:29; 13:25; 14:6, 19; 15:14; 1 Sam. 10:10; 11:6; 16:13). So too do the prophets themselves refer to the enabling operation of the Spirit in their ministries (Ezek. 11:5; Mic. 3:8; Zech. 4:6; 7:12).

Third, the Spirit of God plays a crucial role in ancient Israel's eschatological hopes, in her dreams concerning the future. The same life-giving Spirit, for example, will restore flesh to parched bones and reestablish Israel (Ezek. 37:14). Furthermore, an anticipated outpouring of God's Spirit upon all people resounds within the prophetic proclamation (Isa. 32:15; 44:3; Ezek. 39:29; Joel 2:28). With this outpouring will come transformation, renewal, and a longed-for spiritual vitality.

Reflected in the OT's depiction of the Holy Spirit, then, is a progression of sorts. What begins with the movement of the Spirit at creation and continues with the empowering of selected individuals eventually gives way to a remarkably comprehensive hope in which the Spirit of God will indwell all of God's people—young and old, men and women. Herein lies a major qualitative difference between the OT and the New. What formerly could only be imagined has now come to pass: God's Spirit not simply coming upon selected individuals, but actually dwelling within the hearts of the members of the entire community of faith (Acts 2; 1 Cor. 3:16; Gal. 5:25).

LOCALIZED ACCOUNTS Repeatedly, the writer of Judges introduces the various individual episodes with references to *the Israelites*. In so doing, he deliberately creates the impression that all members of the tribal confederation participate in each and every event. In a sense, of course, they do, for those things that characterize selected tribes increasingly come to characterize the entire community. In reality, however, each episode originally involves only a segment of the whole.

To illustrate and substantiate this point, the text itself typically specifies what part of the tribal confederation is involved in each account. Never do we find all of the Israelites participating in the proceedings. Rarely are even half of the tribes represented. The stories thus developed in more localized contexts and only later came to describe the Israelites collectively, as charted below:

Oppressor	*Deliverer*	*Affected Tribes*
Cushan-Rishathaim	Othniel	Unspecified (3:7-11)
Moab	Ehud	Benjamin, Ephraim (3:15, 27)
Jabin	Deborah	Naphtali, Zebulun, Ephraim, Benjamin, Machir, Issachar, Reuben, Gilead, Dan, Asher (4:6; 5:14-15, 17)
Midian	Gideon	Manasseh, Asher, Zebulun, Naphtali, Ephraim (6:35; 7:24)
Ammon	Jephthah	presently Gilead, but earlier Judah, Benjamin, Ephraim (10:9; 11:4-6)
Philistines	Samson	Dan, Judah (13:2; 15:9-11)

PROHIBITION AGAINST IMAGES Fashioned images played a significant role in the many religions of the ancient Near East. From Mesopotamia to Egypt, such images stood in worship centers and functioned in sacred rituals. Therefore, the OT's prohibition against idolatry has a remarkably original ring to it. Boecker even argues that this regulation "has no parallel in the history of religion" (145).

In spite of the uniqueness of this prohibition, the OT is both consistent and unanimous in upholding the prohibition and nowhere says anything favorable about images (e.g., Isa. 44:9-20; Jer. 10:1-16; Ps. 135:15-18). This view is maintained in the Apocrypha and in the NT (e.g., Wisd. of Sol. 13–15; Acts. 17:29; Rom. 1:23; Rev. 9:20). From start to finish, idols and the worship of God do not mix. The fundamental question, then, is "Why?" What lies at the heart of idolatry that makes it so undesirable and even dangerous?

To begin with, at least two misconceptions concerning this prohibition need to be dismissed. First, in outlawing images, the OT does not forbid artistic depictions of all varieties (Gutmann: 161-168). The second commandment (Exod. 20:4-6; Deut. 4:15-40; 5:8-10) in no way seeks to establish an expressionless form of either life or worship. One need only recall the relatively elaborate ornamentation of both the tabernacle and the temple to see this point. Rather than preventing visual art, the prohibition regulates it by placing images of God off-limits.

Second, some people have seen in this prohibition a rigid distinction between material and spiritual reality. Accordingly, the commandment emphasizes the superiority of the spiritual world, the essential inferiority of the physical world, and the sizeable chasm between them. This perspective may be at home among Greek and later Western thinkers; yet the Hebrew mind knew little if anything about such categories and classifications. On the contrary, the God of the OT is directly involved in all phases of the material world's creation and ongoing operation.

If neither of these common misconceptions help us adequately understand the prohibition against images, then what alternatives remain? In general, this regulation addresses at least three primary issues:

Controlling God. Of fundamental importance in considering the second commandment and related passages is an understanding of the function of images in ancient Near Eastern religious rituals. In such contexts, idols were not simply symbolic or representational figures. People did not distinguish sharply between image and reality in the same way that moderns typically do. Instead, the image was in some way *connected* to whatever or whoever it represented. The image, therefore, actually was thought to share in the life or divinity of the person or god that it epitomized.

Significantly, what this connection or shared experience meant is that the image could be used in influencing or manipulating the reality that it represented. Precisely this same notion finds expression even today among various cultures and groups who practice black magic. By sticking a pin into the belly of a doll, for example, one intends to inflict pain upon the person whom that doll resembles. Likewise, ancient worshipers often sought to gain some control over the gods by maneuvering and handling their idols. Images, therefore, were supposed to provide access to divine power and influence.

In such a social and religious context, then, at least one reason behind the OT's prohibition of images becomes clearer. The God of the Bible cannot be controlled or manipulated, nor should humans ever attempt to do so. What God does, he does freely and of his own choosing. Similarly, when God acts on behalf of his people, he does so willingly and graciously. Never can the

God of Scripture be forcibly coerced by the manipulative tactics of human beings.

Reducing God. In addition to controlling God, images by their very nature reduce him. Closely connected to the deities that they represented, images in the ancient world almost inevitably gained the adoration of those who possessed them. The image itself became an object of worship and an extension of the deity's presence. Worse yet, the image served to define the character and identity of the depicted god. By worshiping and adoring idols, people increasingly conceptualized the gods in precisely the same way.

Here, then, is the second great danger of fashioning images. The God of Scripture, quite simply, cannot be suitably likened to anything or anyone else. Any image, therefore, automatically reduces God to something far less than what he actually is. As Durham describes this idea,

> Nothing created can serve to represent him, not even in the whole range of the created order, from top to bottom, and even in the realms of the mythopoeic creatures, in the heavens above and in the waters below the earth, because Yahweh has made every thing and every being. . . . No image conceivable to [the Israelites] could serve to represent him. They must worship him as he is, not as they envision him or would like him to be. (286)

The distinction, then, is not between spiritual and physical, but between the Lord and everything else. In short, idols reduce within the human mind a wonderfully irreducible God.

Emulating God. The Israelites themselves were to be God's people, *a priestly kingdom and a holy nation* (Exod. 19:6; cf. 1 Pet. 2:9). They were to emulate God on earth, to serve as his "image" for all of the surrounding nations to see (cf. Gen. 1:26-27; Col. 3:10). Constructing images of wood and stone would therefore constitute a forfeiture of the Israelites' own covenantal calling.

ROLE OF THE JUDGES The book of Judges refers to twelve individuals who in some way lead Israel during this period. The number obviously corresponds to the twelve tribes, although not every tribe finds representation. Six of these individuals, typically designated "major judges," serve as leading characters in various episodes: Othniel, Ehud, Deborah, Gideon, Jephthah, and Samson. Six others, commonly called "minor judges," merely appear on lists: Shamgar, Tola, Jair, Ibzan, Elon, and Abdon. In spite of their titles and designations, however, precisely how each of these figures function within the society remains somewhat difficult to say.

In Hebrew, the verb "to judge" (*šapaṭ*) enjoys a wider range of meanings than in English. Rather than merely designating judicial functions, *šapaṭ* can also mean such things as "to govern," "to act as leader," or "to rule." In the book of Judges, the clarifying passage appears in 2:16. According to this verse, a judge is someone specifically called upon to deliver the people of Israel out of oppression. Therefore, at the simplest level, a judge is a deliverer.

Nevertheless, the noun form of *šapaṭ* never appears in the book of Judges with reference to a named human being. In other words, none of Israel's deliverers are specifically called "judges." Instead, they "judge" (action verb). The noun *judge* is used only once in connection with a particular character, and that one is the Lord himself (11:27). The few other occurrences of the noun are all in a general summary statement void of individual references (2:16-19). By implication, God alone is the true "judge," and Israel's deliverers simply act as judges when God calls and enables them.

Finally, if the writer of the book generally envisions a judge as a divinely summoned and empowered deliverer, then it is at least worth noting two apparent deviations from the norm. First, three of the twelve leaders mentioned do not "judge" Israel, even though each of them has freed Israel from oppressors (Ehud, Shamgar, and Gideon). Perhaps these instances simply constitute variations in terminology. Second and more important, however, none of the so-called "minor judges" other than Shamgar are involved in any military activities. This is so, even though each of the five do indeed "judge" Israel. Since information concerning the role of these minor judges is almost totally lacking, accompanying details were omitted or a second type of leadership is implied here. If the latter, then perhaps these judges provide administrative expertise rather than heroic exploits.

SEA PEOPLES If the stage in Palestine during the Iron Age (1200-586 B.C.) witnessed the urban-rural conflict between the established Canaanites and the just-emerging Israelites, so too did it open its doors for the so-called Sea Peoples *[Canaanites, above]*. Significant upheaval in the Greek world during the thirteenth century B.C. led to the fall of Troy and the destruction of the Mycenean empire. As part of the resulting confusion, groups of people apparently left the area and headed south over the Mediterranean Sea. Although some were rebuffed by the Egyptians, others made successful inroads further north along the coast of Palestine. Among these "Sea Peoples" arriving in Palestine was that notorious group known later as the *Philistines* (e.g., 3:3). The term *Palestine* was derived from their name and first applied to the strip of coastland south of Mt. Carmel (Joel 3:4, KJV).

After their arrival in the area, the Philistines became the third major actor during the period of the judges. Now the Israelites not only must contend with the Canaanites, established inhabitants dwelling in their fortified cities, but also with these newcomers. While the Israelites attempt to come down *out of* the mountains, the Philistines repeatedly seek to extend their holdings up *into* the mountains. In the Palestine of the Iron Age, therefore, the people of Israel experience increased political and religious opposition on virtually all sides. On this rather tense stage, the various judges are called upon to lead Israel out of one difficult situation after another *[Role of the Judges, above]*.

SEPTUAGINT Completed primarily during the third century B.C., the Septuagint is the earliest Greek translation of the Hebrew OT. Due to the expanding influence of Greek culture, Jewish communities throughout the Mediterranean world had increasingly lost their facility with both Hebrew and Aramaic. As a result, such a translation into Greek became essential.

According to legend, the Septuagint was translated in Alexandria, Egypt, by seventy-two scholars during a time period of only seventy-two days! (Letter of Aristeas). The location of Alexandria seems plausible; there was a large Jewish community there, in a Hellenistic milieu. Yet the number of translators and days may be more symbolic. It is somewhat unclear why the completed work is called the Septuagint ("seventy," hence the abbreviation *LXX*). Perhaps the name is a rounded-off form of seventy-two. More likely, it derives from the account that seventy elders accompanied Moses up Mt. Sinai when the law was originally received (Exod. 24:1, 9; some ancient sources say 70 elders translated the LXX).

Many scholars think the LXX was prepared for synagogue reading and instruction in the Jewish community. It also made the Hebrew Scripture available in common Greek for the nations (reckoned to be 72 or 70 in number; cf. Gen. 10; Luke 10:1; 1 En. 17:8). The OT in Greek shows how the Hebrew Bible was understood and interpreted in antiquity. In addition, the LXX was the Bible of the early church and heavily used by the writers of the NT and the church fathers.

The LXX continues to serve an important role in translating and understanding the Bible. What the existence of the LXX means, simply, is that more than one "text" of the OT remains. Furthermore, while it is true that the LXX and the Masoretic Hebrew text are remarkably similar, there are notable differences. The book of Jeremiah, for example, is some 15 percent longer in Hebrew than in Greek. Likewise, various verses appear in differing ways. When translating the OT into other languages, therefore, scholars compare the texts to arrive at the best reading.

In translation work, the Masoretic Hebrew text (established from old manuscripts by the tenth century A.D.) is typically preferred and does serve as the basis for most English versions. Yet the LXX can provide helpful alternatives when certain difficulties arise (e.g., Judg. 7:5-6).

THEOPHANY The term derives from two Greek words and literally means "God shines." With respect to the OT, theophanies are instances in which God reveals himself in dramatic or tangible ways. In contrast to simple speech or quiet gestures, for example, God at times specifically discloses himself through such awe-inspiring means as fire, storms, and earthquakes (e.g., Exod. 3:2-5; 19:16-25; 24:15-18; Deut. 33:2; Job 38:1; Ps. 18:7-8; Ezek. 1:27-28). Appearances of this variety typically accompany noteworthy messages, particularly those declaring God's intentions to act on his people's behalf. As a result, the places where theophanies are experienced often retain a sacred significance.

VIOLENCE AND WAR IN JUDGES For even the casual reader of the book of Judges, violence and killing seem to loom on every page. In the first chapter, the writer presents an extensive catalog of the Israelites' many military opponents. In the closing chapter, war and the annihilation of human beings continue unabated. Much of the same goes on throughout the intervening chapters as well. Just as in various other OT books, violence and war play a major role in Judges.

It is hardly possible to resolve all of the tension that this language of violence and war raises for many people, including Christians who take seriously Jesus' words about loving one's enemies (Matt. 5:44). Nevertheless, it may help to put such language in the following context:

Problem of Assimilation. Throughout the book of Judges, the Israelites are repeatedly accused of coming to terms with the Canaanites. In so doing, they establish ill-conceived covenants, leave standing foreign shrines and idols, intermarry, and indeed embrace a great deal of Canaanite culture and religion (2:2, 11-12, 19; 3:7; 10:13). Significantly, however, the writer of Judges neither specifies the need to terminate the land's inhabitants nor condemns the Israelites for failing to do so. Instead, he makes clear that the Israelites' glaring crime involves intermingling and compromising; they failed to *drive out* the Canaanites. Whether or not there were solutions other than annihilating the "enemy" remains an open question.

Sources of Violence. A great deal of the bloodshed in Judges has nothing whatever to do with God. Instead, it continually grows out of a multitude of human emotions and ambitions. Both Gideon (Judg. 8) and Samson (15:7-8) act violently to attain personal revenge. Similarly, Abimelech crushes countless people in attempts to satisfy his unquenchable thirst for power (Judg. 9), and Jephthah destroys a multitude of Ephraimites out of deep feelings of resentment (12:1-6). Finally, the Israelites collectively commit untold atrocities while searching for solutions to self-instigated problems (Judg. 21). In none of these cases does the Lord genuinely instruct or subsequently praise such activities. On the contrary, these warlike adventures are humanly designed and initiated.

Reverse Aggression. Not only do the Israelites initiate violence against their enemies, but they similarly receive it in return. Such reversed aggression regularly appears in Judges as an act of God in response to his people's constant unfaithfulness. Warfare in the book is not limited, therefore, to Israel fighting against the world. Instead, God at times uses warfare to judge his own people.

God's participation in war, however, does not in itself imply that violence and war, whether against Israel or others, are sacred or even commendable activities. What it does suggest is that God works through the events of human history, including war. God can use even evil activities, individuals, and nations to accomplish his purposes on earth (Craigie, 1978:41-43).

Nature of the Stories. People often read the Bible as though all of its parts are the same. They rarely take account of differing contexts and literary types. In the present case, the book of Judges consists largely of so-called hero stories [Hero Stories, above]. Elsewhere in the ancient world, such stories magnify the battlefield scenes themselves and heap virtually unlimited praise upon various heroic superstars. One need only read portions of the *Iliad* (Greek) or the *Gilgamesh Epic* (Babylonian) for examples. In Judges, while many characteristics of heroic literature appear, they are frequently "toned down." Rather than lavishing human beings with ceaseless praise, various episodes depict God himself as the fighter and victor; the Israelites do little (Lind: 169-174; von Rad: 41-51). In the wars that God initiates, human strength and ingenuity fade in the light of God's own miraculous works.

The Writer's Overall Perspective. It must always be kept in mind that the period of the judges was hardly a time of fond memories for the writer. Indeed, later generations saw here little more than anarchy and increasing disobedience. The writer is therefore not casually recounting sordid stories to encourage his readers to "go and do likewise" (Luke 10:37). On the contrary, he typically assumes that the horror of much of the material will be self-evident.

The Canonical Context of the Book of Judges. The war narratives in Judges do not constitute the Bible's final word on the subject of violence and war. Even in the OT, one senses a progression involving at least three major stages:

• In such books as Joshua and Judges, war narratives at times depict military campaigns in almost comical fashion. Israel's troops are reduced or irrelevant, and God alone secures the victory.

• In Deuteronomy, Samuel, and Kings, monarchical power is greatly restricted, and various kings are harshly criticized for relying upon military might. (Deut. 17:14-20; 1 Sam. 8:9-20; 10:25; 2 Sam. 24; 1 Kings 10:26-29; 11:1-13).

• In the prophetic literature, glimpses appear of a time when peace will reign and war and violence will cease (Isa. 2:1-5; 9:6-7; 11:1-9; Mic. 4:6-7;

Jer. 23:5-8; Zech. 9:9-10). In Isaiah's vision at least, God's people are encouraged to begin modeling that peace in the present world (2:5).

Throughout this progression, a progression *beginning* with narratives such as those in Judges, violence and war are increasingly critiqued. This critique leads the way to a more complete theology of peace based also upon the NT.

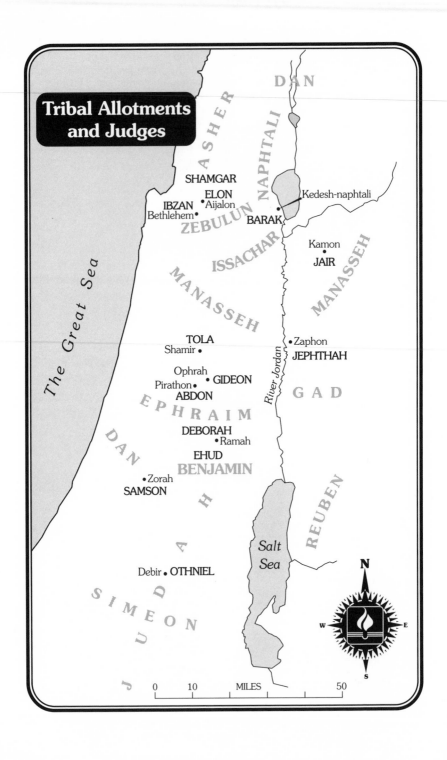

Tribal Allotments and Judges

DAN

ASHER

NAPHTALI

SHAMGAR

ELON
•Aijalon

IBZAN
Bethlehem•

ZEBULUN

BARAK

Kedesh-naphtali

ISSACHAR

Kamon
•
JAIR

MANASSEH

MANASSEH

The Great Sea

TOLA
Shamir •

•Zaphon
JEPHTHAH

Ophrah
•
Pirathon• GIDEON
ABDON

River Jordan

GAD

EPHRAIM

DEBORAH
•Ramah

EHUD
BENJAMIN

•Zorah
SAMSON

DAN

REUBEN

Salt
Sea

J
U
D
A
H

Debir •OTHNIEL

SIMEON

N

W   E

S

0   10   MILES   50

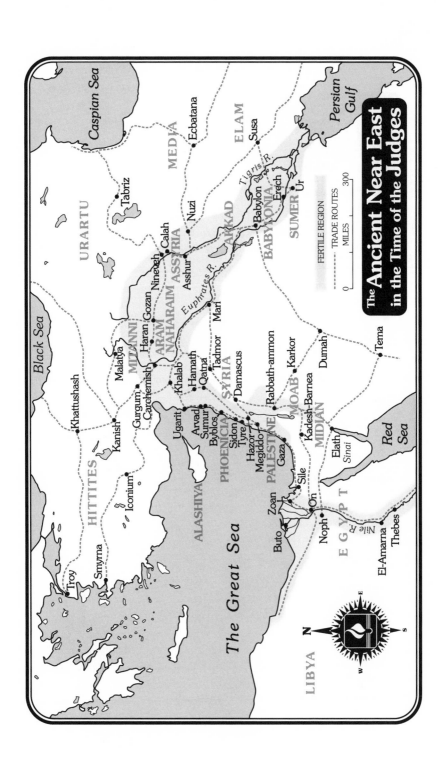

The Ancient Near East in the Time of the Judges

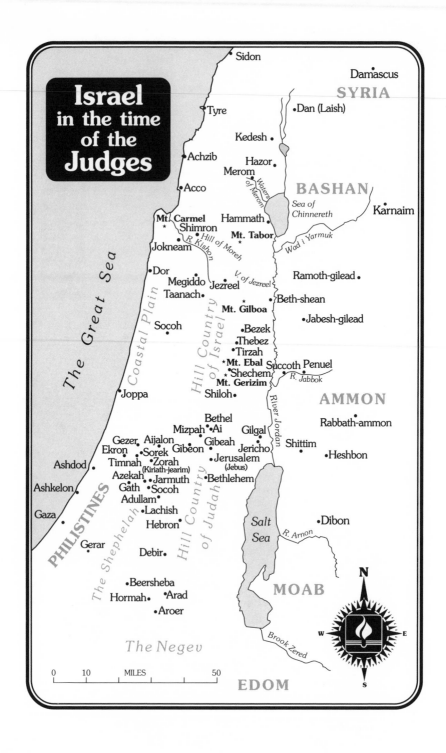

Israel in the time of the Judges

Sidon

Damascus

SYRIA

Tyre

Dan (Laish)

Kedesh

Achzib

Hazor
Merom

Acco

Waters of Merom

BASHAN

Sea of Chinnereth

Karnaim

Mt. Carmel
Shimron

Hammath

Jokneam

Hill of Moreh

R. Kishon

Mt. Tabor

Wadi Yarmuk

Dor

Megiddo
Taanach

Jezreel

V. of Jezreel

Ramoth-gilead

Beth-shean

Mt. Gilboa

Jabesh-gilead

Socoh

Hill Country of Israel

Bezek
Thebez
Tirzah

Mt. Ebal
Shechem
Mt. Gerizim

Succoth Penuel

R. Jabbok

AMMON

Joppa

Shiloh

The Great Sea

Coastal Plain

Bethel
Mizpah Ai

Gilgal

Rabbath-ammon

Gezer Aijalon
Ekron Sorek Gibeon
Timnah Zorah
(Kiriath-jearim)
Azekah Jarmuth
Gath Socoh
Adullam
Lachish

Gibeah

Jericho

Shittim

Jerusalem
(Jebus)

Heshbon

Bethlehem

River Jordan

Ashdod

Ashkelon

Gaza

PHILISTINES

The Shephelah

Hormah
Beersheba
Arad
Aroer

Hebron

Debir

Hill Country of Judah

Salt
Sea

R. Arnon

Dibon

MOAB

The Negev

Brook Zered

N

W E

S

0   10   MILES   50

EDOM

Bibliography

ABD   Ed. D. N. Freedman et al.
   1992   *The Anchor Bible Dictionary.* 6 vols. New York: Doubleday.
Achebe, Chinua
   1988   *Things Fall Apart.* Nairobi, Kenya: Heinemann.
Alter, Robert
   1981   *The Art of Biblical Narrative.* New York: Basic Books.
Amit, Yairah
   1987   "Judges 4: Its Contents and Form." *Journal for the Study of the Old Testament* 39:89-111.
   1990   "Hidden Polemic in the Conquest of Dan: Judges XVII-XVIII." *Vetus Testamentum* 60:4-20.
Andrew, Brother
   1967   *God's Smuggler.* Old Tappan, N.J.: Fleming H. Revell.
Anonymous
   1982   "The War Within: An Anatomy of Lust." *Leadership* 3 (Fall): 30-48.
   1988   "The War Within Continues." *Leadership* 9 (Winter): 24-33.
Armerding, Carl
   1968   "The Heroic Age of Greece and Israel: A Literary-Historical Comparison." Dissertation, Brandeis University.
Bainton, Roland
   1960   *Christian Attitudes Toward War and Peace.* Nashville: Abingdon.
Bar-Efrat, Shimon
   1989   *Narrative Art in the Bible.* Trans. Dorothea Shefer-Vanson. Sheffield: Almond Press.
Baron, Stanley
   1979   "The Locust War." *World Health* (Jan.): 10-15.
Bethge, Eberhard
   1977   *Dietrich Bonhoeffer: Theologian, Christian, Contemporary.* New York: Harper & Row.

Biran, Avraham
  1980   "Tell Dan Five Years Later." *Biblical Archaeologicst* 43:168-182.
  1987   "Dan." In *Archaeology and Biblical Interpretation,* 101-111.
         Ed. L. G. Perdue, L. E. Toombs, and G. C. Johnson. Atlanta:
         John Knox.
Boecker, Hans Jochen
  1980   *Law and the Administration of Justice in the Old Testament
         and Ancient East.* Trans. Jeremy Moiser. Minneapolis: Augsburg.
Boling, Robert G.
  1975   *Judges.* Anchor Bible, 6A. Garden City, N.Y.: Doubleday.
Bonhoeffer, Dietrich
  1955   *Ethics.* New York: Macmillan.
Bonino, José Miguez
  1983   *Toward a Christian Political Ethic.* Philadelphia: Fortress.
Brenner, Athalya, ed.
  1993   *A Feminist Companion to Judges.* Sheffield: Sheffield Academic
         Press.
Brensinger, Terry
  1997   "Nsh." In *New International Dictionary of Old Testament
         Theology and Exegesis,* 3:211-213. Grand Rapids: Zondervan.
Brettler, Marc
  1989   "The Book of Judges: Literature as Politics." *Journal of Biblical
         Literature* 108:395-418.
Brodsky, Harold
  1990   "Locusts in the Book of Joel." *Bible Review* 6:32-39.
Brueggemann, Walter
  1978   *The Prophetic Imagination.* Philadelphia: Fortress.
Buber, Martin
  1967   *Kingship of God.* New York: Harper & Row.
Burney, C. F.
  1903   *The Book of Judges.* New York: KTAV, 1970 reprint.
Campbell, Alastair V.
  1986   *The Gospel of Anger.* London: SPCK.
Chittister, Joan, OSB
  1990   *Wisdom Distilled from the Daily.* San Francisco: Harper.
Cooper, Alan
  1987   "On Reading the Bible Critically and Otherwise." In *Future of
         Biblical Studies.* Ed. R. E. Friedman and H. G. M. Williamson.
         Atlanta: Scholars Press.
Craigie, Peter C.
  1972   "A Reconsideration of Shamgar ben Anath (Judg. 3:31 and 5:6)."
         Journal of Biblical Literature 91:239-240.
  1978   *The Problem of War in the Old Testament.* Grand Rapids:
         Eerdmans.
Crenshaw, James
  1974   "The Samson Saga: Filial Devotion or Erotic Attachment."
         Zeitschrift für die Alttestamentliche Wissenschaft 86:470-503.
Cundall, Arthur E.
  1968   *Judges, Ruth.* Downers Grove, Ill.: InterVarsity.
Day, John
  1992   "Ashteroth." In *ABD,* vol 1.

De Vaux, Roland
  1961   *Ancient Israel.* Vol. 1: *Social Institutions.* New York: McGraw-Hill.
Dongell, Joseph
  1992   "The Bible and Literature." In *Asbury Bible Commentary,* 93-115. Ed. Eugene Carpenter and Wayne McCown. Grand Rapids: Zondervan.
Donovan, Vincent J.
  1978   *Christianity Rediscovered: An Epistle from the Masai.* London: SCM.
Durham, John I.
  1987   *Exodus.* Waco, Tex.: Word Books.
Dyck, Cornelius J., ed.
  1981   *An Introduction to Mennonite History.* Scottdale, Pa.: Herald Press.
Eller, Vernard
  1980   *The Outward Bound.* Grand Rapids: Eerdmans.
Estep, William R.
  1975   *The Anabaptist Story.* Grand Rapids: Eerdmans.
Exum, J. Cheryl
  1980   "Promise and Fulfillment: Narrative Art in Judges 13." *Journal of Biblical Literature* 99:43-59.
  1981   "Aspects of Symmetry and Balance in the Samson Saga." *Journal for the Study of the Old Testament* 19:3-29.
  1990   "The Centre Cannot Hold: Thematic and Textual Instabilities in Judges." *Catholic Biblical Quarterly* 52:410-431.
Fensham, F. C.
  1964   "Did a Treaty Between the Israelites and the Kenites Exist?" *Bulletin of the American Schools of Oriental Research* 175:51-54.
  1977   "The Numeral Seventy in the Old Testament and the Family of Jerubbaal, Ahab, Panammuwa and Athirat." *Palestine Exploration Quarterly* 109:113-115.
Finkelstein, I.
  1985   *Excavations at Shiloh* 1981-84. Vol. 12:123-180. Tel Aviv.
Gaster, Theodore H.
  1969   *Myth, Legend, and Custom in the Old Testament.* New York and London: Harper.
Gevirtz, Stanley
  1963   "Jericho and Shechem: A Religio-Literary Aspect of City Destruction." *Vetus Testamentum* 13:52-62.
Gill, David W.
  1995   "Violence." *New Dictionary of Christian Ethics and Pastoral Theology.* Ed. David J. Atkinson and David F. Field. Downers Grove, Ill: InterVarsity.
Ginzberg, Louis
  1913   *The Legends of the Jews.* Vol. 4. Philadelphia: Jewish Publication Society.
Globe, Alexander
  1974   "The Literary Structure and Unity of the Song of Deborah." *Journal of Biblical Literature* 93:493-512.

Goricheva, Tatiana
    1986   *Talking About God Is Dangerous.* New York: Crossroad.
Gottwald, Norman
    1985   *The Hebrew Bible: A Socio-Literary Introduction.* Philadelphia:
            Fortress.
Gray, John
    1986   *Joshua, Judges, Ruth.* Grand Rapids: Eerdmans.
Green, A. R. W.
    1975   *Role of Human Sacrifices in the Ancient Near East.* Missoula:
            Scholars Press.
Gutmann, J.
    1961   "The 'Second Commandment' and the Image in Judaism."
            Hebrew Union College Annual 32:161-174.
Halpern, Baruch
    1983   *The Emergence of Israel in Canaan.* Society of Biblical Literature
            Monograph, 29. Chico: Scholars Press.
    1988   "The Assassination of Eglon: The First Locked-Room Murder
            Mystery." *Bible Review* 4:33-41.
Hamlin, E. John
    1990   *Judges: At Risk in the Promised Land.* Grand Rapids:
            Eerdmans.
Hanson, R. M.
    1995   "Abuse." *New Dictionary of Christian Ethics and Pastoral
            Theology.* Ed. David J. Atkinson and David F. Field. Downers
            Grove, Ill: InterVarsity.
Heschel, Abraham J.
    1962   *The Prophets.* New York: Jewish Publication Society.
Hobbs, T. R.
    1989   *A Time for War: A Study of Warfare in the Old Testament.*
            Wilmington: Michael Glazier.
Hollyday, Joyce
    1995   "Finding a Way Out of the Brokenness." *Sojourners* 24:29.
Honeyman, A. M.
    1953   "The Salting of Shechem." *Vetus Testamentum* 3:192-195.
Horsman, Sarah
    1989   *Living with Stress.* Cambridge: Lutterworth.
Hubbard, R. Pearce S.
    1966   "The Topography of Ancient Jerusalem." *Palestine Exploration
            Quarterly* 98:130-154.
Hymnal: A Worship Book.
    1992   Prepared by Churches in the Believers Church Tradition.
            Scottdale, Pa.: Mennonite Publishing House; et al.
Janzen, Waldemar
    1994   *Old Testament Ethics.* Louisville: Westminster John Knox.
Keil, C. F., and F. Delitzsch
    1973   *The Book of Judges.* 10 vols. Vol. 2. Trans. J. Martin. Grand
            Rapids: Eerdmans, reprint.
Kenyon, Kathleen
    1974   *Digging Up Jerusalem.* London: Benn.
Kitchen, Kenneth
    1992   "The Exodus." In *ABD,* vol. 2.

Klein, Lillian R.
1989   *The Triumph of Irony in the Book of Judges.* Sheffield: Almond
        Press.
Lactantius
1871   *Works.* Ed. Alexander Roberts and James Donaldson. Vol. 2.
        Edinburgh: T & T Clark.
Lasine, S.
1984   "Guest and Host in Judges 19: Lot's Hospitality in an Inverted
        World." *Journal for the Study of the Old Testament* 29:37-59.
Levin, Meyer
1964   *The Fanatic.* New York: Simon and Schuster.
Lewis, C. S.
1965   *The Weight of Glory.* Grand Rapids: Eerdmans, reprint.
Lind, Millard C.
1980   *Yahweh Is a Warrior.* Scottdale: Herald Press.
Lindars, Barnabas
1983   "Deborah's Song: Women in the Old Testament." *Bulletin of the
        John Rylands University Library of Manchester* 65:158-175.
Livy
1969   *Livy.* 14 vols. Vol. 5 (books 21-22). Trans. B. O. Foster. Loeb
        Classical Library. Cambridge: Harvard Univ. Press.
Long, V. Philips
1994   *The Art of Biblical History.* Grand Rapids: Zondervan.
Luther, Martin
1960   *Works.* Vol. 35. Ed. E. Theodore Bachmann. Philadelphia:
        Fortress.
1967   *Works.* Vol. 54. Ed., trans. Theodore G. Tappert. Philadelphia:
        Fortress.
Malamat, Abraham
1960   "Hazor 'The Head of All Those Kingdoms.'" *Journal of Biblical
        Literature* 79:12-19.
1968   "King Lists of the Old Babylonian Period and Biblical
        Genealogies." *Journal of the American Oriental Society*
        88:163-173.
1970   "The Danite Migration and the Pan-Israelite Exodus-Conquest: A
        Biblical Narrative Pattern." *Biblica* 51:1-16.
Martin, James D.
1975   *The Book of Judges.* Cambridge: Cambridge Univ. Press.
Matthews, Victor H.
1991   "Hospitality and Hostility in Judges 4." *Biblical Theology
        Bulletin* 21:13-21.
1992   "Hospitality and Hostility in Genesis 19 and Judges 19." *Biblical
        Theology Bulletin* 22:3-11.
Mayes, A. H.
        1985 *Judges.* Sheffield: Journal for the Study of the Old
        Testament Press.
Mazar, Amihai
1990   *Archaeology of the Land of the Bible: 10,000—586 B.C.E.*
        New York: Doubleday.
McClendon, James William Jr.
1995   *Making Gospel Sense.* Cleveland: Pilgrim Press.

McKenzie, John L.
  1966   *The World of the Judges*. Englewood Cliffs, N.J.: Prentice Hall.
Menno Simons
  1984   *The Complete Writings of Menno Simons*. Trans. Leonard Verduin. Ed. J. C. Wenger. Scottdale, Pa.: Herald Press.
Miller, J. M.
  1974   Mistaken Identity." *Zeitschrift des Deutschen Palästina-Vereins* 90:115-127.
Moeller, Bob
  1995   "The Sex Life of America's Christians." *Leadership* 16:30-31.
Moltmann, Jürgen
  1967   *Theology of Hope*. Trans. James W. Leitch. London: SCM.
  1981   *The Trinity and the Kingdom*. Trans. Margaret Kohl. San Francisco: Harper & Row.
Moore, George F.
  1910   *Judges*. Edinburgh: T & T Clark.
Muck, Terry
  1988   "How Common Is Pastoral Indiscretion?" *Leadership* 9 (Winter):12-13.
Mullen, F. Theodore Jr.
  1984   "Judges 1:1-36: The Deuteronomistic Reintroduction of the Book of Judges." *The Harvard Theological Review* 77:33-54.
Newbigin, Lesslie
  1977   *The Good Shepherd*. London: Mowbray.
Ngien, Dennis
  1997   "The God Who Suffers." *Christianity Today* 41 (Feb. 3): 38-42.
Nouwen, Henri
  1986   *Lifesigns: Intimacy, Fecundity, and Ecstasy in Christian Perspective*. New York: Doubleday.
Nouwen, Henri, Donald McNeill, and Douglas Morrison
  1982   *Compassion*. New York: Doubleday.
O'Connell, Robert H.
  1996   *The Rhetoric of the Book of Judges*. Leiden: E. J. Brill.
Poling, James
  1995   "Reflections on Family Violence in Central America." *The Journal of Pastoral Care* 49:417-422.
Polzin, Robert
  1980   *Moses and the Deuteronomist: A Literary Study of the Deuteronomic History*. New York: Seabury.
Pritchard, James B., ed.
  1955   *Ancient Near Eastern Texts Relating to the Old Testament*. Princeton: Princeton Univ. Press.
Religious New Service
  1996   "Meeting Focuses on Domestic Violence." *Christian Century* (Dec. 11): 1223-1224.
Reynold, William J.
  1995   *Songs of Glory: Stories of 300 Great Hymns and Gospel Songs*. Grand Rapids: Baker Books.
Ruiv, M.
  1966   "The Government of Shechem in the Amarna Period and in the Days of Abimelech." *Israel Exploration Journal* 16:252-257.

Sarna, Nahum
1971 "Gideon." In *Encyclopedia Judaica*. Ed. Cecil Roth. Jerusalem: Keter.
Simon, Maurice, and Israel W. Slotki, eds.
1980 *Hebrew-English Edition of the Babylonian Talmud*. New York: Traditional Press.
Simons. *See* Menno
Singer, Isaac Bashevis
1968 *The Slave*. New York: Avon Books.
Soggin, J. Alberto
1981 *Judges*. Philadelphia: Westminster.
Stager, Lawrence, and Samuel Wolff
1984 "Child Sacrifice at Carthage—Religious Rite of Population Control?" *Biblical Archaeology Review* 10:30-51.
Sternberg, Meir
1985 *The Poetics of Biblical Narrative*. Bloomington: Indiana Univ. Press.
Stone, Lawson Grant
1988 "From Tribal Confederation to Monarchic State: The Editorial Perspective of the Book of Judges." Dissertation, Yale University.
Tertullian
1950 *Apologetic Works*. In *The Fathers of the Church*. Ed. Roy Joseph Deferrari et al. Vol. 10.
Thomas à Kempis
1960 *The Imitation of Christ*. London: Dent, reprint.
Trible, Phyllis
1984 *Texts of Terror*. Philadelphia: Fortress.
Vachss, Andrew
1998 "A Hard Look at How We Treat Children." *Parade* (Mar. 29): 4-5.
Van Braght, Thieleman J.
1938 *Martyrs Mirror*. Scottdale, Pa.: Herald Press.
Vanhoozer, Kevin
1986 "The Semantics of Biblical Literature: Truth and Scripture's Diverse Literary Forms." In *Hermeneutics, Authority, and Canon*. Ed. D. A. Carson and J. D. Woodbridge. Grand Rapids: Zondervan.
Van Nieuwenhuijze, C. A. S.
1971 *Sociology of the Middle East: A Stocktaking and Interpretation*. Leiden: Brill.
Van Selms, A.
1950 "The Best Man and Bride: From Sumer to St. John, with a New Interpretation of Judges, Chapters 14 and 15." *Journal of Near Eastern Studies* 9:65-75.
Von Rad, Gerhard
1991 *Holy War in Ancient Israel*. Trans. Marva J. Dawn. Grand Rapids: Eerdmans, reprint.
Walsh, J. P. M.
1987 *The Mighty from Their Thrones*. Philadelphia: Fortress.

Webb, Barry G.
    1987   *The Book of Judges: An Integrated Reading.* Sheffield: Journal
          for the Study of the Old Testament Press.
Wesley, John
    1985   *Works.* Vol. 2. Ed. Albert C. Outler. Nashville: Abingdon.
    1989   *Works.* Vol. 9. Ed. Rupert E. Davies. Nashville: Abingdon.
Wright, G. E.
    1965   *Shechem: Biography of a Biblical* City. New York: McGraw-Hill.
Yadin, Yigael
    1972   *Hazor: The Head of All Those Kingdoms.* London: Oxford
          Univ. Press.
Yancey, Philip
    1994   "The Lost Sex Study." *Christianity Today* 38 (Dec. 12): 80.

Selected Resources

Boling, Robert G. *Judges*. Anchor Bible, 6A. New York: Doubleday, 1975. Gives primary attention to background and linguistic matters. Provides a fresh translation. Somewhat technical and includes little in terms of theological reflection.

Cundall, Arthur E. *Judges, Ruth*. Tyndale Old Testament Commentaries. Downers Grove, Ill.: InterVarsity, 1968. Offers brief, informative, evangelical explanations of the text that are intended for the nonspecialist.

Gray, John. *Joshua, Judges, Ruth*. The New Century Bible Commentary. Grand Rapids: Eerdmans, 1986. A brief commentary focusing largely on geographical, historical, and linguistic issues.

Hamlin, John E. *Judges: At Risk in the Promised Land*. International Theological Commentary. Grand Rapids: Eerdmans, 1990. Compact explanations containing rich theological insights. These explanations, geared to the average reader, include many helpful contemporary examples gained from the author's varied international experiences.

Klein, Lillian R. *The Triumph of Irony in the Book of Judges*. Sheffield: Almond Press, 1989. Examines the literary nature of the book, paying particular attention to the author's use of irony.

Long, V. Philips. *The Art of Biblical History*. Grand Rapids: Zondervan. A helpful discussion of what it means to speak of the Bible as a historical document.

Mayes, A. H. *Judges*. Sheffield: Journal for the Study of the Old Testament Press, 1985. A short but insightful examination of the setting and context of the book. Pays some attention to anthropological and sociological issues.

O'Connell, Robert H. *The Rhetoric of the Book of Judges*. Leiden: E. J. Brill, 1996. A technical analysis of the artistic qualities of the book. Intended primarily for specialists.

Soggin, J. Alberto. *Judges*. Old Testament Library. Philadelphia: Westminster, 1981. A detailed unit-by-unit examination of the text. Combines both analysis and reflection in a helpful way.

Webb, Barry G. *The Book of Judges: An Integrated Reading*. Sheffield: Journal for the Study of the Old Testament Press, 1987. A wonderful analysis of the literary structure of the book. Acquaintance with Hebrew is helpful but not essential.

Index of Ancient Sources

OLD TESTAMENT

Genesis
1:1—2:4 123
1:2.....................233
1:26-27 235
2:16-17 44
2:23.....................198
3:5.......................118
3:6.......................189
4:1...............40, 197
4:1-8 189
4:10-12 108
4:23-24 103
6:1-7 126
6:6.......................126
8:20.....................133
10 237
11:1-9 189
11:4.....................118
11:30...................149
12:1.......................93
12:6.....................107
12:7.......................83
12:8.......................32
12:11-20 58
15:8-21 86
16 215
16:7-12 34
16:13.....................82
18:1-15........148-149
18:10...................146
19 247

19:3.....................153
19:5.....................197
19:12-13 34
19:37.....................55
20:2-18 58
21:1-7 ....146, 149
21:8.....................153
22 ....42, 135
22:1-19 139
22:2.....................133
23:15...................164
24:3-4 151
24:47...................101
25:2.......................78
25:6.......................78
25:19-26 149
26:34-35 151
27 58
27:41-45 209
28:19.....................32
28:20-22 138
29:15-30 123
29:31...................149
29:31-35 29
30 58
30:1-6 186
30:1-24 149
30:22-24 146
31:19...................176
31:34-35 176
32:13.....................82
32:22-32 97
32:30...........82, 148

33:18...................107
33:20.....................83
34 112
34:1-4 167
34:7.....................203
35:4 107-108
35:7.......................83
37:12...................107
37:25-28 101
37:29...................134
37:34...................134
37:36...................101
38 58
38:2-3 167
38:15-18 167
38:17...................156
39:1.....................101
39:7-20 168
41 90
41:1-36 123
44:13...................134
45:8.....................178
46:13...................116
46:14...................142
46:27.....................98
49:8.....................104

Exodus
1:8.........................41
2:23.......................42
3—4 ....52, 68
3—12 42
3:2.........................82

3:2-5 237
3:11....................82
3:12....................81
4:1-9 86
14:21-22 65
14:24..................90
15:1-18 73
15:20..................63
15:20-21 134
17:7....................85
17:16..................31
18:1....................78
18:8-11 70
19:5....................36
19:6..................235
19:16-25 237
20:4...........176, 179
20:4-6 ....234, 246
20:19..........82, 148
20:23................176
20:24................177
21:22-25 30
21:23-25 103
24:1..................236
24:9..................236
24:15-18 237
28:6-8 101
28:30................101
28:41................177
29:9..................177
29:20..................29
29:24................177
29:41..................82
31:3..................233
32 ......179, 209, 215
33:1-6 126
33:11..................40
33:20................148
34:13..................83
34:15-16 151
35:4-29 35
38:8..................136

Leviticus
1 207
1:4....................133
2:1.....................82
7:11-18 207
7:16..................138
8:23...................29
8:33..................177

11:24-25 152
11:37-40 152
16:32................177
18:21.........135, 140
19:18.........103, 180
20:1-5 135
20:2..................140
20:10................194
22:18................138
22:21................138
24:14-16 84
24:17..................99
24:20................103
25:2-7 123
26:1..................179

Numbers
3 177
6:1-4 146
6:5.....................70
6:9-12 146
10:29-32 31
11:1..................126
11:25-29 233
12:9..................126
13—14 183
13:8...................92
13:21................186
13:26-29 184
14:6...................31
14:11-12 126
14:12..................68
14:22..................85
15:1-16 148
15:3..................138
20:14-21 130
21:1-3 138
21:4...........126, 130
21:10-13 130
21:21-31......130-131
21:21-35 125
21:26................131
22—24 55
22—25 132
22:4-7 78
22:21-35 34
25 201
25:1-18 79
25:3..................226
26:23................116
26:26................142

27:21..................29
29:39................138
30:1-16 138
30:2..................138
31:1-12 79
31:6..................201
32:39-42 117
32:41................117
35:1..................131
35:1-5 178
35:6-34 99
35:9-28 103

Deuteronomy
1:5....................131
2:2-18 130
2:34..................208
3:6....................208
3:14..................117
4:15-40 234
4:16...........176, 179
4:25..................179
5:1.....................36
5:8....................179
5:8-10 234
6:5....................180
6:25...................36
7:3....................151
7:5........83, 179, 185
7:25...........179, 185
8:17-18 118
9:2.....................30
9:18...................41
10:2..................206
10:5..................206
12:3...........179, 185
12:6..................138
12:31 ..135, 139-140
13:12-18 208
17:6...........203, 205
17:14-20 238
18:9-10........139-140
18:10................135
18:10-12 177
19:21...........99, 103
20:8...................88
21:15-17 198
22:13-21 194
22:21................203
23:21-23 138
24:1-4 156

25:4......................97
26:19..................104
27:12-13 109
27:15..................179
28 39
29:23..................114
31:16....................43
31:20-21 43
32:15..................118
32:35..........100, 103
32:42....................70
33:2..............70, 237

Joshua
1:1.......................27
1:5.......................81
1:7.......................36
2 183
2:1-21 33
2:10-11 70
3:14-17 65
5:10....................35
6 59
6—7 208
6:17..............31, 208
6:22-25 33
7:12....................31
8:30-35 109
9:6......................35
10:6-9 35
10:11..................65
10:15..................35
10:43..................35
11 62
13:1....................26
13:27..................96
14:6...........35, 147
15:13..................31
15:13-19 31
15:14..................30
15:63..................30
16:10..................28
17:2....................81
18:1..................187
18:22..................32
18:23..................81
18:26................128
19:1....................29
19:15................142
19:37..................64
19:40-46 183

19:40-48 145
19:42.........142, 151
19:47.........145, 183
19:51................187
21:2..................187
21:9-16 178
21:24................142
22:10-34 201
22:12................187
22:20..................31
24:26................108
24:28..................40

Ruth
2:1.......................81

1 Samuel
1—4 214
1:1.....................92
1:1-28 149
1:11..................139
1:19-20 146
1:21..................139
1:24..................82
2:1-10 73
2:12..................197
2:27..................147
3:1........95, 149, 215
3:7......................40
4 188
4:3......179-180, 187,
   206
5:1-7 165
5:4....................229
5:9....................108
7:2....................184
7:3....................225
7:4....................225
7:9....................133
7:10....................65
8 ....100, 209
8:1....................145
8:9-20 238
9-31..................168
9:1-2 201
9:6....................147
10 134
10:10................233
10:20-21 201
10:25................238
10:26................195

10:27......82, 94, 197
11 ....124, 213
11:1-11 58
11:2..................124
11:3..................137
11:6...........104, 233
11:7..................201
11:8....................29
11:11..................90
11:12-13 94
12:10................225
12:26-31 134
13—14 145
13:1..................229
13:6..................114
13:17..................81
14:1....................89
14:3..................101
14:6.............89, 151
14:33-35 108
14:41-42 29
15:4-6 31
15:11................126
15:22-26 126
15:32-33 30
16:10................118
16:11..................95
16:13................233
16:14................111
16:15-19 118
16:18..................81
17 145
17:4-7 86
17:26................151
17:36................151
17:39..................86
17:40..................59
17:42..................86
17:54..................92
18:6....................73
18:6-7 134
19 118
19:11-17 58
19:13................176
21 201
22:2....129, 136, 167
23:9-12 101
24 189
25:10-13 94
27—31 145
27:1-4 129

28:6............101, 209
28:7.................209
30:7-8 101
31:1-6 188
31:4.................151
31:11-13 213

2 Samuel
1:1....................27
1:1-16 188
2:1.................209
2:17-23 99
3:12.................188
3:26-30 58
3:27.................99
3:30.................99
5:5.....................30
5:6-10 30
5:6-16 195
5:10.................209
5:17-25 145
5:19.................209
6:12-19 206
8:1....................145
8:18.................177
10:6.................186
10:6-13 129
11..............189-190
11:1...........131, 229
11:1-5 167
11:21.............115
12:1-7 109
12:1-14 117
12:26-31....124, 131,
  229
13:1-22 ......167, 198
13:12.............203
13:19.............134
13:23-29 119
13:31.............134
14:2-3 67
14:4-24 117
14:25.............119
14:28.............198
15:1-6 119
15:6.................119
15:8.................139
15:10-12 119
15:13.............119
17:8.................185
17:11.............201

18:1—19:8 99
18:33.................135
20:4-10 58
20:16-22 67
21:2-6 99
21:14.................201
22:1-51 73
23:30.................142
24 238
24:2.................201
24:24.................164

1 Kings
1:4...............40, 197
1:33.................117
2:5.....................99
2:13-46 ......118, 209
3:1—11:43 168
3:10.................126
4:7-28 216
4:13.................117
4:21.................82
4:25.................201
6:1 227-229
9:15.................108
10:1.................153
10:26-29 ......93, 238
11:1-8 163
11:1-13 238
11:5.................123
11:7.................123
11:26.................92
11:27.................108
11:33.................123
12 209
12:1.................107
12:25.................107
12:25-33 ......52, 203
12:28-30......32, 101,
  179
12:29.................188
12:30..188, 190, 216
13:1.................147
13:1-5 87
13:18.................34
13:33.................177
15:3.................52
15:11.................52
15:13.................225
15:18.................108
15:25-26 52

15:26.................190
15:27.........118, 209
15:34.................52
16:10.................209
16:13-14 209
16:15-19 209
16:21-28 131
16:24.................117
16:25.................203
16:26.........188, 190
17:24.................147
18:16-46 72
18:19.................225
19:1-8 159
20:39-42 117
20:42.................31
22 118
22:8.................209
22:32.................41
34 190

2 Kings
1:2-3 226
1:3-4 34
1:11.................147
2:12...........134, 178
3 55
3:11.................209
3:27.................139
4:7.....................147
5:13.................216
5:20-27 168
6:8-23 94
6:21.................178
8:8.....................82
10:1.................98
10:29.................188
11:1-13 216
12:3.................36
12:20.................108
13:14.................178
13:20.................55
14:3.................52
14:4.................36
14:9.................109
14:9-10 117
15:4.................36
15:29.................187
15:35.................36
16:3.........135, 140
17:3-6 187

17:17............41, 140
18:3.....................52
18:15-16 108
20:8-11 86
21:1-9 ....187, 216
21:1-18 190
21:6...................140
21:7............179, 225
21:11.................203
22—23 16
22:2.....................52
22:13.................209
22:14...................63
22:14-20 67
22:18.................209
23 216
23:4...................225
23:6...................225
23:13.................123
23:15...................32
23:24.................176
23:26.................216
23:26-27 190
24:2.....................55
25 27

1 Chronicles
2:22-23 117
4:41...................125
6:54-81 178
6:69...................142
7:1......................116
7:10.....................58
7:12...................212
7:15...................212
8:6.......................58
10:4...................151
10:10.................165
10:14.................209
11:8...................108
11:31.................142
12:2.....................56
12:18...................84
12:40...................79
19:1—20:3 134
23:12-15 178
27:14.................142

2 Chronicles
9:1......................153
11:6...................157

11:10.................142
17:5.....................82
18:1-27 118
18:7...................209
18:11-27 209
24:20...................84
25:2.....................36
26:7...................125
26:14-21 118
32:5...................108
32:31...................43
33:7...................179
33:9...................203
34:2.....................36
34:21.................209
34:26.................209
35:25...................67

Ezra
7:1-10 216

Nehemiah
2:1-18 216
4:6.......................35
6:14.....................67
6:15...................216
7:67.....................67

Esther
5:6.....................153
9:19.....................29

Job
1:1-5 44
1:5.......................88
1:8.....................126
1:20...................134
2:3.....................126
2:9.....................155
7:17-18 44
21:4...................126
27:3...................233
29:14...................84
33:4...................233
35:9...................118
38:1..............65, 237
42:12-17 44

Psalms
1:4.......................81
4:4.....................104

5:6.......................59
8 139
10:10.................118
12:6...................123
18 ....73, 139
18:7-8 237
18:9-15 65
22:5.....................41
22:25.................139
24:10.................209
30 73
33:6...................233
37:8...................104
45 73
46:1.....................87
49:4...................153
50:14.................138
51:11.................232
55:23...................59
56:12.................139
61:5...................139
65:1...................139
66:13.................139
68:8.....................70
68:32...................70
78:18...................85
78:58.................179
83:11...................92
92 73
96:1.....................73
97:7...................179
98:1.....................73
101:7...................59
104:30...............233
106:37-38 140
107:34...............114
109:18.................84
115:4.................180
116:14...............139
120—134 73
127:3.................198
132:2-5 139
133:1...................36
135:15-18 234
147:10-11 118

Proverbs
1:6.....................153
2:1-11 215
3:5-6 215
3:21-26 215

7:14....................139
11:2....................103
11:12..................215
11:14..................119
12:18..................140
14:8....................215
15:1......................94
16:9....................215
16:18..................103
17:1....................210
17:6....................198
18:12..................103
20:20..................198
20:25..................138
23:22..................198
25:21..................103
25:28..................168
28:6....................189
29:23..................103
31:10..................198
31:28..................104

Ecclesiastes
1:2....................229
4:1....................118
5:4-5 138
9:16..................118
12:8..................229

Isaiah
1:3....................203
2:1-5 238
2:5....................239
3:21..................101
5:1-2 168
5:1-7 118
5:3-4 168
6:5..............82, 148
7:1-17 92
7:10-17 87
7:13..................126
8:3......................67
9:6-7 238
10:1-4 209
10:26..................92
11:1-9 238
15—16 56
19:21..................139
26:17..................41
31:1-9 209
32:15..................233

36:22..................134
41:15....................97
42:17..................179
43:24..................126
44:3....................233
44:9-17 179
44:9-20 234
44:25..................177
47:4....................209
47:12-15 177
52:15....................70
57:13....................41
58 180
59:17....................84
63:10-11 232

Jeremiah
1:4-10 68
2:19..................209
3:1......................41
5:1....................203
5:31..................118
7:4....................180
7:12-15 187
7:31............135, 140
8:10-12 194
9:23-24 118
10:1-16 234
10:14..................179
14:12..................133
14:14-16 118
17:6..................114
17:9..................203
19:4-6 140
21:2..................209
23:5-8 239
26:6..................187
26:7-9 209
26:13..................125
26:28..................209
28 118
32:9..................164
32:30....................41
32:35..................140
35 146
37:7..................209
38:1-13 209
41:5..................134
44:25..................138
48 56
48:9..................114

48:10....................72

Lamentations
1:5......................44
1:14....................44
3:8......................41
3:21-24 44
3:39....................44
3:40-42 44
4:12..................180

Ezekiel
1:27-28 237
6:9....................126
11:5..................233
13 118
15 118
16:12..................101
16:20-21 140
17 118
19 118
20:1..................209
20:3..................209
23 118
23:37-39 140
24:3-14 118
27:8..................119
37:14..................233
38:11....................29
39:29..................233
44:20....................70

Daniel
1:5....................153

Hosea
1:2ff. 41
1:2....................151
2:1-8 226
5 92
6:6....................180
9:9....................203
10:9..................203
10:11....................97
12:4....................97
12:14....................41

Joel
1—2 79
2:28..................233
3:4..................236

Amos
1:3......................98
1:13-15 124
2:6-8 209
2:11-12 146
3:15..................216
4:4......................32
5:11-12 216
5:14..................209
5:21-24 180
7:10-17 209
7:14..................95
8:3......................74
8:10..................74

Jonah
1:16 138-139
2:9......................139
3:10..................125
4 160

Micah
1:7......................179
3:8......................233
3:11..........180, 194
4:6-7 238
5:13..................179
6:4......................67
6:7......................180
6:7-8 140
6:8......................180

Nahum
1:14..................179

Habakkuk
2:18..................179
3:3......................70

Zephaniah
2:8-11 56

Haggai
1:5......................209

Zechariah
2:8......................29
4:6................53, 233
7:12..................233
9:9......................117
9:9-10 239

11:8-9 126

Malachi
1:6-8 203
1:14..................138
2:15..................198

APOCHRYPHA

Apocrypha 234

1 Maccabees
10:83..................165
11:4..................165

Wisdom of Solomon
13—15 234

NEW TESTAMENT

Matthew
1:18-25 149
4:1-11 44
4:8-10 189
4:18..................95
5—7 180
5:9......................94
5:22..................104
5:33-37 139
5:38-42 103
5:38-48 30
5:44..................237
6:2......................104
7:15..................216
7:24-27 215
7:26-27 68
7:29..................216
9:15..................153
10:22..................36
11:20-24 127
12:1-8 180
12:25..................211
12:38-39 87
14:14..................204
15:4-6 139
15:19..................203
16:1-4 87
17:17..................127
18:1..................210
18:4..................93
18:15-20 12

18:21-22 123
19:16-22 93
19:26..................86
20:20-28 210
20:27..................118
21:12-13 104
21:33-46 118
22:1-14 68
22:37-39 180
25:24-30 68
26:14-16....168, 189,
   215
26:39..................189
26:69-75 ....137, 189
27:1-5 189
27:3-5 168
27:3-10 44

Mark
3:24..................211
6:17-18 167
6:31..................160
7:1-23 180
7:6-7 36
7:9-13 ....139, 198
7:22..................59
8:11-12 87
9:33-37 210
9:34..................118
9:35..................118
10:17-22 93
10:27..................86
10:44..................118
11:15-18 104
12:1-12 118
13:35..................90
14:10-11 215

Luke
1:5-25 ....146, 149
1:8-25 86
1:26-38 149
1:37..................86
1:46-55 74
1:57..................146
1:57-66 149
2:1-7 149
8:1-3 67
9:41..................127
9:46..................210
9:51-56 103

9:54.....................94
10:1.....................237
11:17.....................211
18:18-23 93
18:27.....................86
19:40.....................68
19:45-46 104
20:9-19 118
22:4-6 215
22:24.....................118
22:26.....................118
23:55-56 67
24:10.....................67
24:49.....................120

John
3:29.....................155
4:17-18 167
4:48...............87, 120
5:5.....................86
5:14.....................160
8:1-11 167
8:11.....................160
9:1.....................86
11:39.....................86
12:43.....................103
13:3.....................120
13:4-5 120
13:35.....................210
14:12.....................204
15:1-11 60
17:20-21 210
17:21.....................36
18:15-27 44
19:30.....................36
21:15-19 44

Acts
1:8.....................120
2 233
2:16-21 67
5:1-11 ....58, 176
7:51-53 216
8:9-25 188
13:6-11 177
17:29.....................234
18:18.....................139
19:13-20 177
21:23.....................139
23:14.....................139
27:11.....................119

Romans
1:23.....................234
1:29...............59, 204
3 ....67, 180
3:21-26 204
5:12-21 204
6 67
6:15.....................37
8:13.....................159
12:1-2 215
12:8.....................119
12:17.....................103
12:18-19 103
12:19.....................100
13:3.....................104
15:5.....................36
16:1.....................67

1 Corinthians
1:10-17 210
1:22.....................120
1:26-31 ....59, 95
3:16.....................233
4:13.....................95
4:16.....................52
5:1.....................204
5:1-5 167
5:6.....................190
6:18.....................168
9:24-27 36
11:2-16 67
12:28.....................119
13:11.....................36
14:29.....................11
14:34-35 67
16:19.....................67

2 Corinthians
6:15.....................197
12:9.....................94

Galatians
1:7.....................216
1:10.....................104
3:28.....................67
5:6.....................180
5:23.....................168
5:25.....................233

Ephesians
4:3.....................36

4:17-19 167
4:26-27 104
5:10.....................126
5:19.....................74
5:21—6:4 198

Philippians
2:1-11 52
2:2.....................36
2:3.....................93
2:7.....................93
2:19-20 52
3:1-11 180
3:8.....................40
4:3.....................67

Colossians
1:10.....................126
3:5.....................159
3:10.....................235
3:16.....................74
3:18-21 198

1 Thessalonians
2:4-6 104
2:7.....................94
5:6-8 168

1 Timothy
3:6.....................104
5:8.....................198

2 Timothy
2:24.....................94
3:3.....................168

Titus
1:8.....................168
3:2.....................94

Hebrews
9:4.....................206
12:14.....................94

James
1:2-3 44
1:19-20 104
2:1-13 210
3:17-18 94
5:12.....................139

1 Peter
1:13............168, 215
2:9.....................235
2:14...................104
3:7.....................198
4:7.....................168

2 Peter
1:20.....................11

1 John
4:7-12 210

Revelation
2—3 123
3:16...................127
5:9-14 74
9:20...................234
14:3....................74
18:17.................119
22:15.................177

CHURCH FATHERS

Lactantius..........104

Tertullian
125 45

PSEUDEPIGRAPHA

1 Enoch
17:8...................237

Jubilees
49:10...................90

Letter of Aristeas
.........................236

OTHER JEWISH SOURCES

Babylonian Talmud
.........................187

Josephus 141

OTHER SOURCES

Amarna Letters ..17,
  107, 195, 223

Egyptian Execration Texts ..107, 183-184,
  195, 223

Gilgamesh Epic
.........................238

Heroic Literature
..................69, 231

Iliad 238

Mari 184

Moabite Stone
.................131, 224

Pritchard, *ANET*
.............................86

Ugaritic Texts....224

The Author

Terry L. Brensinger is a professor called to preach. Never one to leave the Bible in an academic vacuum, his primary calling is to explore the meaning and relevance of the Old Testament for the contemporary church. His speaking engagements take him to churches and conferences throughout the country, both within and outside his own denomination.

Brensinger serves as professor of biblical studies and chair of the Biblical Studies, Religion, and Philosophy Department at Messiah College, Grantham, Pennsylvania. Before he began teaching at Messiah in 1985, he pastored churches in Columbia, Kentucky, and in New York City. In 1992-93, he served as visiting professor of biblical studies at Daystar University in Nairobi, Kenya. In 1992-93, he was a scholar in residence at the Ecumenical Institute (Tantur) in Jerusalem.

Born in Allentown, Pennsylvania, Brensinger received his B.A. from Messiah College, an M.Div. from Asbury Theological Seminary, an M.A. in Near Eastern Archaeology from Drew University, and his M.Phil. and Ph.D. in Old Testament studies, also from Drew. In addition, he has studied at Jerusalem University College, Princeton Theological Seminary, and the Jewish Theological Seminary of America. He is a member of the American Schools of Oriental Research and the Society of Biblical Literature.

Brensinger has published *Simile and Prophetic Language in the Old Testament*. He and E. Morris Sider edited *Within the Perfection of Christ: Essays on Peace and the Nature of the Church*. His work has also appeared in *The Asbury Bible Commentary, The Anchor Bible Dictionary, The New International Dictionary of Old Testament Theology and Exegesis,* and various scholarly journals and church magazines.

Terry and Debra Brensinger are active members of the Grantham Brethren in Christ Church. They are the parents of three children: Timothy, Jordan, and Julie.